Published by Straight Talk Books
P.O. Box 301, Milwaukee, WI 53201
800.661.3311 • timeofgrace.org

Cover image: RichVintage/iStock

Printed in the United States of America
ISBN: 978-1-942107-10-1

RESTART

Promises new every morning to jump-start your day

Introduction

I have some books in my personal library that I enjoyed reading very much, but I have no intention of reading them again. I now know the plot line, so the suspense is gone, and then there are my favorite detective novels that are so well-written, with such great dialogue and character development, that they are fun to read over and over.

Into which category does the Bible fit in your life? Do you feel that you know all the basics? Does setting aside time for reading it seem like a waste of your time? Or does each time you pick up the Book yield new delights, new insights, new wisdom, new comfort?

It is my hope through these daily Grace Moments to whet your appetite for the Word. I hope to reveal new ways of thinking about treasured and familiar passages, and perhaps I can introduce you to some that are new to you.

May these moments together inspire you to marvel all over again at the Father's magnificent works, Christ's wonderful redemption, and the Spirit's powerful working in your life.

january

Those who hope in the LORD will renew their strength.
They will soar on wings like eagles; they will run and
not grow weary, they will walk and not be faint.

Isaiah 40:31

When goals let you down
Diana Kerr

Happy New Year! I love the fresh start of a new year because I love setting goals, and I love helping my clients set them too.

However. I'll be the first to admit that striving after goals can make you feel pretty empty. Goals are like anything else that we rely on too heavily: they will let you down.

Goals can fail you even if you succeed at accomplishing them. How? Because many of the achievements we seek after are good things that aren't the *ultimate* thing. To make things worse, our motives are often a little messed up—a guaranteed way to decrease your satisfaction in achieving your goals. (For example, losing weight to be skinnier than your sister-in-law or seeking a promotion to get more money so you're happier.)

As you go into this year, ask yourself if your goals really matter in the scope of eternity. If not, throw them out or adjust them. Ask yourself the *why* behind your goals. What's your motivation? For your sake and for the sake of the Lord who loved you enough to lay down his life for you, make sure you're not laboring in vain (Psalm 127:1) and keep 1 Corinthians 10:31 in mind: **"Whether you eat or drink or whatever you do, do it all for the glory of God."** No big goal means anything without God in the equation, and no *small* goal is insignificant if it's done to the glory of your Savior-God.

I want to be more joyful, less resentful

Pastor Mark Jeske

My life experience has been that pain memories are more intense than pleasure memories. That can be good—pain memories can serve as warnings not to do certain dumb things a second time. But they can also overwhelm and crowd out happy thoughts and leave you feeling blue.

Peter Pan wants people to think that happy thoughts can make them fly. Well, they can. Not *literally*, of course. But choosing to let your mind dwell on God's amazing outpouring of blessings into your life can give wings to your spirit and help lift you out of an emotional hole. St. Paul agrees: **"Rejoice in the Lord always. I will say it again: Rejoice!"** (Philippians 4:4).

The gospel of Christ makes us all optimists. The great enemies of mankind have been defeated: *Satan*, the old dragon, has been defanged. Now mortally wounded, he rages about but his destiny is fixed. Your *sin* was put in its entirety on Christ, and you bear it no more. The *grave* is now only a resting place for your tired old body and will have to yield it up when the archangel Michael's trumpet blows. *Hell* was experienced for you by Christ on his cross, and you will never know what its torments are like. Even *death*, that grim reaper, may look like he's winning, but in fact the death of a Christian only means that your spirit has now fled into the presence of Christ.

The more you ponder Christ's mighty work on your behalf, the more your soul rejoices.

God justifies the wicked
Pastor Mark Jeske

The core of the Christian message is dramatically counterintuitive.

It goes against everything you think you know about how the world is supposed to work. The sprinter with the fastest time is supposed to get the blue ribbon. It's the people who haven't committed crimes that stay out of jail. The political candidate with the majority of votes gets elected. Eternal life in heaven is the grandest prize of all, and you would expect that it will be awarded to those who have earned it and deserve it.

That would be nobody. If Christ had not come, judgment day would be like an Olympics where no medals are awarded since every competitor is disqualified. Since mankind turned out to be in such wretched straits, God opened up another way to his heavenly home: faith in Christ. **"To the one who does not work but trusts God *who justifies the ungodly*, their faith is credited as righteousness"** (Romans 4:5). Seriously! Only in God's court does faith in the Savior reverse expectations: an innocent Man was condemned and executed and the ungodly are justified.

When you have a chance to share your faith with people who may be atheists or agnostics or followers of some non-Christian religious system, don't get tangled up in trying to clean up their lives. Just tell them that God loved them so much that he gave his one and only Son and that all the ungodly people who believe in him are justified; they will not perish but have eternal life.

Cohabitation: Sinful or smart?

Pastor Mark Jeske

One of the great ironies of late is the legitimization of gay marriage at the same time that heterosexual couples increasingly are choosing *not* to be married. Social scientists estimate that today over 60 percent of young couples living together are not married. Is this really a good idea? Consider this: a child born to a cohabiting couple has only a one in three chance that both parents will still be around by the time he or she turns 12.

There are plenty of life decisions where God does not have mandates—type of car to drive, buy vs. rent, one career vs. another. But he has intense interest in what people do with his foundational designs for family, gender, and marriage. In the Sixth Commandment (see Exodus 20), he expressly forbade sexual activity outside of a committed marriage bond. It's his will in New Testament times too: **"Marriage should be honored by all, and the marriage bed kept pure, for God will judge the adulterer and all the sexually immoral"** (Hebrews 13:4).

Cohabiting (i.e., sharing a home and a bed) is a bad idea for that reason alone. Why deliberately insult the God who made you and who has given you so much? Isn't your life hard enough without inviting God's anger over what he terms adultery? Can't you trust him to have designed a way of life that will bring you happiness?

We need to support the vulnerable couples who are choosing to wait. In today's culture they might be feeling pretty lonely.

Believing he's good

Diana Kerr

If you're a fan of Tony Robbins or other self-help gurus, you may have heard this concept: What you focus on becomes your reality.

It's pretty accurate. Focus on your kids being a burden, and they will be. Focus on thinking that a certain person dislikes you, and you'll believe it. Our brains seek out truths—reference statements—to support whatever we focus on.

So I want to know: What are you believing about God these days? Are you focusing on his goodness, faithfulness, love, grace, promises, and protection? Or are you focused elsewhere, blinded to these things because you're distracted or you're believing lies?

Psalm 34:8 encourages us to acknowledge the goodness of God: **"Taste and see that the Lord is good; blessed is the one who takes refuge in him."**

Taste and *see*. I love that. This makes me want to really open my eyes, quiet myself and the outside world, be present with the Lord, and focus on the reality that he is good and he is a precious refuge for my weary body, overwhelmed mind, and sin-stained heart. We're missing out on so much when we journey through life believing a reality other than this.

I know this is easier said than done, so can I give you some practical tips? Start a gratitude journal. Turn off the music in the car and be present in your surroundings. Wake up five minutes earlier to sit with the Lord. You will quickly discover that he is so good!

Names of God: LORD (Yahweh)

Pastor Mark Jeske

What's in a name? In mine, not much. The name itself, Mark, just refers to a pencil check in a box or a blemish on a surface or an identifying sign. I was named after a biblical character, but the name itself has no hidden meaning.

Not so in Hebrew—it seems as if every Hebrew name is designed to have a special message. Samuel, for instance, means "heard by God" and was given to her little boy by a grateful woman who feared she was permanently infertile. No surprise, then, that the proper name by which our God revealed himself to his Israelite believers would have a powerful meaning. There is no English equivalent; the closest we can get is "The LORD." The proper name, transliterated as *Jahveh* (i.e., *Jehovah*), or *Yahweh*, is a verbal variation of the Hebrew verb *I* AM.

The name emphasizes God's eternal existence and his rock-steady purpose. He once explained that dual nature of that purpose to his champion Moses, letting him see the intensity of his glory from behind as he passed by: **"He passed in front of Moses, proclaiming, 'The LORD, the LORD, the compassionate and gracious God, slow to anger, abounding in love and faithfulness, maintaining love to thousands, and forgiving wickedness, rebellion and sin. Yet he does not leave the guilty unpunished'"** (Exodus 34:6,7).

Does that sound like a paradox? It is. On Calvary the LORD both punished and forgave the world's sin.

Exclusivity

Pastor Daron Lindemann

Jesus once said, **"I am the way and the truth and the life. No one comes to the Father except through me"** (John 14:6).

The exclusivity of Jesus as the only Savior is a truth we are blessed to believe, but sometimes we forget it.

In fact, sometimes we're tempted to treat Jesus as if he's in our way. We grow enamored with our own opinion as truth. And the life that possesses our souls is this earthly life. But when Jesus isn't our only way, our only truth, and our only life, then he isn't our Savior.

Jesus brings you to the Father, who is so glad that you are no longer detoured or dead-ended by your lesser ways and who is so strong to forgive and bless. "I am the way," he promises. He doesn't just show you the way. Jesus *is* the way.

Jesus communicates with you in the Bible. He doesn't demand that you resolve every problem. "I am the truth," he promises. Make everything in your life a spiritual issue, and you will find the answers that you need.

Jesus makes you first place and gives you everything he has, even his life. In his dying and rising, Jesus awakens you to a new life of your own dying to your sinful self and rising too. "I am the life," Jesus promises.

If those who are troubled by the exclusivity of Jesus can observe him as the only Savior, they will be troubled no more.

Income inequality envy

Pastor Mark Jeske

One of the most disagreeable parts of a political campaign season is listening to candidate speeches that stoke people's fears, resentments, and envy. Negative emotions always seem to motivate people better than happy thoughts; angry voters are more likely to go to the polls than contented voters.

One of the issues that has resonated profoundly with the electorate in recent years is resentment over "income inequality." Getting all the people who feel they've been cheated out of the prosperity they deserve to gravitate toward your political party has been working as a campaign strategy. I fear that strategy though. All of us, me included, are vulnerable enough to Satan's temptations to be discontented with our lives, and we don't need to throw any more wood into the fire under that boiler.

The psalm writer Asaph had his own problems with income inequality resentments: **"I envied the arrogant when I saw the prosperity of the wicked. They have no struggles; their bodies are healthy and strong. They are free from common human burdens"** (Psalm 73:3-5). Everybody else is doing so well—why do I always get the short end of the stick?

The truth is that other people have their own miseries. All of us have been blessed by God. We have more than we need, and we know that soon we'll have to leave it behind anyway. Envy is a black hole with no bottom. Let's spend our energy cultivating contented hearts and rejoice that we have enough to share.

I want to be more generous, less selfish

Pastor Mark Jeske

Everybody, and I mean everybody, at every age, at every income level, at every rung of the personal balance sheet ladder has a reason not to be a giver. You can claim poverty, youth, debts, growing family, mortgage and auto loan payments, business exposure, impending retirement, fixed income, and many other reasons, and you can talk yourself into holding onto every dime.

It seems like an iron law of economic logic: The more I give, the less I will have. The less I give, the more I will have. Logical, but false. Completely false, because it defies God's structure of economic convection.

God himself is incredibly generous. He pours love and mercy and resources into people's lives, and when his generosity ignites a fire in people's lives and they become generous, *he sends them even more! Seriously!* **"One person gives freely, yet gains even more; another withholds unduly, but comes to poverty. A generous person will prosper; whoever refreshes others will be refreshed"** (Proverbs 11:24,25).

What makes God's generosity convection system work is that it's not a closed system. He enjoys injecting more resources into the lives of his children. He's a God of abundance, not scarcity. He loves it when you trust his Word and expect his promises. He loves it when you and I show the same generosity toward other people that he has shown to us.

Say it with me: the more I give, the more I have.

"God works in mysterious ways"
Pastor Mark Jeske

People will be telling a story about how some good fortune came to them in the strangest way and they will smile, shrug, and say appreciatively, "God certainly works in mysterious ways." And they will be right. He does indeed, but that phrase was not drawn from Scripture.

It comes from the British poet William Cowper (pronounced "Cooper"), whose marvelous little poem appeared in England in 1774:

> *God moves in a mysterious way*
> *His wonders to perform;*
> *He plants his footsteps in the sea*
> *And rides upon the storm.*

Cowper continued with another five stanzas that found delight in God's hidden plans that always work out for the good of his children.

Cowper was absolutely right. In the moment, God's ways can seem frustratingly opaque.

"Why am I suffering like this?" "Why are my prayers unanswered?" "Why is my life so full of setbacks and my unbelieving neighbor's so easy?" But all things work together for the good of those who love the Lord, and in the end we can look back and marvel at how God stitched everything together in a beautiful tapestry.

"Oh, the depth of the riches of the wisdom and knowledge of God! How unsearchable his judgments, and his paths beyond tracing out! 'Who has known the mind of the Lord? Or who has been his counselor?'" (Romans 11:33,34).

Speak up while there's time

Pastor Mark Jeske

I can't get too angry with people who aren't motivated by the urgency of Scripture's call to repentance, warnings of hell, and the soon coming of the day of judgment. Every day we are bombarded with advertisements urging us, "Call now!" "Time is running out!" "Hurry!" We have all figured out long ago that all that urgency is contrived. We don't have to hurry at all.

But God means it. Life is short and uncertain, and eternity is long. People who are connected to Christ in faith will rise again to glory in heaven. People who have no time for God during their earthly lives will find that God has no time for them when they are judged. "Apart from me, evildoers, into the fire prepared for the devil and his angels," they will hear.

You and I are part of God's rescue team. Your words to the lost ones really do matter: **"My brothers and sisters, if one of you should wander from the truth and someone should bring that person back, remember this: Whoever turns a sinner from the error of their way will save them from death and cover over a multitude of sins"** (James 5:19,20). Don't hold back. Your personal eloquence is not the difference maker. When you speak God's words, the power and persuasiveness come from God.

Do you know even one person who hasn't heard the gospel? Speak up while there's time.

Undivided heart

Pastor Mark Jeske

It's a cowboy movie cliché. An American Indian chief sits in a war council, listening to the proposals that a federal agent is bringing. He isn't liking what he's hearing. His deep voice rumbles gravely, "Paleface speak with forked tongue." Everybody knows what he means—that the government representative is saying one thing but actually planning the opposite.

Saying what you mean and meaning what you say is called *integrity*. It means your word can be relied upon. It means people can trust you. It means people will know your true intent by what you say.

You know, it's possible to attend church worship with a forked tongue. It's possible to sing words of praise you don't mean, nod agreement to a sermon you don't agree with, and say prayers that don't come from your heart. It's not too hard to fool fellow parishioners, but God cannot be mocked. King David knew that and feared his own capacity for double-mindedness: **"Teach me your way, Lord, that I may rely on your faithfulness; give me an *undivided* heart, that I may fear your name"** (Psalm 86:11).

Integrity in worship means that when you confess your sins, you are truly sorry for offending God and hurting other people. It means that you really do see Jesus Christ as your only hope of forgiveness and immortality. And it means that you truly do intend to amend your sinful life.

No forks in your tongue and no divide in your heart.

Eager for the Lord's Supper

Pastor Daron Lindemann

What if you had only one day to live? What would you do? Jesus had one day left to live, and he shared his Holy Supper with his disciples.

Even though Jesus' disciples argued over who was the greatest. Even though they secretly sinned, were slow to believe, and would publicly deny him and abandon him, Jesus spoke to his disciples in the upper room: **"I have eagerly desired to eat this Passover with you before I suffer"** (Luke 22:15).

Think of a time when you just couldn't wait for an upcoming event, an appointment with a new client, a date, a job interview, a vacation. It probably distracted you from the daily routine so you couldn't focus on much of anything else. Jesus says he felt this same way about eating with his disciples *before* he suffered. Later wouldn't do.

Waiting for them to better understand, better behave, better believe was not an option. Jesus didn't need that. He wanted to—eagerly desired to—share this intimate, personal moment with these slackers and sinners the way they were right then.

No changes were necessary for them. No changes are necessary for you.

Jesus is eager for you to join him in the Lord's Supper, instructed in his Word and invited by his grace. Eat and drink. As you are, repentant sinner. And when you do, you'll find that instead of you changing for the Lord's Supper . . . the Lord's Supper changes you.

Vulcan salute

Pastor Mark Jeske

The television series *Star Trek* produced only three years' worth of shows and was then canceled by NBC. But the show had developed a passionate fan base and soon went into more or less permanent syndication, spinning off movies, graphic novels, and fan conventions. One of the iconic characters, a part-human part-Vulcan named Mr. Spock, often gave the traditional Vulcan blessing upon departing: "Live long and prosper." To give the greeting properly, you need to hold up your right hand, palm outward and thumb extended, with a big gap between your third and fourth fingers.

It's a sweet thing to say to a departing friend. It needs to be acknowledged, however, that the *Star Trek* scriptwriters stole that idea from the Bible. Repeatedly in Scripture God promises to intervene in the lives of his believers when they believe his words and put them into practice: **"My son, do not forget my teaching, but keep my commands in your heart, for they will prolong your life many years and bring you peace and prosperity"** (Proverbs 3:1,2).

That doesn't mean all believers will live to age 100 and be wealthy. It does mean that God promises both to improve the quality and increase the length of our lives on earth. He will delay attacks of illness and deflect major injuries. He will send extra resources and people to help us along. His Word helps us find joy and rid our souls of the toxic sludge of bitterness and self-pity.

Best of all—we get to boldly go beyond the stars where all the saints are waiting.

Tent living
Diana Kerr

What do you want to improve about your living space? Personally, I have Pinterest boards full of ideas. If you're a dude, maybe you have a mental list of some guy projects you'd like to undertake: build a deck, put a workbench in the basement, etc.

I get sucked into the home improvement world easily. I honestly try to avoid watching HGTV, even though I adore a good episode of *Fixer Upper* as much as the next person.

The problem is that I expect too much of my home. I set the bar too high for something that 1) exists here on the soil of this earth and 2) is not going to last. I'm just setting myself up for disappointment, distraction, and even idolatry.

Scripture verses like this snap me back to reality: **"We know that if the earthly tent we live in is destroyed, we have a building from God, an eternal house in heaven, not built by human hands"** (2 Corinthians 5:1).

Did you see what word was used there? *Tent.* The Bible uses this word multiple times when talking about our homes and about our bodies. Picturing my home as nothing more than a tent *majorly* reduces my expectations of how great it should be and what it should provide me. It's temporary.

So who cares about earthly tents? I've got an eternal mansion waiting for me that Jesus bought for me. I'm asking for God's help to focus on *that* instead.

I want to be more confident, less worried

Pastor Mark Jeske

Anxiety is like a contagious disease. It's everywhere. Just look at how many people in our country regularly use antidepressant medication to get through their days. Think of how many others self-medicate with alcohol or "recreational" drugs. People's lives are full of stress, fear, anxiety, and worry. There is violent unrest all over the world. Even economic geniuses can't figure out what's going on with our national economy, and where does that leave the little guy? People are worried about their health and their retirement savings, and they're even more fearful about their children.

Imagine if you were plucked up off your couch and temporarily set into the living room of a family 150 years ago. Would you be surprised to hear those family members fretting over the country's economic and military situation? Think of how reassuring you could be that everything was going to work out all right.

Jesus has the advantage of having seen all the world's history. When you are connected by faith into the family of the triune God, you have the protection and resources of the almighty God behind you. Jesus once counseled his stressed disciples: **"Therefore I tell you, do not worry about your life. . . . Look at the birds of the air; they do not sow or reap or store away in barns, and yet your heavenly Father feeds them. Are you not much more valuable than they?"** (Matthew 6:25,26). This is how valuable you are to your Father: he sent his divine Son to die for you.

Breathe.

Free from anxiety and worry
Diana Kerr

Let's talk about the Proverbs 31 woman.

I know she has a tendency to induce guilt and inadequacy. Whether you are a woman or a man, I get that you probably don't want to be held to the standard of the Proverbs 31 woman with all that she accomplishes in a given day. So rather than focusing on how well this fictitious superwoman tackles her to-do list, what if we first focused on her *attitude*? See, nothing that she accomplished would mean much if she went about it in a stressed-out, frantic, high-anxiety, snapping-at-her-family kind of way.

Proverbs 31:25 describes this woman's approach to life, it says, **"She can laugh at the days to come."** My self-study Bible says this means, "She is free from anxiety and worry." Whoa. How's that for a healthy attitude? How is it even possible that this ultra-busy woman is free from anxiety and worry? Did Prozac exist in Bible times?

What does it take to live free from anxiety and worry? It takes trust that God can accomplish through you what he needs to in the time that's available, even though it never seems like enough. It takes deep confidence in his promises that he's got everything under control and that no matter what happens, *he is enough*. It takes an eternal perspective that this life is more than to-do lists but about a God whose grace changes the way in which we approach everything we do on earth as we both work and rest to his glory.

Empirically verifiable doctrine

Pastor Mark Jeske

British author G. K. Chesterton once noted that the scriptural doctrine of original sin was the only one that is empirically verifiable: "Certain new theologians dispute original sin," he said, "which is the only part of Christian theology which can really be proved." "Original" sin is that which inheres in people already at birth, or as David writes in Psalm 51, even from conception itself. Thus it is a condition of the soul even before it expresses itself in sinful thoughts, words, and deeds.

You sure don't need to be a Christian to be convinced that evil exists on a massive scale on earth. The cruelties and barbarities of war and crime cannot be shrugged off—they march on century after century. However, at least some people may need persuading that evil lives in them.

St. Paul leaves us with no such illusions: **"There is no one righteous, not even one; there is no one who understands; there is no one who seeks God"** (Romans 3:10,11). I am morally no better than you, and you are no better than your neighbor. We are all in this mess together. But we have all been equally redeemed by Christ, whose shed blood is sufficient to wash clean all humanity: **"He is the atoning sacrifice for our sins, and not only for ours but also for the sins of the whole world"** (1 John 2:2). Alas, the doctrine of the grand redemption is not empirically verifiable.

But it is found in the Bible. Do you believe it? Will you share it?

Grow your vocabulary: Atonement

Pastor Mark Jeske

The Bible is a collection of sacred writings that spans more than 16 centuries. Its writers used quite a variety of genres and styles—history, law, sermons, poetry, proverb, musical libretto, letters, and prophecy. The New Testament begins with five books of stories, and then come the epistles (letters) that explain what happened and apply those truths to people's lives. Thus the epistles are a little more abstract; they are couched in the language of doctrine.

Want to grow your biblical vocabulary? Let's start with the word *atonement*. Example: **"For this reason he had to be made like them, fully human in every way, in order that he might become a merciful and faithful high priest in service to God, and that he might make *atonement* for the sins of the people"** (Hebrews 2:17). Here's a word that for once doesn't come from Hebrew, Greek, or Latin. In fact its roots are from English itself.

It is the grave dilemma of the human race that our terminally sinful condition is inherited by our children. Their little bodies bear the curse even before they learn to speak. All humanity by birth is *at odds* with God. It is the great work of Christ to make us *at one* instead. (Get it? "At one"?) He allowed himself to be forsaken by his Father on a cross so that he might bring us back together.

This great atonement embraces the greatest of all paradoxes: Christ died to make us alive.

The joy of the Lord

Pastor Mark Jeske

Sometimes the Bible's message makes you sad. God's holy law demands a level of purity and holiness that makes us feel dirty by comparison. **"If you, Lord, kept a record of sins, Lord, who could stand?"** (i.e., guiltless before you) says Psalm 130:3.

But God's mercy triumphs over judgment, and his gospel has the last word over the law's condemnation. That's why rejoicing and celebration are always the dominant emotions in a believer's heart. Nehemiah did not want the Israelites' shame over their past failings to cloud their confidence in their Savior-God: **"Then Nehemiah the governor, Ezra the priest and teacher of the Law, and the Levites who were instructing the people said to them all, 'This day is holy to the Lord your God. Do not mourn or weep.' For all the people had been weeping as they listened to the words of the Law. Nehemiah said, 'Go and enjoy choice food and sweet drinks, and send some to those who have nothing prepared. This day is holy to our Lord. Do not grieve, for the joy of the Lord is your strength'"** (Nehemiah 8:9,10).

The gospel of our Savior Jesus is the source of strength for the way in which we live our lives. Shame, guilt, pressure, and nagging bring nothing but grudging, short-term bursts of better behavior, and we soon lapse. What changes hearts and inspires a life of love is the gospel message of forgiveness, favor, and immortality in Christ.

The joy of the Lord is our strength.

Names of God: Paracl

Pastor Mark Jeske

I love the richness and historical sweep of the story of the Christian church. But I hasten to add that I feel a little compassion for newbies to the faith who run into a multilingual buzz saw when they hear the liturgy and sing the old hymns for the first time. It must sound like insider talk only for those who know Hebrew, Greek, and Latin.

One of those obscure but beautiful terms is Jesus' special name for the Holy Spirit, which admittedly sounds like a set of track shoes. On the night of his betrayal and arrest, he gave his nervous disciples big news about a coming gift: **"All this I have spoken while still with you. But the Advocate** [Greek *Parákletos*]**, the Holy Spirit, whom the Father will send in my name, will teach you all things and will remind you of everything I have said to you"** (John 14:25,26).

The Greek verb on which this unique name is built means to function as a coach. What do good coaches do for their players? They teach. They plan. They prepare. They yell. They encourage. They console. All that is *exactly* what the Holy Spirit does for believers. The Paraclete comes to live in you the moment you are baptized and begins his coaching work. You too can expect teaching, scolding, encouragement, guidance, pushing, and comfort from the third person of the Trinity.

He does all that not to beat you down or drive you crazy. He does all that to develop the gifts he's given you.

Without faith you can't please God

Pastor Mark Jeske

Who are the people most admired in your community? Star athletes—yeah, probably. Wealthy socialites and top businesspeople—yep. Organizers of human relief projects—certainly. Who are the "good people" on your block? You know—the ones with tidy lawns and a fairly recent paint job . . . don't have loud drunken parties . . . keep their dog on a leash . . . kids don't run wild.

Does God think you're a good person? If you want something from the Almighty, how do you mentally justify your request? Do you rehearse all the good things you've done lately? Save your breath. The key is faith, faith in Christ your Savior. **"Without faith it is impossible to please God, because anyone who comes to him must believe that he exists and that he rewards those who earnestly seek him"** (Hebrews 11:6).

Jesus taught that nobody can approach the Father except through him. It is not your performance that makes God approve of you but Christ's performance. All his obedience and his holiness are now attributed to your account. All the good and selfless and servant-hearted things you've done for the past month aren't to work your way into his favor but are gestures of love and appreciation for what God has already done for you. Through Christ's work we now can approach God not as distant, quirky royalty surrounded by an impenetrable bureaucracy, but as our Daddy.

That close. That dear.

I want to be more spiritual, less worldly
Pastor Mark Jeske

Here's one of our dilemmas as Christians: God made a beautiful world for us to live in. It is full of treats, attractions, and sensory delights, all of which he made to bring us pleasure. Travel, golf, cabernets, gardening, web surfing, scotch, dancing, and zip-lining are all great fun. But all of them can also turn into time wasters, money pits, addictions, and ultimately harmful distractions from developing our relationship with God.

How do you know when your love for these things is getting unhealthy? When they stoke your own self-absorbed narcissism. When you're too busy to go to church. When there is no time in the week for reading your Bible. When your life is too full to accept a ministry role in your congregation. When your relationships with other family members are fraying. If you are not sure if any of these things applies to you, ask someone in your family.

What to do? **"Like newborn babies, crave pure spiritual milk, so that by it you may grow up in your salvation"** (1 Peter 2:2). Take inventory of the things that you know really matter. Is God where he belongs in your life—on the throne? Is your spouse still your number-one person? Are you risking your job and income with your passions? Are you spending enough time with your children?

Grow in your ability to enjoy God's treats without becoming worldly. How would you live if you knew you had only a week left?

Extravagant worship

Pastor Mark Jeske

Even a casual reading of the life of Christ in the gospels reveals great humility of lifestyle. The Lord who reigned from his sapphire throne in heaven, attended by 10,000 X 10,000 angels, made sure his disciples knew about livin' small. His messages counseled his followers to live generously and care for the poor. Still true today.

But there is a place for extravagance, and that is in worship. The care and sacrifice that the Israelites put into the construction of the great temple in Jerusalem sent a message to all visitors of how much the Israelites valued their relationship with their God. Jesus himself had some striking things to say about a woman who spent a fortune on a single act of worship: **"Then Mary took about a pint of pure nard, an expensive perfume; she poured it on Jesus' feet and wiped his feet with her hair. . . . 'Leave her alone,' Jesus replied. 'It was intended that she should save this perfume for the day of my burial'"** (John 12:3,7).

It is good to learn the disciplines of living modestly, even humbly. It is even better to be free with your time and money in giving a hand up to other people who are struggling. It is grandest of all to be generous, even extravagant, in worshiping the God who has given you everything, both now and in eternity.

Our kind Father, loving Savior, and mighty Spirit are worthy of your best. Your *best*!

In government we trust?

Pastor Daron Lindemann

The U.S. currency motto "In God We Trust" has incited debates since it first appeared on a two-cent coin during the Civil War. President Teddy Roosevelt ordered the phrase removed from new gold coins in 1907. New secular sentiments threaten it further.

Is America "going to hell in a handbasket" if we can't keep God on our money? if we can't pray publicly in public schools? if the Ten Commandments aren't flanking the doorways of every courthouse? Some say yes. The Bible says no. **"The authorities that exist have been established by God. For the one in authority is God's servant for your good. But if you do wrong, be afraid, for rulers do not bear the sword for no reason. They are God's servants, agents of wrath to bring punishment on the wrongdoer"** (Romans 13:1,4).

It is not the God-given duty of earthly government to teach the Bible or proclaim the gospel. That's the job of Christians (Matthew 28:18-20). The government's purpose is to enact laws, use force, and keep peace and order for the common good. They "bear the sword" as "agents of wrath"; they don't bring good tidings of great joy from the mouth of God.

Leave that to Christians who trust in the only true God and all the teachings of his Word. Thank God for our government and our religious freedoms. Thank the government for doing its job. And take time to do yours.

"Actions speak louder than words"

Pastor Mark Jeske

"People lie; actions don't," they say. How true. So is this: "Actions speak louder than words." Talk sometimes really is cheap. It costs nothing and can't be verified in and of itself. Deeds matter. It's there that you will find the truth.

That proverb sounds as if it came from the Bible, but it didn't. In that specific wording it goes back at least to 1736 in a letter from one Boston gentleman to another. But the truth of the proverb aligns with any number of Bible passages. Jesus himself urged his followers not only to evaluate the content of the messages of people who claimed to be religious leaders but to pay attention to their deeds as well: **"Watch out for false prophets. They come to you in sheep's clothing, but inwardly they are ferocious wolves. By their fruit you will recognize them. Do people pick grapes from thornbushes, or figs from thistles?"** (Matthew 7:15,16). Evil deeds invalidate the spiritual credibility of the speaker.

On the flip side, positive deeds *gain* credibility for those with the Christian message. When new Christian missions are planted in third-world countries, they often get rooted more quickly when they have a humanitarian component. The mercy ministries that help people with health care, water engineering and purification, and education make the gospel message more believable to skeptical onlookers.

Does your congregation have visible ways for people to help one another and serve your community?

Leaning on a spider's web

Diana Kerr

Tell me about your biggest stressors, the things you strive for, and the things you're attached to, and I bet I can tell you what it is that you trust in this life. Many of us are unconsciously led by these misguided reliances and beliefs.

Some of us lean on our marriages or our families, believing that the key to a good life is a strong family unit. Some of us lean on money, believing that financial stability will pave the way to peace. Some of us lean on our accomplishments, believing that we're worth more when we cross off a bunch of stuff on our to-do lists.

We all do this in some form or another. Our sinful hearts are not as allegiant to God as we think they are and as we want them to be. So we lean on earthly things, often good blessings from our Lord, but those things are so much less reliable than we realize.

The book of Job talks about this challenge and describes the actions of those who have forgotten God: **"What they trust in is fragile; what they rely on is a spider's web. They lean on the web, but it gives way; they cling to it, but it does not hold"** (8:14,15).

Friend, what are you clinging to that's as weak as a spider's web? What if you put that thing back in its rightful place in your heart and lean on God? I promise you it'd be a game changer.

Only if or even if

Pastor Daron Lindemann

David Livingstone, a legendary missionary to Africa in the 19th century, was contacted by a mission society eager to send a few good men to help. They asked if there was a good road to the missionary's current location.

Livingstone wrote back, "If you have men who will come only if there is a good road, I don't want them. I want men who will come even if there is no road."

When Jesus called his first disciples, they didn't set up conditions like politicians who stuff their little pet projects into bills as a condition for voting yes. "Jesus, I'll follow you only if . . ." They left their nets, their jobs, even their families, and followed.

When Jesus predicted that Peter would disown him, **"Peter insisted emphatically, 'Even if I have to die with you, I will never disown you.' And all the others said the same"** (Mark 14:31). Sure, in the moment Peter was confident, and then in another moment he didn't have the courage. But maybe later he remembered these words, their heartfelt intent, and the grace of Jesus to hear them once again.

"Even if . . . I have to endure a hardship . . . I have to control my lust . . . I have to say no to my boyfriend . . . I have to give until it hurts . . . I have to die, I will, Jesus. You came into my life with no conditions. So I will follow you, even if there is no road."

Racial reconciliation:
Guess who's coming to dinner?

Pastor Mark Jeske

Are you a Harry Potter fan? Then you know what a "Mudblood" is. The pure-blooded wizards could be very arrogant, looking down at a young wizard or witch who might have a non-magical parent (a.k.a. a "Muggle"). When Draco Malfoy called Hermione a Mudblood, it was a racist term of contempt.

Harry Potter is fictitious. Moses is real. And there is tribal pride in real life too. Moses had married a woman named Zipporah, and she was not an Israelite. Moses' brother and especially his sister resented the woman for her racial background: **"Miriam and Aaron began to talk against Moses because of his Cushite wife, for he had married a Cushite"** (Numbers 12:1). The land of Cush is located between the second and third cataracts of the Nile, today's Sudan. The Greeks called the people who lived there Ethiopians (i.e., "burnt faces") because of their dark skin. Though Zipporah was from the Sinai Desert region, Miriam must have believed her to be part African because of her dark skin.

Our country has a long and bitter history of fear of miscegenation, i.e., mingling of the races through intermarriage. Has anybody in your close family dated or married outside the tribe? You can be God's agent of racial reconciliation by making "other" people in your family to feel welcomed and respected.

After all, everybody on earth is descended from the same parents. The only race that really matters is the human race.

Racial reconciliation:
Accept people not like you

Pastor Mark Jeske

The congregation in Rome must have been very diverse, as diverse as the huge metropolitan area in which it was formed. In the long list of people whom Paul greeted by name in the last chapter of his letter to them are found Hebrew, Greek, and Latin names; men and women leaders; travelers and locals. There would have been both slaves and freemen in the congregation. When left to themselves, people *always* clump together with those just like them, so there needed to be extra glue added to the mix to bring and keep people together.

That's why Paul found it necessary to state some important things that should have been obvious but weren't: **"Accept one another, then, just as Christ accepted you, in order to bring praise to God"** (Romans 15:7). The gaps that seem to separate people of different races, languages, geographical regions, cultures, ages, economic and social classes, and genders are nothing compared to the enormous gap between a holy God and his sinful ex-children.

Christ solved that problem by coming to earth in person and becoming not just like us but one of us. His incarnation bonded him to us forever. In that way he was able to represent us as our holy Substitute before the Father, bringing us the holiness and righteousness we could never earn. In that way he also demonstrated for us how to treat people not like us—with respect, love, and acceptance.

How accepting is your congregation?

Racial reconciliation:
They hate sheepherders

Pastor Mark Jeske

prej•u•dice (prĕj´ə-dĭs) *n.* An adverse opinion or judgment formed beforehand, without knowledge of or examination of the facts.

It's fairly easy to spot prejudice in others, not quite so easy in yourself. Prejudice comes from arrogance of tribe, laziness of inquiry, desire for power over others, and unwillingness to share a place in the game. Satan despises the human race, and it brings his twisted mind a sick joy to get us to do the same.

Prejudice has been around a long time. Assistant Pharaoh Joseph, originally from Canaan and now residing in the royal palaces of Egypt, explained to his Canaanite brothers why the Egyptians would leave them alone if they moved to the Nile delta region of Goshen: **" . . . you should answer, 'Your servants have tended livestock from our boyhood on, just as our fathers did.' Then you will be allowed to settle in the region of Goshen, for all shepherds are detestable to the Egyptians"** (Genesis 46:34).

Why pick on sheepherders? What's not to like about wool and lamb chops? Prejudices aren't logical. But they are certainly hurtful. As God's agents of reconciliation in his broken world, you and I can make a difference in our circles by opening up our minds to see value in people not like us. Each of us has gaps and holes in his or her cultural heritage. By bonding with others, we become richer and more complete.

february

Love one another. As I have loved you,
so you must love on another.

John 13:34

Stop talking so much

Diana Kerr

The title of the book sounds iffy, but overall I love *How to Win Friends and Influence People*. Basically, this book teaches you how to make people feel appreciated, liked, and understood, which in turn also makes life better for you.

One of the book's hardest lessons is this: stop talking so much. That's not easy! All of us have a bit of an ego, and most of us like talking about ourselves more than we like listening.

Not surprisingly, the Bible was touting this concept of listening more and talking less *way* before Dale Carnegie got around to writing about it. Proverbs is full of juicy, applicable advice on this topic (which, if you saw me in social situations, you would see I am not the best at following). Proverbs 12:23 hits me hard, right where it hurts the most: **"The prudent keep their knowledge to themselves, but a fool's heart blurts out folly."**

My heart's convicted by the missed opportunities God may have placed before me to build people up or grow a relationship with them that I ruined because I couldn't shut up, even though I thought I had interesting knowledge to share. If you're in the same boat as me, let's pray that before we go into each social situation God would help us focus on *others* and remember that the wisest person in the room is *not* usually the one talking the most.

Use what you've got
Pastor Mark Jeske

"Do what you can, with what you've got, where you are." Thus spoke Theodore Roosevelt in his autobiography, and he is dead on. If you give in to the temptation to belittle your resources, envy others, make excuses for your inaction, blame others, and pity yourself as an endless victim, you will waste your life, deprive others of your actual abilities, and insult the God who blessed you in the first place.

The apostle Peter wanted each of his readers to feel like part of God's team: **"*Each of you* should use whatever gift you have received to serve others, as faithful stewards of God's grace in its various forms. If anyone speaks, they should do so as one who speaks the very words of God. If anyone serves, they should do so with the strength God provides, so that in all things God may be praised through Jesus Christ"** (1 Peter 4:10,11).

Why aren't people doing this? Because they don't like their gifts and wish they had those of others. Because they listened to the whisperings of the evil one and think they have nothing. Because they are lazy and willing to coast on the labors of others. Stop! You are gifted! You are needed! If you are unsure of your gifts, ask other people at your church what they value in you. State out loud what you're passionate about.

Ask the Holy Spirit within you to speak up just a little bit louder.

If you can't find happiness

Pastor Daron Lindemann

Today eight out of ten Americans believe that enjoying yourself is the highest goal of life and to find happiness you need to look within yourself. But what do we see in there? New studies suggest that it's not good.

Consider the new pressures of social media. Previously the home was a place to relax. We could forget about our acne or bad hair or out-of-date clothing. Nobody was watching. There was no competition or comparing.

Now wherever we go—even at home—social media is buzzing, and the competition and comparing goes with us. Everybody is always watching. We're on display, and the pressure is stressing us out. There is always someone better looking, more organized, or living the dream that we're not. It can be depressing.

"I know that there is nothing better for people than to be happy and to do good while they live. That each of them may eat and drink, and find satisfaction in all their toil—this is the gift of God" (Ecclesiastes 3:12,13).

Happiness isn't a personal experience. Nor is it feeling good on the inside. Happiness is a gift from God. Happiness is being grateful for food and drink from a loving Father. Happiness is believing in divine promises. Happiness is serving others with a fulfillment of God's reflected love.

You can't find true happiness until you look to God for it. Then you will know it's his gift to you.

"Inerrant": Not in the Bible?

Pastor Mark Jeske

You know what's just as bad as taking something out of the Bible or denying what's in the Bible? Adding teachings to the Bible, that's what. In the very last words of Scripture, at the very end of Revelation, God puts a severe curse on anybody who does either.

Does it surprise you that there are some doctrinal terms in frequent use among Christians that do not come from Scripture? Didn't I just say that that was forbidden? Well, perhaps the *word* itself is not found there, but the *concepts* behind the term certainly are. One such term is *inerrant*, i.e., without error. It is a helpful term because it is one-word shorthand for this: **"Prophecy never had its origin in the human will, but prophets, though human, spoke from God as they were carried along by the Holy Spirit"** (2 Peter 1:21).

That passage invites you to see all of Scripture's content as having been provided personally, word for word, by God. The human "authors" had their own vocabularies and life experiences, but the content is 100 percent controlled by God. Scripture is inspired, i.e., "in-Spirited," since the Holy Spirit carried along the prophets, evangelists, and apostles to record what he wanted.

That means you can trust that all the historical events recorded there really did happen, including Noah's great flood and Jonah's great fish. That means all the great things promised through Christ's crucifixion really are yours and all the glories of heaven really are waiting for you.

I'm lonely
Pastor Mark Jeske

You might think with a world population of over 7.4 billion that it would be pretty hard to be lonely on this planet. You might think that there is an army of potential friends just like you ready, willing, and able to be part of your life. You might think that insane new digital technology would make sure nobody got ignored or neglected, that relationships are now so easy to establish that nobody anywhere could feel alone. You might think all of those things, but you'd be wrong.

Truth is, you can be intensely lonely even in a big city, even inside a family: **"Turn to me and be gracious to me, for I am lonely and afflicted. Relieve the troubles of my heart"** (Psalm 25:16,17). (David lonely? Seriously?) How is that possible? A feeling of isolation, even when in a group, comes from fear, fear of rejection and mockery, the assumption that nobody could understand or empathize with what is going on in your life.

It comes from repeated disappointments, from being let down, from frequent criticism, from seldom hearing the magic words: "I love you." "You did well." "I appreciate you." It comes from low self-esteem—if I don't like myself, why should anybody else like me? The best feeling of connectedness is built on the ultimate connection—our loving heavenly Father's unconditional love: **"Though my father and mother forsake me, the Lord will receive me"** (Psalm 27:10).

Do you have any idea of how valuable and beautiful God thinks you are?

Make a difference: Be a teacher

Pastor Mark Jeske

When I think about the people, aside from my parents, who have had the greatest impact on my life, there would be a lot of teachers in the top ten. Multiplying that influence would be all the teachers who also coach. There may be no adult more significant in the life of a middle school or high school kid than his or her athletic coach.

Teachers open up new worlds to their students. They give them a new vocabulary. They encourage dreams and help to identify passions and strengths. They push students to excel beyond what the kids thought possible. They set a bar for excellence and show how to get there. Coaches help their athletes find their roles, bring out the best in them, encourage the weary, yell at the lazy, and pump energy into them all.

The most valuable of all the teachers and coaches are those who can do their work in the name of Christ, both in regular school and Sunday school. God values them too: **"Those who are wise will shine like the brightness of the heavens, and those who lead many to righteousness, like the stars for ever and ever"** (Daniel 12:3). Imagine the impact—not only for students' lives but for their eternity. Are you the right age to consider teaching or coaching as your life's work? Do you know some young people with the gifts and personalities to be great teachers or coaches?

Make a difference. Be a teacher.

What Jesus learned can teach us

Pastor Daron Lindemann

A championship basketball team doesn't have to be undefeated in the regular season to win the final tournament—sometimes they're even better prepared for the tournament because they've learned from a loss or two earlier in the season. Likewise, Jesus won salvation for us because trials and troubles along the way prepared him for the intense suffering and sacrifice.

"Son though he was, he learned obedience from what he suffered" (Hebrews 5:8). Jesus knew from eternity that he must obey God the Father because of his position as a son, just like all children know it's their duty to obey their parents. Then Jesus developed beyond that. He learned to obey his Father despite being tempted otherwise. He learned how much his Father loves him. Then he trusted him even more. He submitted his holy desires to those of the Father, and those desires merged to become one. That loving obedience developed more extensively in Jesus over time because of what he suffered.

If the Son of God can learn obedience because of suffering, can't suffering lead us to become more obedient as well?

Being made complete, Jesus "became the source of eternal salvation for all who obey him" (Hebrews 5:9). Jesus' painful prayers, tearful cries, and human suffering all helped to make him a complete Savior.

So now the question isn't *if* suffering teaches you but, rather, *how much*. And the Bible has the answer: completely. For salvation.

Names of God: Elohim

Pastor Mark Jeske

In the ancient Semitic languages of the Middle East, the main word for God is *El*, masculine plural *Elohim* (pronounced ello-HEEM). The root meaning seems to be power, majesty, and authority; all of which make him worthy of worship. The word occasionally may be used for government magistrates and angels, but its chief use is for the supreme deity. *Elohim* takes a plural verb when it is used for the heathen gods of other nations, but when used for the God of Israel, it takes a singular verb. *Hmm* . . . isn't that interesting?

The concept of the Trinity, three persons/one God, is more fully expressed in the New Testament, but there are plenty of hints and clues in the Old. Already in the first chapter of the Bible, Elohim is the all-powerful Creator, speaking his mighty words and watching his creation leap into being at his command. On the sixth day came these words: **"Then God** [Hebrew: *Elohim*] **said, 'Let *us* make mankind in our image'"** (Genesis 1:26). The rest of the Bible fills in more of the story—that Father, Son, and Spirit all participated fully in the plan and execution of creation week.

Every time you see that little three-letter word, *G-O-D*, remember the insanely enormous blast of energy that made all the matter of the universe out of nothing and then put it into beautiful and intricate order. Remember also that he will destroy it when he returns for judgment and that he will re-create a new world where he and we will live together forever.

Worship is praying

Pastor Mark Jeske

God realizes that he has you at a bit of a disadvantage. He can see you, but you can't see him. He can hear you plainly and directly, but you can hear him only indirectly. He's aware of the stress that places on you, and he makes allowances for it.

You honor him when you pray. Christian prayers acknowledge God as omnipresent, caring, omniscient, and all-powerful. Prayer accepts the posture of humility. We don't stand eyeball-to-eyeball, jawing and positioning ourselves in a contest of strength. Prayer isn't a debate. Prayer means we accept our relative smallness; we accept his design of human life, accept his ways, accept his wisdom and plans, and respect the enormous reservoirs of resources at his command.

And it means that we confess our need. **"Look to the Lord and his strength; seek his face always"** (1 Chronicles 16:11). It's not as though he's clueless to our needs, but he *wants* us to articulate them to him, so that when he helps us we will make the connection and give him the glory. He wants to hear our words of sorrow over sin so that he can assure us of his love and steady forgiveness in Christ. He *wants* us to bring the needs of others to him—not because he couldn't figure it out without our help, but because it is such a beautiful exercise of love and compassion. He loves to respond *because we prayed*.

He waits to be asked. Got a minute for him right now?

Freely give
Diana Kerr

We humans can be really stingy sometimes, can't we? Stingy with our possessions, stingy with our time, stingy with forgiveness . . .

It's like we think we've earned all the blessings and gifts we hoard, like *we* did something to build up this stockpile of love, grace, and riches we claim as our own.

Crazy enough, we actually have done literally *nothing* to deserve grace and forgiveness, so they are certainly not ours to hoard. And as far as physical blessings, yes, some things in this life require effort on our part, but honestly no matter how hard we work, we get zero results unless they're given to us by God.

How does this realization change things? How does it change the way we view that homeless person by the freeway exit ramp, the needs of our church, or that coworker who drives us crazy?

Jesus sent out his disciples to perform miracles in his name, sharing a beautiful truth wrapped up in a simple command: **"Freely you have received; freely give"** (Matthew 10:8).

In other words, what you've been given you got for free. So give it out freely, for free.

We will never exceed or even match the generosity of our Lord's spiritual and tangible blessings to us. But that doesn't mean we can't keep his generosity and goodness top of mind and then watch how our grip loosens on what we have as we freely pass on to others what he's freely given us.

What's it like to be right all the time?
Pastor Daron Lindemann

Do you know anyone who thinks she is right all the time? She actually is, if she believes in Jesus. The Bible has a word for that: *Righteous.*

It refers to an acceptable performance. It makes a person right. Like a résumé says, "I'm right for the job." This is a natural expectation not just about jobs but about God. We instinctively believe we are getting it right with God when we are performing acceptably.

This becomes self-righteousness. We all naturally seek our own righteousness in working or parenting or how responsible we are or how many friends we have. It makes us a "good person." Ah, but not good enough.

"But now apart from the law the righteousness of God has been made known. . . . This righteousness is given through faith in Jesus Christ to all who believe . . . for all have sinned and fall short of the glory of God, and all are justified freely by his grace through the redemption that came by Christ Jesus" (Romans 3:21-24).

"But now" there is another performance. The redemption performance of Christ Jesus is for us, not from us; given to us, not gained by us; created outside of us, not inside of us.

Believe it, and your struggle for acceptance ends, your craving for approval is filled, and your need to accomplish a list of things to feel good about your day is checked off. You're right. All the time.

Forgiveness that never ends

Diana Kerr

Have you ever worked really hard to forgive someone only to have him or her disappoint you *again*? Goodness, I definitely have. Let's be honest: as sinners who carry pride and bitterness, sometimes it takes us years to get over stuff and soften our hearts toward someone.

And then that person we worked so hard to forgive does something that requires us to forgive all over again. I have naively fallen into the trap of thinking that if I forgive someone once, it will be smooth sailing from there on out. However, our flawed, imperfect world doesn't always work that way.

The Jewish leaders of Jesus' time said you should only forgive someone three times. Jesus (our sinless Savior who has forgiven each of our sins an embarrassing amount of times), shattered that rule.

"Then Peter came to Jesus and asked, 'Lord, how many times shall I forgive my brother or sister who sins against me? Up to seven times?' Jesus answered, 'I tell you, not seven times, but seventy-seven times'" (Matthew 18:21,22).

In other words, our Lord wants us to forgive endlessly, over and over and over again. If by grace we are forgiven countless times, then that grace compels us to pass on that limitless forgiveness. Note that forgiveness doesn't mean you can't set boundaries or that you are condoning an action, but it does say, "I forgive you now, completely and unconditionally, and I will forgive you over and over again."

Make a difference: Be a leader

Pastor Mark Jeske

When people give some thought to leadership in the church, the first role to pop into their heads is probably that of pastor. Of course. Churches desperately need strong pastors who can speak the Word of God clearly, teach and counsel with love and care, recruit and manage volunteers, and inspire a culture of outreach.

But the church needs strong lay leaders *just as much*. Any healthy business needs a good balance between governance and management, *and the church does too*. Lay leaders evaluate the work of the pastoral staff; help set the mission, vision, and agenda; oversee the finances; own and manage the property; and approve the program of work. Lay leaders watch over the interests of the members of the congregation—after all, it's *their* church, not the pastor's church.

Has God given you the gifts for leadership? **"We have different gifts, according to the grace given to each of us. If your gift is . . . to encourage, then give encouragement. . . . If it is to lead, do it diligently"** (Romans 12:6,8). Leaders release energy in others, set the bar with personal buy-in and generosity, bring new workers onto the team, and know how to say thank you.

Don't be afraid to get involved. Choose a mentor and ask for advice to navigate the organization. Put up your hand and volunteer. Step up. Reach up. Serve like a leader and lead like a servant.

Make a difference. Be a leader.

The glamour of love

Pastor Daron Lindemann

Glamour Shots is a photo studio specializing in makeover photography. I've been in the homes of everyday-looking people, notice their Glamour Shots pictures, and think they should be magazine models for perfume or jeans.

But beware! If you have a Glamour Shots picture of yourself looking down on you from the mantle, it sometimes says, "Hey, why are you so ugly? You ought to look like this every day!" Something similar happens with wedding pictures. Couples struggling with needy kiddos or aging through the empty nest years wonder, *"Why is love so hard? Sometimes so ugly? What's wrong?"* It's just not glamorous anymore.

God experienced this when he came to earth. The smelly animal feeding trough didn't quite compare to his eternal paradise of heaven. The mess of people problems. Sin. Death. Evil spirits. So ugly.

For a moment, at his transfiguration, Jesus would look glamorous. **"The appearance of his face changed, and his clothes became as bright as a flash of lightning"** (Luke 9:29). This was a temporary impression, not everlasting good looks. The beauty of Jesus would soon be seen in his ugly suffering for sinners and his determination to wrestle with cursed death.

Valentine's Day is momentary glamour. The roses, the sweet whispers, warm hugs, and romantic dinners. Love won't always be this pretty, and that's okay. Enjoy it while you can. Soon love will sacrifice, struggle, and get messy again. True beauty. And Jesus smiles.

There is a greater power with us

Pastor Mark Jeske

Adolf Hitler kept the German people fighting and hoping longer by releasing rumors that his scientists had perfected a secret weapon that would tilt the war in their favor. The V1 and V2 rockets did cause a stir and some panic in England, but they did very little to change the outcome of the war.

As God's beloved children, you possess a number of secret weapons that give you major life advantages. The Word of the Lord guides you in life's major decisions. The angels of the Lord protect you from the ravages of the evil one. The Spirit of the Lord fills your heart and sustains you in trouble and adversity.

King Hezekiah knew these things and gave a brave and confident address to the people of Judah at a time of terrible national crisis: **"'Be strong and courageous. Do not be afraid or discouraged because of the king of Assyria and the vast army with him, for there is a greater power with us than with him. With him is only the arm of flesh, but with us is the LORD our God to help us and to fight our battles.' And the people gained confidence from what Hezekiah the king of Judah said"** (2 Chronicles 32:7,8).

Jesus really did defeat Satan. Heaven really did triumph over hell. Good is really mightier than evil. Light is really more powerful than darkness. Believe in the victory that Jesus has already won for you.

It's your secret weapon.

Sin is sin is sin
Diana Kerr

Let's talk real for a minute. We are often way more concerned about certain sins than others.

I rarely see Christians worked up about the spiritual dangers of overeating, gossip, worry, or excessive spending. However, homosexual attraction? College partying? Living together before marriage? There is loads of judgment doled out in these areas. Sadly, we even get more worked up about things that *aren't* sin—how to worship, vote, or raise kids—than we do about some of the "lesser" sins.

I get that it makes sense practically speaking to get more worked up about certain sin than others. But all sin is dangerous. It all separates us and distracts us from our loving, amazing God. The scary thing is that the seemingly less intense sins can cause these results just as easily as the "big" ones because they're so sneaky. We don't expect them to cause a rift between us and God, but they can and will.

Jesus warned his disciples, **"Be careful, or your hearts will be weighed down with carousing, drunkenness and the anxieties of life, and that day** (judgment day) **will close on you suddenly like a trap"** (Luke 21:34).

Every time Jesus lists out a sin like worry right along with the classic big, bad sins, I feel uncomfortable. I should. I want to watch myself carefully, own up to the fact that even my "little" sins are a big deal, and then run to Jesus for forgiveness.

I'm overwhelmed

Pastor Mark Jeske

It's a great feeling to be on top of all your responsibilities and jobs. It's misery to feel overwhelmed.

Maybe you overpromised, and now people are demanding work that is only partially complete. Maybe people you were counting on quit on you. Maybe you had some nasty personal reversals—a stretch of serious illness, investments gone sour, family crisis, or layoff of a breadwinner. Maybe you bit off way more than you could chew and are feeling pretty inadequate. The feeling is like when you're standing on tiptoes in deep water and you're afraid that the water level will soon reach your nose. Panic begins.

David was a tough fighter, military leader, and skilled organizer. But he had his moments of terror too: **"I waited patiently for the LORD; he turned to me and heard my cry. He lifted me out of the slimy pit, out of the mud and mire; he set my feet on a rock and gave me a firm place to stand"** (Psalm 40:1,2). In fact the very reason that the Lord let him get into so many deep holes was so that his rescuing mercy would become so obvious. As Jesus once told the grieving parents of a man born blind, those hardships had come so that the work of God might be displayed in his life.

When you are being overwhelmed, cry out to your Savior and watch for his big hand.

Shaken-up comforts
Diana Kerr

We all like comfort and routine to a degree. Even adventurous, spontaneous folks like some degree of predictability or consistency in certain areas of life.

With my hand raised in embarrassed admission, I'll admit that I like comfort, routine, and predictability *a lot*. I idolize an easy life, a life within my control that goes my way. I even prefer the comfort of my own sin to trying to deal with it.

But that's not how my God wants me to operate.

In the course of my life, he's rattled me from my comfort and sin and he's shaken up my plans much more than I ever wanted. Same for you too?

Most times, I found myself clinging to the security blanket of my previous life. There's risk and unease in the new and unknown. Frankly, we don't always believe God's big enough to handle it.

I see my own mistrust mirrored in the Israelites' cries to Moses: **"Didn't we say to you in Egypt, 'Leave us alone; let us serve the Egyptians'? It would have been better for us to serve the Egyptians than to die in the desert!"** (Exodus 14:12).

Like the Israelites, we don't know the ending of God's story for us. But the God who is powerful enough to free and protect the Israelites is the same God who watches over you in times of change and discomfort. He is enough, and he offers more than our old comforts ever could.

The paradox of causality

Pastor Mark Jeske

We all like nice, neat, tidy logical systems. We like categories and straight lines of cause and effect. Life is messy, however, and so are the causes of why things happen the way they do.

Should the extraordinary results of St. Paul's long and productive missionary ministry be attributed to him or to God? Yes. His work and God's work were twined together, just the way God likes it: **"Therefore I glory in Christ Jesus in my service to God. I will not venture to speak of anything except what Christ has accomplished through me in leading the Gentiles to obey God by what I have said and done"** (Romans 15:17,18). Can leaders in the church have personal vision, hard work, drive, strategy, organization, and flexible execution and still give all glory to God? Yes. **"By the grace of God I am what I am, and his grace to me was not without effect. No, I worked harder than all of them—yet not I, but the grace of God that was with me"** (1 Corinthians 15:10).

This is the paradox of causality. It pleases God to have made us miniature versions of himself, who would love what he loves and share in his work. Does the rescue of sinful people through the proclamation of the gospel depend on God or on us? Yes. Is that a little confusing? Yes. Is the solution to work really hard and praise God for what he accomplished? Yes.

Make a difference: Be a missionary
Pastor Mark Jeske

The growth of the Christian faith over the centuries has taken many paths. It is shared through families; it migrates as people move; it is picked up by travelers and carried along. But one of the most powerful forces is the intentional sending of missionaries.

Really the Great Commission of Christ makes all of us missionaries, called to make disciples of all nations. All of us are called to engage our communities with the gospel. But there is a special calling for those who choose to live as foreigners in another country in order to make Christ known.

St. Paul grew up in the eastern Mediterranean region, but the Spirit of the Lord led him westward, through what is now Turkey, Greece, and Italy: **"From Jerusalem all the way around to Illyricum, I have fully proclaimed the gospel of Christ. It has always been my ambition to preach the gospel where Christ was not known, so that I would not be building on someone else's foundation. Rather, as it is written: 'Those who were not told about him will see, and those who have not heard will understand'"** (Romans 15:19-22).

Does the call to bring the Word to people of a faraway land stir your blood? Could you serve as a lay administrator, or do you have the stuff to learn another language fluently enough to teach? Could you plant the idea in the head of a young person you know with language talent and a spirit of adventure?

Make a difference. Be a missionary.

The idol of work

Pastor Mark Jeske

The very first of God's Ten Commandments forbids idolatry, but honestly I would have to say I can't ever remember someone confessing that sin to me in private counseling. In fact, even the word *idol* appears to have lost its fear factor and has become a *desirable* term! The Fox TV show *American Idol* stayed on the air an incredible 15 seasons, including 8 straight years as the number-one U.S. television show. Insane! America loves idols.

But God doesn't. He calls it terrible sin when anything or anybody takes his place in the center of a person's life. An idol is a false god, something Satan uses to distract us and seduce us. An idol is anything we love or trust more than God, and they're all bad. Idols can be good things in and of themselves, but when they displace God they become poison to our souls.

Take work, for example. Scripture tells us how noble and important work is, that anyone who won't work shouldn't eat. Work without connection to God is empty: **"My heart took delight in all my labor, and this was the reward for all my toil. Yet when I surveyed all that my hands had done and what I had toiled to achieve, everything was meaningless, a chasing after the wind; nothing was gained under the sun"** (Ecclesiastes 2:10,11).

Get control of your pace of work. Make sure there's time for family; make extra sure there's time for worship.

The idol of money

Pastor Mark Jeske

All of us work to make money (or if unemployed would very much like to work to make money). How is it possible to pursue financial gain, though, without money then becoming our master? Aye, there's the rub, as Hamlet said.

Money is not evil in and of itself. It is just a tool. But it also represents portable power, the ability to get other people to do things for us. Money-love can be as addictive and enslaving as any narcotic. I can sure see and smell materialism in other people—when I see friends with maxed-out credit cards or others obsessed with day trading, bingo, the slots, and online poker, for instance. Respect its seductive appeal! **"Wealth is worthless in the day of wrath, but righteousness delivers from death"** (Proverbs 11:4).

I'm a little less sharp in detecting materialism in myself, and so I need to listen to the people God put around me. Not a single investment, not a single dollar, will make a bit of difference to my destiny on judgment day. The only asset from my personal balance sheet that I can take with me is the righteousness I have from Jesus Christ.

Whatever money I have right now really belongs to God, and it needs to be used according to *his* agenda. When I am generous with him, when I take care of my family and help other people first, I can then be trusted to spend on myself.

The idol of sports

Pastor Mark Jeske

What is it with kids' soccer leagues and their Sunday morning games anyway? Are those leagues run by total heathens? Or do the parents ask for that time slot because they're not going to go to church anyway?

Sports for people of all ages are awesome! Leave it to Satan to find a way to take something good and morph it into something bad. You know sports is becoming an idol when . . . you skip church so that you can watch two hours of NFL pregame shows plus all three games . . . you get violent and abusive to your family when your team loses . . . you spend more money on sports gear than you would ever put into a collection plate . . . you think nothing of driving your kids to out-of-town basketball tournaments every weekend . . . your family's lives are falling apart but you don't notice because you're playing golf all the time.

St. Paul used sports analogies to encourage believers to focus! **"Everyone who competes in the games goes into strict training. They do it to get a crown that will not last, but we do it to get a crown that will last forever. Therefore I do not run like someone running aimlessly; I do not fight like a boxer beating the air. No, I strike a blow to my body and make it my slave so that after I have preached to others, I myself will not be disqualified for the prize"** (1 Corinthians 9:25-27).

If you have the slightest suspicion that your sports life is out of balance, have a family meeting today.

The idol of gaming

Pastor Mark Jeske

It seems like just yesterday that the coolest arcade game ever was *Pong*, but I doubt that anybody ever got addicted to a slow bouncing ball and an electronic paddle. Today's hi-res graphics, special effects, compelling story lines, and wham-bang game action have created armies of glaze-eyed near zombies who find their own preferred reality in the virtual world.

How can you tell if you (or others in your family) love gaming too much? Do you know you spend too much time in front of the screen but can't stop? Have you lost interest in human relationships because you're so deep into the virtual world? Do you lie to others about what you're up to? Are you risking your grades or job performance because of time spent gaming? Are you getting enough sleep to care for your body (a.k.a. the temple of the Lord)? Do you spend way too much money on consoles, games, upgrades, and online play? Do you care more about your progress in the game than progress in your life? Does reading your Bible now seem too boring and tame by comparison?

Games can be fun, but reality has to come first. **"Those who work their land will have abundant food, but those who chase fantasies have no sense"** (Proverbs 12:11). Are you a gaming addict? Do you have the courage to ask other people in your family if they think you have a problem? Is there someone you can trust to give your game controllers to for a week while you detox?

The idol of the body

Pastor Mark Jeske

The root of all idolatry really is the worship of self, so it's no surprise that one of the forms idolatry can take is an unhealthy self-absorption with your body and appearance. We all want to look nice when we step out of the house. But expensive clothes, designer accessories, makeup, jewelry, and hair care and all the time they take can become an exhausting competition. Do you feel judged? inadequate and insecure in how you look? Whose approval for your appearance do you most desire?

And what's not to love about personal fitness? God certainly wants us to care for our bodies; much of our personal health (or lack thereof) is within our control. How do you know when attention to exercise and diet (good things) become dysfunctional obsessions (i.e., bad things)? Is it your dream to have a buff bod as your number-one self-identifier? Are you vain about your six-pack abs? Worse—are you depressed and self-hating because of your midriff softness?

The Word of God demolishes all idols if we but pay attention to it. Do you want to feel better physically? Did you know that a good relationship with God will actually improve your health and help keep your self-image in balance? **"In all your ways submit to him, and he will make your paths straight. Do not be wise in your own eyes; fear the LORD and shun evil. This will bring health to your body and nourishment to your bones"** (Proverbs 3:6-8).

Don't cave to peer pressure

Pastor Mark Jeske

Man, it's not so hard to ignore your parents, but it's really, really hard to say no to your friends. Who over the age of 14 has not felt the riptide pull of peer pressure? Nobody wants to be mocked for being weak, being a loser, being left behind, being chicken. Everybody wants to belong. Strong leaders pull the people in their group behind them, sometimes to terrible deeds.

Peer pressure wasn't invented in recent times—it's always been around: **"You have spent enough time in the past doing what pagans choose to do—living in debauchery, lust, drunkenness, orgies, carousing and detestable idolatry. They are surprised that you do not join them in their reckless, wild living, and they heap abuse on you"** (1 Peter 4:3,4). When people have decided to carouse, they want everybody else to join them so that they won't feel guilty and so that there won't be any innocent ones left to rat them out. If they do get busted, at least they'll have company in whatever leper colony they end up in.

It all comes down to whose approval you need to feel good about yourself. Are your friends number one in your life? Do you crave their approval more than anything? If so, know that you have made them an idol. Know also that they're not really your friends if they goad you into doing things that are sinful or illegal or both.

When you are being squeezed, ask Jesus what he'd like you to do.

Make a difference: Be a connector
Pastor Mark Jeske

Levi was a tax collector. His fellow Jews hated and resented him and his associates more than people today dislike the IRS for extracting so much money from us. The tax collectors were franchisees of the Roman Empire, so that made them collaborators with the enemy. They also were known as cheaters.

As he passed by Levi's revenue collecting booth, Jesus did an amazing thing. He called Levi to quit his job and follow him. An even more remarkable thing happened—Levi accepted the invitation. And then he did something wonderful. He invited his friends to meet Jesus: **"While Jesus was having dinner at Levi's house, many tax collectors and sinners were eating with him and his disciples, for there were many who followed him"** (Mark 2:15). Levi wanted his friends to know why he was giving up the lucrative business they were all engaged in, and perhaps he was hoping that Jesus' powerful teachings would have the same effect on them.

Do your friends know where you stand with the Lord Jesus? Do they know your faith story and why it is so powerful in your life? Levi was on to something. Do you have opportunities to bring the gospel to them or bring them to the gospel? Have you ever shared a print piece with any of them? passed on a digital devotion or video? invited them to church 'n' brunch?

Make a difference. Be a connector.

"Trinity": Not in the Bible?

Pastor Mark Jeske

Trinity has to be the most famous non-Bible Bible word ever. Thousands of congregations all over America have chosen it as their name. But even though the term isn't in Scripture, the ideas behind the term are everywhere, and not just in the New Testament. The Old Testament too is full of references to the Spirit of the Lord. And it has an abundance of messianic prophecies, foretelling how the divine Son of God would be born on earth as a man.

Christians long ago desired a simple term that could summarize what they believed about the identity of their God, and so they made up a word that combined the Latin word for three—*tri*—with the word *unity*. There are examples of the term all the way back to the second century A.D.

How our God can be three and one at the same time is a mystery. It is a mathematical paradox. Scripture reveals these things to us not so much that we understand as just believe. The three persons each have their separate works—only the Son was incarnate, for example—but overall they function in unity toward their grand goal of gathering believers.

Each person of the Trinity touches your life in a special way. St. Paul concluded his second letter to the Christian congregation in Corinth with a trinitarian benediction: **"May the grace of the Lord Jesus Christ, and the love of God, and the fellowship of the Holy Spirit be with you all"** (2 Corinthians 13:14).

march

My comfort in my suffering is this:
Your promise preserves my life.

Psalm 119:50

Forty days—repent!

Pastor Mark Jeske

It happened at least two dozen times in the Bible that when God was going to do something special in advancing his plan of salvation, he chose the number 40. The Israelites were sentenced to that many years of wandering in the desert. Jesus spent that many days fasting and praying as his public ministry began, and for 40 days he showed himself alive to stunned and delighted disciples after his resurrection.

Forty days was God's solemn deadline to the people of the Assyrian imperial capital Nineveh for a major change in their attitudes and actions. He sent his prophet Jonah to warn them of their doom:

"Jonah obeyed the word of the LORD and went to Nineveh . . . proclaiming, 'Forty more days and Nineveh will be overthrown.' The Ninevites believed God. A fast was proclaimed, and all of them, from the greatest to the least, put on sackcloth" (Jonah 3:3-5).

Somewhere back in the very early years of the Christian church, it occurred to spiritual leaders that a season of spiritual preparation before Easter would be a helpful discipline for people. For 40 days (Sundays as feast days excepted) Christians would reflect on their sins, their guilt, and the terrible dilemma that necessitated Christ's suffering and death. It is a time for confession, humble requests for forgiveness, and solemn resolves to live a new and holier life.

Towering over all the faithful during Lent is the cross—symbol of all that's wrong with us and all that's wonderful about Jesus Christ.

A holy mission: Reduce conflict

Pastor Mark Jeske

It doesn't take much intelligence to start or continue a fight. It's easy—just let your emotions take over. There's a powerful adrenaline rush to being angry, isn't there? As Emperor Palpatine said to Luke Skywalker, "I feel your anger. Your hate has made you powerful."

Peacemaking, as opposed to starting and continuing fights, is God's work. It is hard because it goes against nature. It is learned behavior, and as a mind-set it must be chosen. Choose it. **"Make every effort to live in peace with everyone"** (Hebrews 12:14). Peacemaking means ascribing the best possible motives to the actions of others instead of concluding the worst. Peacemaking means de-escalating an argument instead of amping it up.

Peacemaking means helping two adversaries to reconcile instead of enjoying watching them go at it and egging them on. Peacemaking means not being so cocksure that you are right all the time and listening better to see if the other person has a point. Peacemaking means that you can suppress your own ego and cheerfully let other people win sometimes. Peacemaking means being willing to go first in saying, "I'm sorry." "It was my fault." "Will you forgive me?" "Let's start over."

As incentive, ponder how Jesus Christ absorbed injustice in his body and soul in order to reconcile you and me with God. The One who forgave his enemies from the cross invites us to do the same. The Prince of peace would like us to love peace as much as he does.

Shalom.

You have been chosen
Diana Kerr

My family is unapologetically in love with all the *Toy Story* movies. (My mom cheered, clapped, and cried in the theater during *Toy Story 2*.) Remember the first movie when Buzz and Woody end up inside a claw machine at the arcade and Sid picks them up with the claw? "He has been chosen! He has been chosen!" all the toy aliens left behind inside the machine repeat. They're totally psyched for Woody and Buzz; being "chosen" is a big deal.

You can probably guess where I'm headed with this. You and I are chosen too, but by our gracious God, not by some kid at an arcade. Most of the time, though, we have identity amnesia, and that's a problem. See, 1 Peter 2:9 says, **"You are a chosen people, a royal priesthood, a holy nation, God's special possession, that you may declare the praises of him who called you out of darkness into his wonderful light."**

Chosen. Royal. Holy. God's special possession. This is what we are. One of the problems when we forget this lies in the second half of the verse. We were meant to declare God's praises, but we obviously don't do this much when we forget our identity.

Read the verse again and let it soak in. Your identity is *incredible* and wonderful, and you have done nothing to deserve that. You have been chosen and redeemed by a God who's crazy about you. Own that identity, acknowledge the gift that it is, and go praise God publicly.

He turned water into wine
Pastor Daron Lindemann

Here are some things we can learn from Jesus turning water into wine (John 2).

1. Invite Jesus to your wedding and to your marriage.
2. If we care about something, Jesus cares too.
3. God performs miracles in our lives often without us noticing.
4. Listen to your mom.
5. Jesus transforms our outward rituals (like jugs at a wedding used for ceremonial washing or the rituals of life like washing dishes) into spiritual blessings filled with faith and love.
6. God is not just found in church but in all of life's activities.
7. The humble carpenter from Nazareth is the heavenly Savior-God.
8. God isn't frugal. He provides for us lavishly. In turn, honor him with your best.

Savior Jesus, be my guest and attend the events of my life as you attended the wedding at Cana. Bring joy and gladness now as you did then. Replenish me in my needs and fill me up with your abundance—your way. By the miracle of your gracious love, strengthen my faith in you. Lead me to be generous to others as you are to me. Finally, visit all who are married with your gracious presence and providing. Amen.

Enough
Diana Kerr

I know we *much* prefer to sweep these under the rug, but I want you to think about your worries and fears. Think about the what-ifs, the worst-case scenarios, the things that feel like they would be the end of the world if they happened to you.

Infertility. Life-changing illness. Job loss. A cheating spouse.

Those things would be tough. So tough. And if I wasn't a Christian, I'd be *terrified* at the thought of those things.

But you and I are different. In the midst of our pain, the God whose blood was enough to redeem us is also a God who is enough to comfort us, enough to bring us peace and joy, enough to help us get through each day. See, at the root of our fears and worries is often an unconscious belief that God isn't enough, that if you lost one of the most important things in your life you couldn't get through it. But God *is* enough.

I hear God's words to Paul in my head in my moments of struggle or worry: **"My grace is sufficient for you, for my power is made perfect in weakness"** (2 Corinthians 12:9). When I'm feeling weak or fearful, I whisper or pray, "God, you are enough. I know you are enough." I do this over and over, reminding myself of how his power shines in my weakest moment and that, no matter what, he is sufficient and I'll be okay, not to mention that my place in heaven is secure.

Come to the upper room—and be warned

Pastor Mark Jeske

Jesus knew that his time of public ministry was just about over. The grim thunderclouds of evil were concentrating in Jerusalem, and his bitterest enemies, aided by insider information from his disciple Judas, would be arresting him in a few hours. He spent those hours carefully, leaving his disciples with powerful memories of a humble foot washing, last Passover meal, and first-ever Lord's Supper.

And he taught them. In painfully clear language he showed them what they were in for as his disciples, trying to prepare them for the coming assaults of Satan and his evil host. He had special words of warning for his impetuous student, Simon Peter, who would boast that evening that he would never leave Jesus: **"Simon, Simon, Satan has asked to sift all of you as wheat. But I have prayed for you, Simon, that your faith may not fail. And when you have turned back, strengthen your brothers"** (Luke 22:31,32).

Well Simon's faith did fail. Satan did sift him, and he denied his Savior three times. But Jesus did restore him to faith and to his old job, and for the rest of his life he humbly and fearlessly carried out a ministry of forgiveness and restoration to other sinners.

Don't waste this Lenten season. Let Jesus' words of warning register in your brain and strike your heart. You are under demonic assault too. But let Jesus' gracious words of unconditional love inspire you to love him all over again.

What's in your wallet?

Pastor Mark Jeske

Everybody is chasing something. People follow their appetites. Some want power over other people. Some want fame, recognition, and celebrity. Some want sexual gratification with someone other than a spouse. Some are chasing business success at all costs—anything to close a deal. Some are plotting revenge; others are plotting how to climb the corporate ladder faster. Some crave the pleasure of travel, shopping, lounging, and being pampered. It's moneymoneymoney that makes those things happen.

What are you chasing? Be honest—what are your appetites? **"Keep your lives free from the love of money and be content with what you have, because God has said, 'Never will I leave you; never will I forsake you'"** (Hebrews 13:5). What's in your wallet? What are the assets in your life that you most prize? Your financial portfolio? Real estate? Position in the company? Where does your family play in? How close is God to the top?

It's not that money, property, position, and renown are bad things. They are all potentially good. But without faith in God they become gods themselves to those who have them, who chase them, who are controlled by them. They can give only a short-term buzz and soon are taken away.

If you have God, you have everything—peace, a healthy life agenda, forgiveness for yesterday, and eternal hope for tomorrow. Everything you can touch is temporary. Only God can say, "Never will I leave you."

Acknowledging the power of the Spirit

Diana Kerr

I don't normally go about my day conscious of the fact that my heart is pumping, but it is. I also don't tend to journey through the day constantly aware that the Holy Spirit is dwelling within me, but he is.

Whether I pay attention to these things or not, they're happening at all times. I don't need to be conscious of my beating heart to receive the benefits it provides, but when it comes to the Holy Spirit, I'm missing out if I forget he's with me. Yes, he's by my side even when I'm not thinking about him, but when I *am* thinking about him, the moments of my day-to-day look very different.

Second Timothy 1:7 says that **"the Spirit God gave us does not make us timid, but gives us power, love and self-discipline."** Um, don't you want all those blessings in your corner during the day? I do.

I'm realizing more and more that God's power within me isn't as effective if I completely ignore it and try to be strong enough on my own. Ask me how good I was at avoiding stress eating or standing up to fear when I tried to accomplish them with my own strength. (Not so good.)

Acknowledging the Spirit's strength and power within me not only takes some of the pressure off of me, but it empowers me to know that I am stronger than I realize, only through him.

True compassion

Pastor Mark Jeske

I don't have to explain to you that it's a dog-eat-dog world out there. Every man for himself. A jungle. Social Darwinism—survival of the fittest. Kill or be killed. No quarter. Take no prisoners.

Into that world walked Jesus Christ and changed everything. Instead of dishing out abuse as he was abused, instead of retaliating with even greater force, he absorbed the biggest blow that evil could give him, absorbed it without hating back. In fact, his first gasped sentence from the cross was a prayer for forgiveness upon those who had treated him most cruelly. His mercy was hurled forward across the centuries and has washed over you and me as well.

Christ now invites us to broker that same mercy to other people. For instance, Scripture urges us to show compassion to others. That word *compassion* comes from two Latin words that mean "to suffer along with," to share someone else's pain. Like this: **"Continue to remember those in prison as if you were together with them in prison, and those who are mistreated as if you yourselves were suffering"** (Hebrews 13:3). It's easy to blame the poor and miserable of this world, easy to walk away, easy to avert your eyes. True compassion lives in a heart willing to open itself to another's pain.

You can start by practicing on the people you live with. Shock them. Ask them how they're doing and take the time to let them tell you how they really are.

40 days
Pastor Daron Lindemann

Periods of 40 days or years in the Bible provide a pattern for Lent. They speak about persevering through turmoil and temptation, to prepare for triumph.

The flood (40 days and 40 nights of rain) brought death then life, with waters that destroyed the wicked but delivered those righteous by faith (Genesis 7).

Prophets of God struggled with their own weaknesses but found mountainous strength in God. Moses spent 40 days with God on the mountain **"without eating bread or drinking water"** (Exodus 34:28) and receiving the Ten Commandments. Elijah **"traveled forty days and forty nights until he reached Horeb, the mountain of God"** (1 Kings 19:8).

The spies explored the land of Canaan for 40 days (Numbers 13). This tested their faith as they found reason to fear for their lives. The Israelites repeatedly rebelled against God so that he finally disciplined them—to bring them back to their spiritual senses, as recalled by Moses: **"Remember how the LORD your God led you all the way in the wilderness these forty years, to humble and test you"** (Deuteronomy 8:2).

For 40 days the giant, Goliath, cursed God until young David risked everything to defend the Lord's reputation (1 Samuel 17). Jesus himself triumphed over temptation in the wilderness for 40 days (Luke 4:2). This prepared Jesus for the battle at the cross.

During Lent, practice repentance and prayer, Bible reading, and special midweek worship. These prepare you for Easter and help you persevere.

The power of pride
Pastor Mark Jeske

Have you ever noticed how terrible a disease it is to be obsessed with being in control? We see it more quickly in other people, not so quickly in ourselves. God sees it all the time as people try to control their lives and get what they want *without him*.

Asa, king of Judah from 910 to 869 B.C., wanted relief from pressure from the rival kingdom of Israel along his northern border. He did not bother to consult the Lord but chose to loot the temple treasury and attempt to buy mercenary services of Aram (Syria), Israel's neighbor to its north. Oops. The prophet Hanani blistered his ears: **"You relied on the king of Aram and not on the Lord your God. . . . The eyes of the Lord range throughout the earth to strengthen those whose hearts are fully committed to him. You have done a foolish thing, and from now on you will be at war"** (2 Chronicles 16:7,9).

Why do we not ask God for help? Because we are proud enough and stubborn enough and vain enough to want to do it ourselves . . . because we want to claim the success . . . because to ask for help sounds in our little brains like begging or being weak or incompetent . . . because we want action . . . because we don't want to wait for God's time.

You can work hard, plan wisely, take responsibility, and strive to be self-reliant. But always keep God in your plans, listen for his voice of guidance, and give him more glory than you give yourself.

You can't plead ignorance

Pastor Mark Jeske

I was driving along a dark suburban road on a second date with a girl I was desperately trying to impress. To my horror I saw rotating red lights in my rearview and had to pull over. The cop informed me that I was traveling 36 mph and asked if I knew the speed limit. I didn't, but I thought I was fine. But as I looked up through the windshield, I realized that I had come to a stop 20 feet away from a big road sign, now brightly lit by my headlights, reading SPEED LIMIT 25 MPH. Oops. My admitted ignorance of the law was unfortunately no excuse.

God will surely hear millions of protests on judgment day made by sad-faced unbelievers, protests that they just didn't know. Will God accept ignorance as an excuse? **"The wrath of God is being revealed from heaven against all the godlessness and wickedness of people, who suppress the truth by their wickedness, since what may be known about God is plain to them, because God has made it plain to them. For since the creation of the world God's invisible qualities—his eternal power and divine nature—have been clearly seen, being understood from what has been made, so that people are without excuse"** (Romans 1:18-20).

Christians must not water down the hard news of God's law. The wrath will fall. It is unimaginably bad. Only through faith in Christ will people escape an eternity in hell.

Come to the upper room— and be comforted

Pastor Mark Jeske

It's one of the mysteries of human existence that sometimes it's in the bleakest of moments that wonderful things can happen. An injured child in the hospital leads a husband and wife to stop arguing and draws them back together . . . a mortal threat to a business stops staff bickering and gets the team spirit going again . . . a son gets arrested and suddenly has time and ears for the old man's advice.

In the darkened upper room where Jesus ate his last Passover meal with his disciples, oil lamps flickering, they heard hard predictions from the Master of suffering and persecutions to come. But they heard also heartwarming words of comfort from the One who knew he would emerge victorious in three days: **"I no longer call you servants, because a servant does not know his master's business. Instead, I have called you friends, for everything that I learned from my Father I have made known to you"** (John 15:15).

Is there a term or name that you could wish for that is more desirable than being called a *friend* of Jesus? It cost Jesus his life to give you that status. You can wear that badge every time you pray, and through Christ the Father will listen to you. You can wear that name tag when you step into court on judgment day, and the Judge will acquit you immediately because all your misdeeds have been wiped from your record.

Say it with gratitude and pride: "I am Jesus' friend!"

Sweet dreams

Pastor Mark Jeske

A friend shared one of his main business strategies: "Always tell the truth—then you don't have to be so smart." His point, of course, was that the more lies you tell, the harder you have to work to remember which lie you told to whom.

To toss and turn in your bed, dreading that your misdeeds will be found out, is a miserable experience. All of your problems remain in the morning, and now you're exhausted and draggy as the day begins. Too late you remember your parents' warnings: "Think before you act!" "Be careful of the company you keep." "Say what you mean and mean what you say." "Accept responsibility when it's your fault." "Cheaters never prosper." "Always keep your word." "Do what you say you're going to do."

King Solomon had seen a lot of the world and understood the human condition really, really well. He offered some very good advice to his own children: **"My son, do not let wisdom and understanding out of your sight, preserve sound judgment and discretion. When you lie down, you will not be afraid; when you lie down, your sleep will be sweet"** (Proverbs 3:21,24).

It truly is a wonderful feeling to lie down at the end of a long day, work done, enjoying the favor of your God, and at peace with everyone. And with yourself.

Hit the dirt

Pastor Daron Lindemann

Dropping to the ground, or hitting the dirt, is a survival tactic, whether you're a soldier or a farmer trapped in a tornado. You don't proudly stand tall to defy bullets or 100 mph winds. You get dirty, but survive.

Dirt and *dust* in the Bible are metaphors for the humility of faith that saves. Sinners repent and realize that without God we're dead, much like Adam was merely a clod of dirt until God breathed into him. Job thought he had all the right answers; then he finally admitted, **"I despise myself and repent in dust and ashes"** (Job 42:6).

The season of Lent features the ashes and dust of humble repentance. This is good for any of Adam's children. **"Let him bury his face in the dust. . . . It is good to wait quietly for the salvation of the LORD"** (Lamentations 3:29,26).

The humble repentance of Lent helps discipline our proud and stubborn selves, who need to be kicked to the ground and told, "You're not in charge here!" Earthly treasures sooner or later deteriorate into dust, but **"because of the LORD's great love we are not consumed, for his compassions never fail. They are new every morning; great is your faithfulness. I say to myself, 'The LORD is my portion; therefore I will wait for him'"** (Lamentations 3:22-24).

Lower yourself and hit the dust of Lenten humility. You'll survive and see what is truly great: the faithful love of the Lord.

You've been warned
Pastor Mark Jeske

The estrangement of creation from its Creator is the central human dilemma. All of the hurtful things in our lives—infidelity, crime, war, disease—have erupted from that first rebellion. Readers of the Old Testament have a profound advantage over everybody else on earth. They have clear insights into how God operates. How he means business with his commandments. How he holds people accountable, following through with merciless judgment when his warnings are ignored.

We need to learn from those stories. **"See to it that you do not refuse him who speaks. If they did not escape when they refused him who warned them on earth, how much less will we, if we turn away from him who warns us from heaven?"** (Hebrews 12:25). The historical records of God's wrath and punishment are recounted not to beat us down and make us want to run away from God. They are intended to get our attention and lead us to welcome his rescue plan in Christ Jesus. **"Therefore, since we are receiving a kingdom that cannot be shaken, let us be thankful, and so worship God acceptably with reverence and awe, for our 'God is a consuming fire'"** (Hebrews 12:28,29).

Time is short. Not a one of us knows with certainty if we'll even be alive tomorrow. People of all ages are dying every day, little children included. Take God's warnings seriously! But take seriously also his kind and gentle gift of the forgiveness of your sins through the shed blood of your Savior.

march 17

Craving God
Diana Kerr

They say sugar is addictive; the more you get of it, the more you want it. Some people say love's the same way; singer Kesha even wrote a song comparing love to drugs.

It makes sense to want more of good things, to crave them. God did create us to crave after all.

So how much are we craving *him*?

Can you relate to the writer of Psalm 42? **"As the deer pants for streams of water, so my soul pants for you, my God. My soul thirsts for God, for the living God"** (verses 1,2). Do you thirst for and crave God as much as you crave dark chocolate or seeing the spouse you missed?

I haven't always thirsted after God. For many years, I didn't realize how much my life was lacking if I didn't spend time with him. These days, the more I get of God, the more I want. I have an unquenchable thirst to be with him, to learn about him, to have him speak to me through his Word, to commune with him throughout the day, and to go to him in prayer.

No matter what your relationship with God looks like, he wants you to go further and deeper. If you aren't craving God, start with getting to know him more. The good news is he'll give you what you crave: peace, rest, forgiveness, love, acceptance, joy, security, identity, and on and on.

Grow your vocabulary: Redemption

Pastor Mark Jeske

The world of the Roman Empire, in which Christ and the apostles lived and carried out their saving ministry, was just as thick with slavery as pre-1865 America. The slave population continuously swelled because of the steady influx of military captives and insolvent debtors. At least in the Roman system slaves could be redeemed if someone could pay the stiff ransom price, in the neighborhood of 500 *denarii* (a *denarius* was the equivalent of a day's wage for a workingman).

Scripture teaches that we are all born into bondage, the slavery of sin. But here's the terrible difference—the Roman slaves could accumulate money and buy their way out. We can't. Money won't pay for our sins, and neither will our good intentions, religious observances, sacrificial acts, self-justification, excuses, blaming, or earnest efforts. Our only hope is that God himself would find a way to make the ransom payment.

So great was the Father's love for his lost children that he did find a way. He blamed, punished, and executed his own Son in our place, and in this way the payment was made in full. **"In him we have *redemption* through his blood, the forgiveness of sins, in accordance with the riches of God's grace"** (Ephesians 1:7). This is the very heart of the wonderful gospel message.

There's only a little time left—believe it! Share it!

You are not the judge

Pastor Mark Jeske

One of the things agnostics and atheists hate most about church people is that "they're so judgmental." Well, are we? On the one hand, all believers do have a prophetic ministry in their lives to speak God's words of both law and gospel, both warning and forgiveness. The words of condemnation that we speak about evil behaviors are not ours but God's.

On the other hand, no less an authority than Christ himself laid into the church people of his day with strenuous warnings not to be judgmental: **"Do not judge, or you too will be judged. For in the same way you judge others, you will be judged, and with the measure you use, it will be measured to you"** (Matthew 7:1,2). So what's the difference between criticizing evil and judging? These are the whisperings of a judgmental heart: "I'm better than he is." "I'm more worthy of God's blessings than she is." "Sinners are so disgusting—they deserve everything they're getting." "I will get a higher place in heaven and, frankly, I deserve it."

If you have your life more together than some other people, if you are enjoying financial security, if your family is still intact, if none of your relatives is in jail, don't boast. With a humble heart thank God for blessings and strength.

And if you need to straighten out another sinner, someone who needs Jesus just as you do, remember to speak the truth in love.

Come to the upper room—and be fed

Pastor Mark Jeske

Imagine that you are one of Jesus' disciples in the upper room late on Maundy Thursday evening and you hear these words: **"He took bread, gave thanks and broke it, and gave it to them, saying, 'This is my body given for you; do this in remembrance of me.' In the same way, after the supper he took the cup, saying, 'This cup is the new covenant in my blood, which is poured out for you'"** (Luke 22:19,20).

Jesus' disciples could not possibly have understood what was going on when they experienced Holy Communion for the first time. In their fear and confusion that night, Jesus' words about eating his body and blood must have sounded strange and more than a little creepy. The physical elements of the Eucharist—bread and a sip of wine—must have seemed too tame and ordinary for the amazing things Jesus claimed to be giving through them.

Weeks later, when the disciples had witnessed the resurrection and received the Spirit's Pentecost outpouring, they grasped the enormous significance of Jesus' gift. Though he had ascended into heaven with his human body, he was still present among them in spirit through his Word and physically present through the Eucharistic meal. What a royal feast we can enjoy at the Lord's Table! The assurance of the forgiveness of our many sins, the promise of God's everyday favor, and the bright hope of a place at God's banquet in heaven are ours.

Can't wait till Sunday.

You can't hide

Pastor Mark Jeske

It really isn't that hard to fool your teacher, your boss, or your local police. The majority of plagiarism, fraud, and crime goes undetected and unsolved. And hey—if you're not caught, it never happened, right? There's no proof!

Don't try to pull that stuff with God. His eyes are better than all the security cameras in the world put together. His memory is better than all the Google and Facebook server farms operating in tandem. And he's a God who cares. He has data on every single man, woman, and child who ever lived, and he holds each one accountable for the way in which he or she lived. **"Nothing in all creation is hidden from God's sight. Everything is uncovered and laid bare before the eyes of him to whom we must give account"** (Hebrews 4:13).

That is terrifying news if you are planning to represent yourself in God's great court on the Last Day. Just one day's worth of sins is enough to send you off to eternal damnation, for no sinner may enter God's holy heaven.

But if you believe in Jesus Christ as your Savior, if you are wearing the robes of holiness that he bought for you, then the Last Day will not be a day of terror for you, running with others for cover that can't hide. Your Brother is coming to introduce you to his Father.

It will be a family reunion.

Names of God: El Shaddai

Pastor Mark Jeske

Perhaps you know the words *El Shaddai* as the title to an Amy Grant song. Written by Michael Card in 1981, the song gained huge popularity for both, including several Dove awards (i.e., a Christian music industry Grammy). Pronounced Ale-Shud-DYE, the words are drawn from God's self-description at an intensely dramatic moment in Abraham's life.

"When Abram was ninety-nine years old, the Lord appeared to him and said, "I am God Almighty [Hebrew: *El Shaddai*]**; walk before me faithfully and be blameless"** (Genesis 17:1). The word *Shaddai* appears to refer to a mountain, which was quite appropriate since on that hill, Mt. Moriah, God instructed Abraham to slay his son Isaac as a sacrifice to him. Pained and crushed in heart, Abraham moved to obey, but God stopped him before he used the knife, providing for the sacrifice a nearby ram whose horns were caught in a thicket. Second Chronicles 3:1 tells us that it was that very site where the magnificent temple of Solomon was later constructed.

El Shaddai does indeed seem to like mountains as locations for some of his significant acts in human history. It was on Mt. Sinai that he gave the law to Moses. It was on Mt. Carmel that the Lord demonstrated forcefully that the Canaanite god Baal was a fraud and Baal's prophets were too.

And it was on Mt. Calvary that the Son of God died to make us sons and daughters of God.

Idle idol

Pastor Daron Lindemann

An idol is anything we turn to in place of God to make us feel approved, content, or in control. People, things, opinions, or desires can be our idols. All of these may be good things, but as idols they become ultimate things.

"They lift it to their shoulders and carry it; they set it up in its place, and there it stands. From that spot it cannot move. Even though someone cries out to it, it cannot answer; it cannot save them from their troubles" (Isaiah 46:7). Our idols can't help. It's like the guy who screams at his TV during a football game, "Just catch the ball!" Nothing happens.

"Like a scarecrow in a cucumber field, their idols cannot speak; they must be carried because they cannot walk. Do not fear them; they can do no harm nor can they do any good" (Jeremiah 10:5). Ask a scarecrow to walk to a Redbox and pick up a movie for you. Is it going to happen? No. Because it can't walk. It can't hear. It's not going. You're still on your own.

What is your idol? Here's the good news. Your most powerful idol cannot control you without your permission. Next time it calls, consider the true Savior who was lifted up on a cross to save you. You didn't manufacture him, but he created you. He lives, he speaks, and he acts. Throw away your idol and turn to the true God.

A beautiful void
Diana Kerr

In 2016 a documentary called *Minimalism* hit select theaters across the U.S. I went to see it, and one line from an interviewee still rings in my head to this day. It went something like this: "You will never have enough of what you don't actually want." I elbowed my husband and was like, "Whoa! That is so biblical!"

You will never have enough of what you don't actually want. What are you after that you think you want? Like the people in the documentary, is it stuff—physical possessions? or money? or recognition? or quality relationships? or success? or physical attractiveness? or the end of your to-do list?

You may think you want those things, but I'm here to tell you that you actually don't. You were designed by God and for God and with a void only he can fill. This isn't a bad thing; it's actually a beautiful gift! Striving to fill yourself with the stuff of this world will never feel as good as you think it will. (Does anyone actually feel good when he or she leaves an all-you-can-eat buffet?)

"I say to myself, 'The LORD is my portion; therefore I will wait for him'" (Lamentations 3:24). This is the much easier option, friends, and the one that actually works—filling yourself up with the Lord. (P.S. He's so crazy about you he *died* for you. Your garage full of stuff will never love you that much.)

What is leadership?

Pastor Mark Jeske

Ask any real estate agent which are the three main factors that determine a home's price, and each will give the same answer: location, location, location. Not so in business, church planting, and the military, where the three main determiners of success are leadership, leadership, leadership.

King David waited patiently for those loyal to his predecessor Saul to come over to his side after Saul's death. Each tribe listed the number of infantrymen who joined David's army—all except the tribe of Issachar. It's almost as though the Israelite West Point was located in their region. Look how their contribution is described: **"These are the numbers of the men armed for battle who came to David at Hebron to turn Saul's kingdom over to him, as the Lord had said: from Issachar, men who understood the times and knew what Israel should do—200 chiefs, with all their relatives under their command"** (1 Chronicles 12:23,32).

I have never heard a better definition of what makes a good leader. First, it's a person who understands the times, who has the discernment to know which are the top strategic issues and which don't matter as much. Second, it's a person who knows what to do. Good leaders live in the future. They have the ability to identify the best path among many to get the group moving. David got two hundred good ones from the tribe of Issachar.

May you have some in your church.

Welcome, friends!

Pastor Mark Jeske

God invented an ingenious system for bringing fresh water to the plants and animals of his world. He uses the radiant heat of the sun to drive convection, moving water up through evaporation and down through rainfall. Brilliant!

He also created a personal resource convection system for believers. He pours out gifts, energy, love, money, and talents on us to see what we'll do with them. How delighted he is when we give offerings back to him. How delighted he is when we are as generous to others as he has first been to us. It inspires him to pour even more resources into our lives so we can be even more generous.

He loves it when we open our homes to others and spend time with them: **"Do not forget to show hospitality to strangers, for by so doing some people have shown hospitality to angels without knowing it"** (Hebrews 13:2). The Christian faith is always shared most effectively through personal relationships, and what better place to build those relationships than in the relaxed atmosphere of one's home? There people can feel safe, appreciated, and heard. There enough trust is built that they may decide to invite you into their home as well.

Our mission in life is not to hide in a bomb shelter, waiting out the chaos until judgment day. We're medics, going out onto the battlefield to tend the wounded. They are the only things in our lives that we can take with us to heaven.

Come to the upper room— and be challenged

Pastor Mark Jeske

It cost you nothing to become a Christian. The conquering of Satan the destroyer, the blood payment, the agony of the cross, the bearing of the heavy load of the sins of the world, the experience of God's rejection and condemnation in your place, suffering the torments of hell itself—all these things Christ accomplished on your behalf without any help from you. And all the benefits of his mighty work are yours through faith, free to all who believe in him and claim them.

But it will cost you everything to be a Christian. Jesus commands and demands nothing less than that you now place *him* on the throne of your life, set aside your personal agenda and replace it with *his*, view all your possessions as really *his*, and submit your giant ego to *his* will. In the dark upper room, just a few hours before the crucifixion, Jesus gave his disciples a serious challenge: **"If you love me, keep my commands"** (John 14:15).

Learning Christ's will and ways and then *choosing to give him your obedience* is a profound act of worship. In some ways it means much more to him than your hosannas and hallelujahs, which after all might be just talk. Obedience to God shows that your faith-statements are real. Second, obedience to God will benefit greatly the people around you, for you will hurt them less.

Obedience to Christ is also the surest path to your own personal satisfaction and happiness in life. Give it gladly.

I want patience, and I want it now

Pastor Mark Jeske

Waiting is work. That's why we don't like to do it. Unfortunately the age in which we live is making the learning of patience harder and harder. Rapid changes in digital technology have sped up the pace of our lives to an insane degree, and it gets worse by the year. The amount of presorted information that you can get over the internet almost instantaneously with a few mouse clicks or finger swipes is nothing less than astonishing.

But working with people will never go that fast. Though technology has changed drastically, human nature has not. People are still as confused, stubborn, opinionated, contrary, proud, and sinful as ever. Scripture counsels a gentle touch and soft words: **"Through patience a ruler can be persuaded, and a gentle tongue can break a bone"** (Proverbs 25:15).

Our incentive to be patient with each other is to reflect on how patient God has been with us. We should be shoveling coal in hell, but instead through Christ we are loved, blessed, and heaven bound. Perhaps our agendas are clear as day in our own minds, but that doesn't mean other people get them. Perhaps we think the brilliance of our plans should receive thunderous applause and immediate implementation by everybody else, but infuriatingly people have the nerve to disagree.

Deep breaths. It shows respect to other people to take your time with them, time to listen to their voices, read their body language, and look into their eyes.

'Tis better to persuade than overpower.

Grow your vocabulary: Justification

Pastor Mark Jeske

If you would interview one hundred people on the street and ask them questions about their religious beliefs about God and salvation, you would hear thoughts about mankind's struggles and how each individual has the ability and obligation to improve himself or herself and learn to be nicer to other people.

The Bible's message is far more intense: **"All have sinned and fall short of the glory of God, and all are *justified* freely by his grace through the redemption that came by Christ Jesus"** (Romans 3:23,24). Did you grasp that powerful double truth? Mankind doesn't just have a few flaws—we have all fallen short of the Creator's righteous expectations. We are all under God's wrath and judgment; we are all candidates for hell.

But the passage's twin truth reveals that God completely on his own did what our deeds could not—he *justified* us. As Christ breathed his last on the cross, the Father declared the world not guilty of its sins. As that powerful message gets to people through Word and sacrament, they come to faith in Christ and believe that his stunning work applies to them personally. Thus they are *justified by faith* and personally receive and experience God's thrilling verdict of Not Guilty!

There is an impulse in each of our hearts to excuse our own failings and justify ourselves by pointing to nicer features of our lives. Fight that urge. Claim the justification that Christ bought for you and then, *then* you will enjoy God's glorious peace.

Stubborn Jesus

Pastor Daron Lindemann

Roger could have been out playing some early season golf today. However, his rotator cuff is still giving him troubles. It's actually been painful for some time, but he's convinced it won't be a problem and, despite his wife's insisting, won't go see a doctor.

What is it about doctors that men hate? Is it the reality that we're not like Superman?

I noticed a billboard that read, "This year thousands of men will die from stubbornness." Very true. Sometimes stubbornness is more fatal than a disease, which could be cured if caught in time.

Jesus died from stubbornness.

Not because he refused to see a doctor for some strange symptoms, but because he refused to say no to his Father's will. Stubbornly, Jesus carried his cross to Calvary and declined the liquid narcotic that would have numbed his full participation in his suffering. Stubbornly, Jesus promised his Father, "Your will be done."

And he did it. He died from stubbornness. **"Here I am, I have come—it is written about me in the scroll. I desire to do your will, my God"** (Psalm 40:7,8). We can thank Jesus no better than to live—stubbornly—as his followers.

Stubborn Jesus, you were so focused on forgiving sinners and fighting off Satan, on healing and helping those in need. Let your hard-minded will to do your Father's will become my will when I fight against temptation. And keep me focused on Christian love, stubbornly refusing my sinful self. Amen.

Jesus the outcast

Pastor Mark Jeske

Outside every major metropolitan area, in the country a small mountain grows every day—a mountain of trash and refuse brought there by a steady stream of garbage trucks. The ancient city of Jerusalem also had a smelly dump just south of the city walls—they called it the Valley of Hinnom, or Gehenna, a place where the fires never went out. It was an eyesore and a nose sore. It was also where the unneeded animal remains from the temple sacrifices were dumped and burned.

Pay attention: **"The high priest carries the blood of animals into the Most Holy Place as a sin offering, but the bodies are burned outside the camp. And so Jesus also suffered outside the city gate to make the people holy through his own blood. Let us, then, go to him outside the camp, bearing the disgrace he bore. For here we do not have an enduring city, but we are looking for the city that is to come"** (Hebrews 13:11-14).

Gehenna's fires made the place a metaphor for the wrath and judgment of God, for hell itself. How fitting that Jesus the Savior became an outcast! Though King of kings, he died like the worst of criminals, suffered hell itself, in order to give us his holiness. Let us go to him, grateful for his humility and sacrifice, willing to bear our struggles and suffering, and inspired to look forward to a better world in heaven.

Where he's waiting for us.

april

He is not here; he has risen! Remember how he told you, while he was still with you in Galilee: "The Son of Man must be delivered over to the hands of sinners, be crucified and on the third day be raised again."

Luke 24:6,7

Limits to technology

Pastor Mark Jeske

Each new technological revolution in communication is greeted with the assumption that it will render obsolete previous technologies. Radio was supposed to supplant newspapers and magazines; TV was supposed to destroy radio; digital video was supposed to be the end of television. Well, none of those things has happened.

And you know what else, none of those miraculous technologies—print, radio, TV, and digital—will ever replace the oldest form of communication: person-to-person, a human voice in a human ear. We are all hardwired for that kind of personal intimacy, since we all heard the human voice for the first time while we were still in our mothers' wombs.

St. John was glad for communication technology but gladder still for one-on-one talk: **"I have much to write you, but I do not want to do so with pen and ink. I hope to see you soon, and we will talk face to face"** (3 John 1:13,14). You know, there is no substitute for congregational life. People whose only spiritual experiences involve reading or TV or the internet are missing out on hugs, eyes, tone, and personal interactivity.

Technology is powering the Word of God all over the globe. Thank him for that! What a gift! But even fiber-optic lightning digital speed cannot replace the splash of baptismal water, the taste of bread and wine in the Lord's Supper, or the touch of a friend as he or she prays for you.

Live at peace
Linda Buxa

I'm not sure if it's intentional, but the day right after April Fools' Day—the day that people in the United States are encouraged to play jokes on, prank, and trick other people—we get to celebrate National Reconciliation Day.

According to the National Calendar Day's website, "This is a day intended to patch up relationships. Misunderstandings, unintended words or actions and simply an unforgiven mistake can tear apart relationships. National Reconciliation Day is the time to take that step and make amends. It's not too late."

You know what I think? Christians should absolutely love this day! After all, we know just how much mistakes can tear apart relationships. When Adam and Eve first sinned, the perfect relationship they were in with God was torn apart—and we all suffer from that too. But God performed the ultimate patch up by sending Jesus to live and to die and to rise in our place. Now, knowing that our most important relationship is at peace, every day in our earthly relationships can be reconciliation day.

From what I can tell in Romans 12:18, the apostle Paul thinks so too: **"If it is possible, as far as it depends on you, live at peace with everyone."**

Not everyone will believe you are sincere, not everyone will accept your apology, not everyone will be kind to you, not everyone will treat you respectfully. But, as far as it depends on you, take the peace you have because of Jesus and pass that along.

It's not too late.

Jesus and hope
Jason Nelson

At a bare minimum, every living thing needs food, water, air, and shelter to survive. But people need something more. People need hope because God created them with the ability to hope. I don't know what goes on in the mind of a chipmunk, but from conception, the mind of every human being develops by yearning for something more. God rewards our first hopes with delivery from a dark, wet, confining space into a big, bright world. God eventually rewards the hope of those who believe in Jesus with delivery into a bigger and brighter existence with him. Hope is the message of Jesus. Hope propels us from one delivery to the other.

Jesus prayed about you and me right before he was arrested. He expressed his hope: **"Father, I want those you have given to me to be with me, to be where I am. I want them to see my glory, which you gave me because you loved me before the world was made"** (John 17:24 GW). Hope drove Jesus to dedicate himself to the saving work the Father sent him to do. Jesus hoped that every disciple God gave him, or would ever give him, would not be lost and would be united with him forever. Jesus' eternal hope is that through him all believers would be joined with the Father like he and the Father are one. Jesus is hoping for unity among women, children, and men and because all will be drawn into the glory of God through him. Hope is what heaven is for.

Jesus and integrity

Jason Nelson

I didn't know about integrity until my junior year in high school. Some of the cool girls drafted me to become class president. I wasn't the kind of guy they would go to prom with, but apparently they thought I was the kind of guy who could make sure there was a prom.

We were turning our gym into a tropical paradise and burning through our class treasury by making a massive papier-mâché volcano. The gym decorating came to a standstill because we were out of money and materials. Some of the guys carried in some shiny new rolls of chicken wire. I found out the wire was stolen. I kept my head down, loaded the rolls into my '61 Ford Galaxie, and took them back to the feed mill where they came from. I apologized to the proprietor. He in turn donated the wire to us. Prom was saved. The next day the principal called me into his office and said, "I heard what you did. That showed a lot of integrity." *Hmm. Integrity.* At a critical stage of my development, my principal gave me a building block for my self-concept. He said I had integrity. He also said I had to find a date for the prom.

Temptation tests our integrity. Jesus faced it like we do. We are vulnerable because we are isolated, spent, and crave acceptance. We have integrity when we can consistently say, **"Go away, Satan! Scripture says, 'Worship the Lord your God and serve only him'"** (Matthew 4:10 GW).

Jesus and justice

Jason Nelson

I love my Savior for spilling his blood to redeem my soul. I admire my Savior for insisting on justice in an unfair world. He laid down his innocent life for the guilty and has untarnished credibility to ask us to do right by others. If we see Jesus only as a champion of justice, we miss the totality of his redeeming work. If we are happy about our personal redemption but never act to end injustice, we miss the totality of his redeeming work.

Justice for undeserving people wouldn't exist had Jesus not arrived on the scene. He made it personal. He said, **"Whatever you did for one of the least of these brothers and sisters of mine, you did for me"** (Matthew 25:40). He was specific so that we can't claim we didn't know what he was talking about. He said whatever you did for the underfed, under clothed, wrongly imprisoned, widows, orphans, and anyone else being unfairly treated you have done for me. We can spend a lifetime believing the right things, but we come up short without seeking justice for those who need it.

Across the globe women and children suffer injustice disproportionately. No one elevated women and children like Jesus did. He was born of a woman, and women were among his closest disciples. He held up children as shining examples of faith. I can only speak for myself. I am sorry for being indifferent to the unjust treatment of so many. I intend to speak up because I am a Christian.

Jesus and service
Jason Nelson

In the upper room, Jesus stripped to the waist and washed his disciples' feet. That event inspired works of art, put an idiom in Christian speech, and demonstrated an irreducible form of service. **"I have set you an example that you should do as I have done for you"** (John 13:15). Jesus taught this core concept of his theology through an act dripping with meaning that his disciples couldn't miss. I am not aware of any other religious leader doing anything like that. I am not aware of any other belief system that reveres a menial task as the enduring standard for serving others. Jesus was on the way to make the ultimate sacrifice for us. He set it up with this humble act and authenticated how he wants us to follow him.

Jesus was selfless by nature. The rest of us need to learn to become that way. So, where do you see yourself in this picture?

We may want to be like Jesus: the Suffering Servant who proved that God came all the way down here to minister to us. We may identify with Peter, who was very self-conscious that his Lord and Savior would handle his gnarly feet. And we may see ourselves in the sponge. Yes, the sponge. We may see ourselves being filled up with the Water of Life repeatedly so that we can be rung out in the hands of Jesus over and over as we serve one person after another.

Pray the name

Pastor Mike Novotny

When I was a kid, I learned a way to pray called the A.C.T.S. Method. It stood for Adoration, Confession, Thanksgiving, and Supplication (asking for stuff). I understood the "I'm sorrys" and "thank you fors" and "please gimmes," but I never really got that first part. Adoration?

But now I get why the best prayer starts there. Adore God. Hallow his name. Meditate on how wonderfully different God is from even the best things in your life. Pray, "God, you are glorious. You created all of this. Your love never fails. You never change. You are always faithful, always forgiving, always in control. You are my hidden treasure, my everything. Earth has nothing I desire besides you."

If you start there, do you know what so naturally comes next? Confession. "But, God, that makes my sin even worse. I forgot your name. I ran to _____ to make me happy instead of to you." And do you know what flows from there? Thanksgiving. "But, Jesus, there is forgiveness in your name! You knew what I would do, but you still died for a sinner like me." Finally, supplication gets spiritual. "God, I want to have a good day, but what I really want is you. I want to remember you, know you, and see you by faith. I don't need anything else. Neither do my friends, my kids, my family. So, God, please open our minds to see you as wonderfully different as you are. **'Hallowed be your name'** (Matthew 6:9). Amen!"

Oh, that's a great way to pray!

Interactive Easter
Pastor Mark Jeske

Ask millennials why they prefer playing video games to watching television and they will give you a quick answer: because the games are interactive. TV is a passive experience. You just sit there. With screen games you participate in the story, become one of the characters, and influence the outcome. Video games are personal.

The incredible events of Holy Week are not only a great drama for us to watch, passively admiring and worshiping Jesus Christ for what he pulled off. Your baptism actually connects you to Christ and puts you into the story: **"We were therefore *buried* with him through baptism into death in order that, just as Christ was *raised* from the dead through the glory of the Father, we too may live a new life"** (Romans 6:4).

Isn't that amazing? Through faith in Christ you are personally involved in the events of his Passion. As he suffered for you, you are there. As he died your death, your sins were being judged and punished. As his lifeless body was gently laid in the tomb, you were buried too. And as he came to live, you and I experienced a spiritual resurrection for a new life.

We gaze in awe and adoration back at those stories, not just as history buffs but to celebrate our new hope, our new identities, and our new energy for service and usefulness.

We'll be alive in eternity. We're alive *now*.

A day to remember
Pastor Matt Ewart

Palm Sunday has become a regularly celebrated event. Some churches decorate their worship space with palm branches. Many churches have the entire service revolve around this one event. Christians make such a big deal about the day that it's worth asking: *What's the big deal about Jesus entering Jerusalem?*

Here's one thing to think about. When you look at the way people cheered for Jesus on Palm Sunday, it gives you a small glimpse of what Jesus rightfully deserved. Masses of people welcomed him into Jerusalem in a way that would be fitting for a king. They honored him in the biggest way they could. If Jesus wanted to, he could've made a kingdom full of people who cheered for him. He earned that.

But as he himself would soon declare to Pontius Pilate, he was after a different kind of kingdom. Though hailed a king on Sunday, his faithful obedience to his Father would mean he would submit to death on Friday. His crown would be one of thorns. His throne would be a cross.

That makes Palm Sunday a big deal. Jesus entered Jerusalem knowing full well what awaited him. This is the day he committed himself to a path of suffering and death. He entered Jerusalem to find you. That makes it a day worth remembering—even to this day.

"Hosanna! Blessed is he who comes in the name of the Lord! Blessed is the coming kingdom of our father David! Hosanna in the highest heaven!" (Mark 11:9,10).

A heart to hear

Linda Buxa

Sometimes when I don't know what to pray for, I take the advice of Jesus' brother James: **"If any of you lacks wisdom, you should ask God, who gives generously to all without finding fault, and it will be given to you"** (James 1:5).

I know I'm not completely wise, and if God said he'd give it to me, I might as well pray for it. After all, doesn't wisdom equal smart and knowledgeable? Who doesn't want that? Then I read Solomon's view of wisdom.

One night, the Lord appeared to Solomon in a dream and said, **"Ask for whatever you want me to give you."** Solomon didn't ask for riches or honor, but instead said, **"Give your servant a discerning heart to govern your people and to distinguish between right and wrong"** (1 Kings 3:5,9).

In Greek, "a discerning heart" means Solomon asked for "a heart to hear." Solomon's view of wisdom leaves less opportunity to display my knowledge and more opportunities to display my love. A heart to hear means that in all my interactions with people, I'm asking for more patience, more awareness of their needs. It means I take the time to listen, which leaves less time to talk and display my wisdom. It means I have compassion to see where other people are hurting and find ways to serve them. A heart to hear requires more of me, because it's not about me.

Ask for a heart to hear, and it will be given to you.

Loving forbearance
Sarah Habben

Makrothumia is a Greek word used to describe one of the Holy Spirit's fruits. *Makro* means "long." *Thumos* means "anger." So *makrothumia* literally means "long to get angry." We would call it patience, or forbearance.

Meet Archer. He goes from zero to boiling in under 60 seconds. He's easily offended. He punches back. He wears a proactive frown. To be fair, Archer is only four. He's a work in progress.

We're well past preschool, but we're still a lot like Archer. We find little virtue in curbing our frustration, holding our tongues, or turning the other cheek. We think spite is our right.

Meet God. *He*, if anyone, has a right to anger. Think of Adam's fateful bite, the grumbling Israelites, the spiritually blind Pharisees, the slow-to-believe disciples, your hair-trigger temper, my mean streak. What has stopped God from slamming heaven's door and pitching humanity into hell's abyss? *Makrothumia*, that's what. God is slow to anger. And what genuine relief that gives us when we **"bear in mind that our Lord's patience means salvation"** (2 Peter 3:15).

God patiently withheld his anger over our sin until his Son hung on a cross—and then God punished Jesus in our place. God still exercises perfect patience. He wants us to repent, not perish, and so he forbears and forgives. He treats us gently, as works in progress.

Thank you, God, for being slow to anger, for not giving up on me. When my own patience is tested, help me bear with others in love. Amen.

Power play

Pastor Matt Ewart

In hockey there's this thing called a power play. Basically when a player is penalized, he is forced to sit in the penalty box while his teammates play a man down. The opposing team members do their best to take advantage of the situation. They attack full force while their opponent is weak.

That concept happens beyond hockey. In fact, it'll probably come into play for you today. There will be situations where you have the upper hand against someone else. You'll have the opportunity to take advantage of someone else's weakness.

Jesus had such an opportunity too. The day before his death, when he was about to celebrate the Passover with his disciples, John includes this detail in his gospel: **"Jesus knew that the Father had put all things under his power, and that he had come from God and was returning to God"** (John 13:3).

What did Jesus do when given a power play? Not what I would do. Probably not what you would do either. He got down on his knees to wash his disciples' feet. And within 24 hours, Jesus would stoop down even lower as he died on a cross to wash away their sins and yours.

Not only was this foot washing a beautiful demonstration of Jesus' love. He wanted this expression of his love to be a model for you. Today when you have the upper hand on someone else, make a power play and serve him or her as Jesus served you.

A palpable pardon

Sarah Habben

The table bore evidence of a feast: bowls smeared with bitter herbs, cooled slices of lamb, torn unleavened bread. A group of men sat with their Master; their fear and worry had temporarily retired to the dark corners of the room. They were observing Passover, recalling that remarkable night in Egypt 1,500 years before when God's death plague *passed over* all those who sheltered behind doorframes painted with lamb's blood.

Jesus, who had earlier kneeled to clean his followers' feet, was not done surprising. He took a piece of bread and broke it. His strange and wonderful words still ring in our ears: **"Take and eat; this is my body."** Lifting a cup of wine, he said, **"Drink from it, all of you. This is my blood of the covenant, which is poured out for many for the forgiveness of sins"** (Matthew 26:26-28).

Soon the blood of God's Lamb would be spilled so that all the world could shelter behind it. Soon God's holy anger would *pass over* sinful humanity and strike down his Son instead. But Jesus' love didn't waver, even at hell's gate. In love, he left his followers of all time a legacy: the sacrament of his body and blood. In it we receive a palpable pardon for all our sins and relief from fear and guilt.

Your Savior has prepared a feast of forgiveness for you in the Lord's Supper, which you won't want to pass over.

You have an advocate

Pastor Jeremy Mattek

A criminal defense attorney once told me that the most frequent question he's asked is: "Why do you defend people you know are guilty?" When I asked him how he normally responds, he said he doesn't consider himself to be a successful attorney only if his client doesn't go to prison. "Truth is," he said, "most of my clients *are* guilty of something. However," he went on, "not every person charged with a crime is treated fairly." Under the law, even criminals have rights; rights that are sometimes violated or ignored during their arrest. His goal is to make sure every person is treated fairly.

In 1 John 2:1 the Bible describes Jesus as an advocate; someone who, like a lawyer, comes to someone's defense. The Bible says that Jesus chooses to defend us; individuals who are most certainly guilty of any number of sins that God's law condemns.

But he not only defends us. He also did something even the best attorney wouldn't do. He volunteered to take our punishment and offered himself as a sacrifice.

He did that because he believes you have rights. Because of Jesus' sacrifice, you have the God-given right to walk through life knowing you are forgiven. You have the right to be released from the guilt you've been carrying and to know God loves you, no matter how you've sinned.

You have the right to know you'll always have an advocate who will come to your defense and will always win.

april 15

Strong tower

Pastor Mike Novotny

I will never forget standing behind the walls of Masada. Just west of the Dead Sea, Masada is an ancient fortress built on a tiny plateau, surrounded by steep drops. When the Roman army toppled Jewish cities and towns, Jewish rebels fled to Masada, the impregnable fortress. Up on that tower they were safe.

How about you? Where do you go when the walls of your life come crumbling down? when a friend won't forgive you? when the surgeon can't guarantee the surgery will work? when you can't bring your husband back from the dead? when you feel like a hopeless failure? When life marches like an army and threatens to kill your peace and take your happiness captive, where do you run?

The name of God! Proverbs says, **"The name of the LORD is a fortified tower; the righteous run to it and are safe"** (18:10). Like Masada, there's a refuge to which you can run. There's a tower so strong and so high that the fiercest enemies can't break in. Jesus Christ shed his blood so that the door to that tower would always be open to you. By washing away your sins, he guaranteed God's name would be a source of comfort and security, a mighty fortress to help you free from every need.

Masada, if you haven't heard, wasn't as strong as the rebels thought. The Romans figured out a way to get in. But not the name of God. That tower will always keep you safe. So, run to it. Run to God.

Crabby church people
Pastor Mark Jeske

In Jesus' famous parable, the prodigal son gets all the main attention, but Jesus has important things to say about the fuming "good boy" who stayed home and worked.

"When he came near the house, he heard music and dancing. The older brother became angry and refused to go in. So his father went out and pleaded with him. But he answered his father, 'Look! All these years I've been slaving for you and never disobeyed your orders. Yet you never gave me even a young goat so I could celebrate with my friends. But when this son of yours who has squandered your property with prostitutes comes home, you kill the fattened calf for him!'" (Luke 15:25,28-30).

It is a miserable facet of human nature that some bad boys and girls are still out in the spiritual cold because they assume that their older brothers and sisters (a.k.a. church people) judge them and despise them. The church is supposed to be the official broker of God's mercy, but sometimes the institution is as cold and suspicious as the older son in this parable.

The hypocrisy reeks. People with their lives more under control are still by nature sinful as well and need Christ's mercy and forgiveness just as much as prodigals. And if they have stayed in church while others ran away, even that is a gift from the working of the Holy Spirit.

Are you ready to risk a fattened calf when a prodigal in your life exhibits signs of repentance?

Spread the word
Linda Buxa

"Many of the Samaritans from that town believed in him because of the woman's testimony, 'He told me everything I ever did.' So when the Samaritans came to him, they urged him to stay with them, and he stayed two days. And because of his words many more became believers. They said to the woman, 'We no longer believe just because of what you said; now we have heard for ourselves, and we know that this man really is the Savior of the world'" (John 4:39-42).

The Samaritan woman had what most would consider a checkered past: four husbands and now living with another. She wasn't exactly welcome in polite company, which is why she was getting water at the well in the heat of the day. Yet Jesus talked to her. She met the Messiah and knew other people needed to meet him too. So she introduced Jesus to the people, and they ultimately believed because of his words, not hers.

That's how it is supposed to work. Most people meet Jesus for the first time through others who already believe in him. After Jesus took God's wrath on the cross and rose from death, he went back into heaven—and told people to make disciples. So get busy.

The people around you will likely first meet Jesus because of your words. Then, just like the Samaritan woman, invite them to meet Jesus through his Word. The Holy Spirit will work through those words, which have authority, power, and are living and active.

Love in action
Sarah Habben

Fruit trees need strong roots. Roots help a tree gather enough moisture and nutrients to eventually bear fruit.

God wants his people to bear fruit too, fruit that is never out of season. And just as the fruit of a tree proceeds from its root, so a Christian's fruit proceeds from the hidden work of the Holy Spirit. Through the gospel of God's love, the Spirit changes us, enabling us to bear "the fruit of the Spirit." One example of that fruit is Christian love.

The love that comes naturally to humans grows from worldly roots. Such love is quick to ripen and quick to rot. Love rooted in the gospel is different. **"This is how we know what love is: Jesus Christ laid down his life for us. And we ought to lay down our lives for our brothers and sisters. . . . Let us not love with words or speech but with actions and in truth"** (1 John 3:16,18).

Of course, laying down our life for someone is not a typical way that we show Christian love. Daily love is not so heroic. But it does require holy strength to lay down our impatience with our whining children, to lay down our own agendas and listen to a friend's worries, to lay down our desire to retaliate when someone hurts us. Such love in action requires the work of the Spirit in our hearts. Such love is only possible because Christ loved us first.

Astonishing peace

Sarah Habben

"Inner peace" is a state of internal calm and self-acceptance. If you have it, you're able to transcend past regrets and future worries. You're unruffled by the behavior of others.

But there's a catch. Inner peace has to come from, well, *within*. It requires a great mastery of self. After all, what "Zen den" is so deep that regret and fear can't claw out? We can train our minds and tether our negativity, but no matter how strong our will, we cannot control it always. Inner peace has limits.

If only our mistakes could be ripped from the ledger, never to raise their accusing voices again! If only, instead of mere acceptance of those mistakes, there was payment for them. If only we had an *outside* voice, not an inner one, reminding us regularly and with great authority, that peace was ours. If only that peace was so formidably fashioned that fear could no longer stalk our hearts and guilt could no longer hold our minds hostage. Wouldn't that just boggle your brain?

There is such a peace. It was forged by Jesus in the furnace of Good Friday. Flourished at his empty tomb on Easter Sunday. Honed by the Holy Spirit whenever we hear God's promise of forgiveness. It stands guard at our hearts and minds so that fear and guilt cannot gain entry. It's not inner peace. It's an astonishing peace.

"And the peace of God, which transcends all understanding, will guard your hearts and your minds in Christ Jesus" (Philippians 4:7).

Inspiring respect
Pastor Matt Ewart

There are two ways to get respect: the easy way and the hard way.

The easy way to get respect is by demanding it. Maybe you've heard someone say something like this: "Don't you know who I am?" or "Don't you know what I can do?" The easy way to get respect means you hold up your position or your title over everybody beneath you.

The hard way to get respect is to not assume you have it automatically. Rather, you act so as to inspire it. You leverage your position or title to serve those beneath you. This is not the easy way to get respect, nor is it the expected way. But the result will be much more genuine.

Here's the surprising part. While God deserves your respect simply by virtue of who he is, he decided to leverage his position to serve you and save you. Although he could have been satisfied to just demand respect from you, it was his plan to inspire it. That plan, prophesied about in Jeremiah, would unfold eventually and beautifully in Jesus: **"I will make an everlasting covenant with them: I will never stop doing good to them, and I will inspire them to fear me, so that they will never turn away from me"** (Jeremiah 32:40).

What titles do you have? What positions do you hold? God inspired your respect even though he could have demanded it. Maybe today he will give you an opportunity to do the same.

The name game

Pastor Mike Novotny

Have you ever played the name game—when you blurt out the first thing that pops into your mind when you hear someone's name? For example, what do you think of when I say . . . Justin Bieber? What about Al Capone? What about your boss?

But what about God? God cares intensely about your answer. Here's why: God's name, for all practical purposes, is what you think about God. It's his reputation in your heart. That reputation might be right or wrong, biblical or man-made, soul-stirring or yawn-producing, but whatever you associate with God's name matters more than anything. It determines your level of peace, your amount of joy, how you deal with drama, and how blessed you will be today. In fact, what we think about God is so important that the Jewish people sometimes referred to him simply as *Ha Shem*, which is Hebrew for "The Name."

That explains why God played the name game with Moses in Exodus chapter 34: **"[The Lord] stood there with [Moses] and proclaimed his name, the Lord. And he passed in front of Moses, proclaiming, 'The Lord, the Lord, the compassionate and gracious God, slow to anger, abounding in love and faithfulness, maintaining love to thousands, and forgiving wickedness, rebellion and sin'"** (verses 5-7).

God wanted the world to think of a lot when it came to his holy name. So meditate on those verses for a few minutes. Then, tell me, what do you think of when I say . . . God?

God's children

Linda Buxa

On July 1, 2015, Sir Nicholas George Winton died at age 106. When he was 30, this British man worked in Prague, Czechoslovakia, in a refugee camp filled with people fleeing from the coming Nazi invasion.

While there, parents begged him to get their children out of the country before the Nazis arrived. He returned to London, raised money to cover the cost of transportation, found foster parents for each child, and secured a 50 pound guarantee for each child—to pay for travel when they eventually left Britain. In nine months, Nicholas Winton managed to evacuate 669 children on eight trains from Prague to London, and a group of 15 were flown to Sweden. And those children came to be known as Winton's Children.

Those children needed Sir Winton. They certainly couldn't save themselves. Their relatives couldn't get them out. They needed someone to step up and make a sacrifice to rescue them.

The war that Satan and sin had waged on the world meant we were just like those children—doomed to death. We couldn't get out of danger on our own. Family and friends couldn't earn salvation for us. All of humanity needed someone to step up and make a sacrifice to rescue us. And that's what Jesus did. Because he stepped up and sacrificed himself, **"see what great love the Father has lavished on us, that we should be called children of God! And that is what we are!"** (1 John 3:1).

The Shepherd's voice

Linda Buxa

"His sheep follow him because they know his voice. But they will never follow a stranger; in fact, they will run away from him because they do not recognize a stranger's voice" (John 10:4,5).

Oh, Jesus, you sacrificed glory in heaven to come to earth for me. You sacrificed glory on earth to die in my place. You showed your glory by coming back to life after being dead. You called my name and made me part of your family.

You have earned the right to be my Shepherd, and I know your voice. Temptations and danger are not from you. It's not like Satan wants to love me. His demons aren't working for my benefit. This world isn't on my side either. Let me not even be interested in or distracted by any of them. In fact, help me run away from anyone who isn't my Shepherd, from anything that hasn't earned the right for my attention.

You, Jesus, are my Good Shepherd. You lead me. You protect me. You give me rest. You are with me. You chase me down with your goodness and mercy. You comfort me. You give me everything I need. You give me courage. You give me peace. You give me uncountable blessings. You give me eternal life.

Let me love your voice. Help me follow you.

And all God's people said, "Amen!"

Overcome! Enjoy eternal life

Pastor Mark Jeske

Everybody wants heaven on earth. Nobody's going to get it until God sends the archangel Michael to blow the celestial trumpet and announce the Great Day of Judgment.

In the meantime, brothers and sisters, you and I are in the middle of a live-fire exercise. It's war. We are under outward assault from Satan, his demons, and all his many human helpers. Worse, we are internally at risk from our own sinful hearts and weak flesh. Over and over God encourages us in his Word to hear his voice, believe his promises, claim his unconditional love and free forgiveness, and *overcome*.

The book of Revelation contains seven mini-epistles to seven congregations in western Asia Minor. Each one concludes with the intense encouragement for the believers to fight their spiritual battles and do whatever it takes to prevail: **"To him who overcomes, I will give the right to eat from the tree of life, which is in the paradise of God"** (Revelation 2:7 NIV84).

Adam and Eve were expelled from the Garden of Eden, among other reasons, in order that they wouldn't eat of the tree of life in their sinful condition and be locked forever in their brokenness. Here is God's wonderful promise to all overcomers, i.e., those who didn't throw their faith away and cave in to Satan's lies: immortality in our original, pristine spiritual condition.

Imagine it: You will never feel more alive. Sickness and death will never trouble you again.

Overcome! No hell for you

Pastor Mark Jeske

Have you ever had your evangelism invitation to another sinner blown off with a remark like, "I'm not concerned about any so-called judgment day; I've already suffered my hell on this earth"? One way or another you have to deliver the hard news: "No, you haven't. You have not remotely begun to experience the wrath that God is going to bring down on Satan, his demons, and all who follow him."

Even people with very hard lives get to enjoy the blessings that a kind God distributes to believers and unbelievers alike: orange and purple sunsets, gentle rain on a June evening, the bracing cold air of winter, melodies from birds overhead. The hell described by Scripture has none of those things—only a misery so intense and persistent that not even a drop of water for parched mouths was to be given to the damned in Jesus' parable of the rich man and poor Lazurus.

Our Savior Jesus experienced hell for us on his horrible cross—supreme physical agony coupled with the dark fury of God's judgment. He suffered all alone, and he suffered enough. Through his precious gospel he gives you and me heartfelt encouragement not to grow weary in our faith: **"He who overcomes will not be hurt at all by the second death"** (Revelation 2:11 NIV84). The first death is the perishing of our bodies, which God will undo with a simple word. It is the second death, condemnation to hell, that is far worse, and Jesus has freed you from it.

Hang on! Just a little bit longer . . .

Overcome! A hidden life awaits

Pastor Mark Jeske

In 1969 Peggy Lee had a hit song called "Is That All There Is?" The lyrics describe a world-weary woman who's seen it all, tried it all, and is left with nothing but disappointment.

I fear that Peggy is speaking for a lot of people. Nothing has worked out for them as advertised. Their hopes, frustrated. Their dreams, crushed. Could you not, right now, without having to think too hard, make a list of ten permanent wounds that you carry? Does it make you sad to see your life slipping away? Do you feel cheated?

The Revelation of St. John helps you see that a magnificent hidden life awaits you in heaven and that it's a gift of God's grace to you just as miraculous manna once fell from heaven to feed the hungry Israelites. **"To him who overcomes, I will give some of the hidden manna. I will also give him a white stone with a new name written on it, known only to him who receives it"** (Revelation 2:17 NIV84).

Group decisions used to be made with white and black stones. A black stone was a veto. A white stone was an affirmation. Think of it—through Jesus Christ your Savior, God has voted you in!

Don't give up! Don't quit! A magnificent hidden life awaits you!

Overcome! There will be justice

Pastor Mark Jeske

Have you recently been the victim of a crime? Which is worse—that the case is never solved and the evildoer remains hidden or that the criminal is caught but is unable to be convicted? Either way the evildoer goes free; either way there is no justice.

Satan and his evil brood seem to be getting away with murder, aren't they? Our human attempts at security, policing, courts, and appropriate punishment and deterrence are flawed and partial. As hard as we try to establish justice, we all know that injustices abound—unsolved crimes, racism and prejudices, graft and corruption, and bribery have never been abolished.

Hang on! Don't be afraid, and don't give up. A time is coming when the great King of heaven will return and hold the world accountable for its deeds. And get this—the believers will share in this divine accountability process: **"To him who overcomes and does my will to the end, I will give authority over the nations—'He will rule them with an iron scepter; he will dash them to pieces like pottery'—just as I have received authority from my Father"** (Revelation 2:26,27 NIV84).

What this means is that you can absorb injustice now, knowing that God will take care of business later. Claim Christ's forgiveness now, so that you can be sure that no outstanding indictments will be hanging over your head in the judgment.

And then you too will be seated with the Judge.

Overcome! Enjoy your heavenly clothes
Pastor Mark Jeske

Why do brides universally prefer to dress in white for their weddings? The color just seems to be perfect for the occasion—purity, a new start, joy, elegance. Dark colors are for funerals. A wedding dress needs to be white.

You and I are heading for a wedding—the Big One, when Christ the Bridegroom comes for the believers, his church, his bride. The heavenly Groom is very particular about his bride's outfit. He wants us to wear the pure and beautiful robes of his holiness, bought for us at the terrible price of his life. In heaven we will not only have our sinful criminal record expunged, but we will personally be cleansed as well. Won't it be wonderful never again to have an evil desire? speak wicked words? offend God with evil deeds?

Overcome! Don't let Satan steal your place at the wedding or persuade you to throw away your clothes. Overcome! The hardships and struggles are soon over and will become a faint memory. Overcome! You can lean all the weight of your hopes and expectations on your Savior Jesus. **"He who overcomes will, like them, be dressed in white. I will *never* blot out his name from the book of life, but will acknowledge his name before my Father and his angels"** (Revelation 3:5 NIV84).

His gift of grace makes you look beautiful to him. Your name in the book of life is in his handwriting.

april **29**

Overcome! Eternal belonging
Pastor Mark Jeske

There aren't many experiences in life worse than being excluded, shut out from a group to which you would like to belong. Middle-school girls learn quickly how much pain they can inflict on another girl by refusing to let her into their circle. Gangs have an eternal allure to young men who desperately want to be part of something big.

Here's a concept—God knows your name and face and life, and he wants you, yes *you*, to be not just an extra in a heaven crowd scene but an important part of his celestial family. He wants you not on the fringes but right in the center of things: **"Him who overcomes I will make a pillar in the temple of my God. Never again will he leave it. I will write on him the name of my God and the name of the city of my God, the new Jerusalem, which is coming down out of heaven from my God; and I will also write on him my new name"** (Revelation 3:12 NIV84).

You may or may not be into tattoos in this life—do you have any ink? But figuratively speaking God is going to put his everlasting claim on you by "writing" his name on you. Imagine—he desires an everlasting relationship with you, the ultimate belonging.

Heaven is even better than being put back into the Garden of Eden, where you would have to endure the serpent's temptations all over again. When we arrive in heaven, we are there to stay!

Overcome! You shall be a co-regent

Pastor Mark Jeske

What is your personal idea of what life in heaven will be like? Do you see yourself as a bored singer going to choir practice for the eight millionth time? lying around on vacation for zillions of years? a cherub in God's angel army? a janitor, happy to sweep up after everyone else?

Get this—Jesus Christ promises his faithful overcomers that they will not only enter heaven but join him at the center of power in the universe. We are not only his loyal subjects—we are also his brothers and sisters, which makes us princes and princesses. We are heavenly royalty. For now we accept that great honor and dignity as an invisible promise. We struggle and suffer; we endure and wait.

But when Jesus returns, the believers will see for themselves how high he will lift them up: **"To him who overcomes, I will give the right to sit with me on my throne, just as I overcame and sat down with my Father on his throne"** (Revelation 3:21 NIV84). Imagine! Co-regents with the Lord of the universe. Who could believe that if it weren't actually written in the Bible? You can look it up for yourself. No matter how small and powerless and insignificant you may feel now, your Savior has amazing plans for an amazing eternity for you.

Hang on! The glory to come is worth every bit of your hardships today.

may

Let us acknowledge the Lord; let us press on to
acknowledge him. As surely as the sun rises,
he will appear; he will come to us like the winter
rains, like the spring rains that water the earth.

Hosea 6:3

Knowing joy
Sarah Habben

We all like being happy. The problem with happiness is that it's circumstantial. Happiness winks on and off like a firefly's backside. Hitting green lights all the way to work makes us happy. Getting rear-ended in the parking lot makes us unhappy. A compliment from a coworker makes us happy. Being criticized makes us unhappy. Happiness hangs out at ball games and family reunions. But it's an infrequent guest at funerals and in ER waiting rooms.

Joy is different. Joy isn't a feeling. It's more of a *knowing*. **"For the joy set before him** [Jesus] **endured the cross, scorning its shame, and sat down at the right hand of the throne of God"** (Hebrews 12:2).

Jesus' joy was knowing he was about to make peace between sinful humanity and our holy God. Did he feel happy when he anticipated the agony of the cross, abandonment by his Father, the weight of our sins, and death? No—he was overwhelmed with sorrow! But even in sorrow he knew the joy of doing his Father's will: presenting the world with the forgiveness we could never earn.

And so a Christian's joy is closely linked to Jesus' joy. His joy was in giving that gift. Ours is in receiving it. We *know*—however dark our circumstance, however we *feel*—we have God's favor and a heavenly home. From that knowledge grows a joy that makes our hearts stand tall even when pummeled by earthly sorrow. A joy that smiles in every circumstance.

Even at red lights.

Glimpses of the gospel

Pastor Mike Novotny

I sinned during the sermon. Although it was not my intention, I said something very personal and very aggressive toward a member of our congregation. She was hurt and confused. I would not have been surprised if she found a new church. But she didn't. Instead she reached out to me and, after my sincere repentance, we reconciled. These days, if you would see the two of us at our church, you would see smiles and laughter and genuine friendship.

Do you know what that is? Not just a Hallmark ending. That is a glimpse of God. When the apostle Paul wrote, **"God's invisible qualities—his eternal power and divine nature—have been clearly seen, being understood from what has been made"** (Romans 1:20), he was telling us that what we see and experience here has a lot in common with the God "up there." If Jesus is the Light of the world and if her forgiveness was "letting her light shine," then what I experienced from her was a glimpse of Jesus himself.

Just imagine the connections. Every word of encouragement is a faint echo of God's voice, prepared to say, "Well done, good and faithful servant!" Every invitation to come to the party is a preview of Jesus, ready to say, "Come and share in your Master's happiness." Every act of love that you simply do not deserve and never would expect is a glimpse of the grace of God.

He showed them

Jason Nelson

One of the unlimited number of things that sets Jesus apart from anyone else wearing skin was the way he taught. He generally didn't get all preachy except on those who should have known better like the Pharisees. He didn't go on and on much *about* God. In his words and actions, he showed us God. So much so that anyone who watched him live and saw him die could arrive at only one conclusion: **"When the centurion and those with him who were guarding Jesus saw the earthquake and all that had happened, they were terrified, and exclaimed, 'Surely he was the Son of God!'"** (Matthew 27:54).

When blind Bartimaeus annoyed people because he was constantly clamoring for any kind of mercy, Jesus asked him one pointed question: **"What do you want me to do for you?"** Bartimaeus answered very directly, **"Rabbi, I want to see"** (Mark 10:51).

When some Greeks visiting Jerusalem wondered what all the fuss was about on Palm Sunday, they approached Philip: **"'Sir,' they said, 'we would like to see Jesus'"** (John 12:21).

Jesus showed himself to his own forerunner: **"Go back and report to John what you hear and see: The blind receive sight, the lame walk, those who have leprosy are cleansed, the deaf hear, the dead are raised, and the good news is proclaimed to the poor. Blessed is anyone who does not stumble on account of me"** (Matthew 11:4-6).

People don't stumble over what they can see.

He picked me
Linda Buxa

In 1846 some Wisconsin residents were trying to choose a name for their small town. No one could agree, so they settled on a solution. They put letters of the alphabet on slips of paper and let a young girl pick them out until the letters formed a name.

Hello, Ixonia! If towns could have feelings, I bet this town would feel pretty special. After all, as the only town in the United States with this name, Ixonia was—literally—handpicked.

Who knew you'd have something in common with a small town in Wisconsin? Isaiah tells you that you do. (And because you do have emotions, the following passage makes you feel pretty special. Just read your name in place of Jacob and Israel.)

"But now, this is what the LORD says—he who created you, Jacob, he who formed you, Israel: 'Do not fear, for I have redeemed you; I have summoned you by name; you are mine'" (Isaiah 43:1).

The God who placed stars in the heavens formed you. He handpicked how he wanted you to be put together, your skills, your gifts, your personality, your appearance. You are exactly who he wants you to be.

So while there are things that concern you in this world, you are so secure in his love and protection that you don't have to be afraid. Because God sent his Son, Jesus, to buy you back from Satan's control, you are now his—and he calls you by name.

Now you can say, "He picked me."

Hallowed be

Pastor Mike Novotny

Hallowed be thy name. Recognize those words? They are the second line (and the first request) in the most famous prayer of all time, the Lord's Prayer. But do you know what they mean? (Would you bet your cell phone on your answer?) *Hallowed?* Not exactly a word we use, well, ever! Is it like . . . *Hallow-een*? Is it the way British gentlemen greet one another? Hallow!

Let me help. *Hallowed* is a verb that technically means "to honor as sacred." But I prefer this definition—"to think of someone as wonderfully different." In this case, God's name (what we think about God). That helps me understand Jesus' famous prayer. The very first thing to pray for, even before daily bread and forgiveness of sins, is for help to think of our Father as wonderfully different. Because if I think of God as different from everything I love in this life, as infinitely better than the best parts of my days, then my soul gets stirred up to worship.

Like this—"Father, open my eyes to see that you are more beautiful than the sun coming up. You are more faithful than my golden retriever. You are more exciting than a last-second touchdown pass. You are more captivating than the little toes of my newborn granddaughter. You are more enjoyable than perfectly cooked pasta. You are more forgiving than my best friend. In a million ways, Father, you are more. You are different. Wonderfully different."

That's what Jesus meant here: **"Our Father in heaven, hallowed be your name"** (Matthew 6:9).

What are you praying *against*?

Linda Buxa

Christians are pretty good at praying *for* something.

We say it all the time, "I'll pray *for* <fill in the blank>." Whatever the blank is, we pray *for* healing, peace, you, help, me, marriage, patience, family, courage, finances.

I don't think I've ever heard a Christian say, "I'll pray *against* <fill in the blank>."

Still, over and over in the Bible, we hear about the concept. In the book of Psalms, King David prayed against evil and specifically said, **"My prayer will still be against the deeds of evildoers"** (Psalm 141:5).

So recently, I started to pray against evil.

I prayed against evil words that belittle people. I prayed against corruption. I prayed against those who defend partially delivering a child, then crushing its skull and vacuuming out its brain. I prayed against the spiritual forces of evil that lead people into depression and suicidal thoughts.

You know what? It was scary and awesome at the same time. We often give sin a softer name, one that seems more culturally acceptable. But sin is evil, and evil opposes the will of God.

So while we are busy praying good prayers for things, we should also pray against some things too. Because while the God of the universe has already won the war, there are still battles to fight.

"For our struggle is not against flesh and blood, but against the rulers, against the authorities, against the powers of this dark world and against the spiritual forces of evil in the heavenly realms" (Ephesians 6:12).

Sacrifices sacrifice something

Pastor Mark Jeske

The worship life of the Old Testament Israelites looked very different from a Christian church service today. When you came to Jerusalem, you would bring a sacrifice, either of your crops or of one of your animals. The head of the family would carry out the slaughter of the animal with the priest and watch the blood flow.

Imagine that you are the farmer or shepherd watching that animal die. Some of your wealth was going down the drain right in front of your eyes! That male animal would never be able to sire offspring. That meat being burned up on the great altar couldn't be eaten to nourish any people. And on the great festivals? **"The next day they made sacrifices to the Lord and presented burnt offerings to him: a thousand bulls, a thousand rams and a thousand male lambs, together with their drink offerings"** (1 Chronicles 29:21).

Those sacrifices really sacrificed something; that is, they really cost the Israelite people something of value. Animals were their wealth. When they slaughtered those animals, they were sending some powerful messages to God: 1) We are obeying you. 2) We love you and appreciate you and want to show it by giving our best. 3) *We have utter confidence that you can and will replace these animals and much more.*

That's also our spirit as we give our sacrificial gifts to the Lord. Lord, you are the Source of everything. We know you will give back to us much more than we ever gave to you.

may 8

Missed use?

Pastor Mike Novotny

When I was a teenager, my mom would always give me the same speech before going out: "No drinking, no smoking, no sex, no drugs." Looking back, I understand why she chose those four. It only takes one night of drunken driving or one act of sex to change a life forever.

But what about God's top ten? No murder, no adultery, no idolatry. I get those. But no **"misusing the name of the Lord your God"** (Exodus 20:7)? Is that really worthy of one of the top spots?

Absolutely. Here's why: The biggest misuse of God's name is the missed use of God's name, when Jesus' name isn't used at all. When we wallow in sin and shame instead of calling on his name. When we feel lonely instead of thinking of the One who promised to be with us always. When we believe our work is worthless despite the promises of the God who said our labor would never be in vain. When we don't think of God at all, when we miss using his name, we misuse his name.

Please do not forget the glorious name of our God. The Lamb of God who takes away the sin of the world. The compassionate Father who is close to the brokenhearted. The Groom who pursues and woos and proposes to live with his Bride in spiritual sickness and health. Think deeply about your Savior, Redeemer, and Friend, and you'll know why your Father never wanted you to go out without a reminder of his holy name.

Mercy for doubters

Pastor Mark Jeske

A waitress at the restaurant where I once worked told me why she wasn't a church member. "I would like to believe," she said. I was stunned. To me faith was obvious and easy. Not to her. She actually kind of wanted to be a believer, but it just wasn't happening for her.

What's not to understand about the coming judgment? How can you not agree with the Bible's teaching of universal evil? What's not to like about a Savior who gives you unconditional love, forgiveness of your sins, and eternal life after death?

Sometimes church lifers like me forget that all faith is a gift from God. We are all born skeptics and doubters. Until Word and sacrament turn on the lights in our brains and bring warmth to our cold hearts, we find the Bible's stories strange and unbelievable. One of the very first fruits of our gratitude for the gift of faith should be patience with those who are not as far along as we have been blessed to come: **"Be merciful to those who doubt"** (Jude 1:22).

It's important that church people don't make inquirers feel stupid. It's important that we take their questions seriously and that we have God's answers for people from God's words, not our own doctrinal opinions. An arrogant and judgmental tone in our voices might keep people frozen in their doubts.

A soft voice, listening ears, and compassionate heart are better. Way better.

To forgive, willingly give
Pastor Matt Ewart

Forgiveness is to give willingly what someone took wrongfully.

There are many definitions of forgiveness out there, but the one above captures why forgiveness can be so difficult to give. It requires a willingness to give away something that was wrongfully taken.

That's the last thing you want to do when someone wrongs you, but that's the essence of forgiveness. You must decide to give what was taken. It doesn't mean the other person was right to take it. It just means you refuse to seek payback.

As you work to apply that definition of forgiveness to your own life, constantly keep in mind how God applied that definition for us. Jesus willingly gave what we wrongfully took. He offered to his Father a payment on our behalf, and the payment added up to his own life. For God to forgive us, he had to willingly give what we wrongfully took. Life for life.

What might forgiveness cost you today? Some pride? Some money? Your place in line? The need to forgive is more of a certainty than a possibility, so always be mindful of what was forgiven for you. The power to willingly give what was wrongfully taken comes from knowing what God willingly gave for you. For times when the cost is hard to deal with, here is a passage that demonstrates God's heart toward you: **"I will forgive their wickedness and will remember their sins no more"** (Jeremiah 31:34).

Don't lose heart

Sarah Habben

I intend to go to the gym at 5:30 A.M., but my pillow is so soft. I sit down to read a devotion, but I find myself on Facebook. A lack of self-control can harm both body and spirit.

An Olympic runner has an iron will. She beats her body into submission because she's aiming for gold. She strives even though she knows her accomplishment is impermanent.

I am in a race toward a prize that will last forever: the crown of eternal life. But my race isn't over. I need spiritual self-control to stay the course, to not be disqualified for the prize. The thing is, when it comes to self-control, I have two "selves" in me. My sinner-self wanders from the course with dangerous indifference. My saint-self runs in step with the Spirit. For as long as I live on earth, my inner sinner and saint will fight for control.

Can I win this race? Only with the Holy Spirit's help. My personal (spiritual) trainer uses God's Word to strip me of my indifference and to recharge my faith. He enables me to keep my eyes on the prize. "Fix your eyes on Jesus!" he urges. "Don't lose heart. Don't drop out. Christ has won the victory, and he has a crown of life for you."

"Everyone who competes in the games goes into strict training. They do it to get a crown that will not last, but we do it to get a crown that will last forever" (1 Corinthians 9:25).

It's what you know

Pastor Matt Ewart

*"Whether you think you can or
think you can't, you're right."*—Henry Ford

People have long recognized the power of belief. As a child you were probably told more than once that *you can do anything if you put your mind to it.*

There might be some truth to that on some level, but God offers you something better than shaping the way you *think* about yourself. In his gift of Baptism, he changes what you *know* about yourself.

No matter how long ago the water was applied to you in the name of God, everything in your past is under the jurisdiction of your baptism. That means the guilt you feel has been washed away. The sin you committed is forgiven. Your identity is tied to Jesus' perfect record. Your purpose is driven by who God says you are, and he says you are his loved child.

Baptism doesn't just change what you *think* about yourself. It's so much better than that. It changes what you *know* about yourself. In this washing with water through the Word, everything Jesus did is poured freely out onto you. In Baptism your past is forgiven and your present is redeemed.

When you know who you are, it changes everything.

"In Christ Jesus you are all children of God through faith, for all of you who were baptized into Christ have clothed yourselves with Christ" (Galatians 3:26,27).

A listening ministry

Jason Nelson

If you're still looking to find your niche in the body of Christ, try a listening ministry. In spite of the admonition that **"everyone should be quick to listen, slow to speak"** (James 1:19), most people would rather talk. I would. I'm a lousy listener, and I did it for a living. It took restraint to let others finish their stories and not tell mine. If you can pay attention like a mute angel, you can make someone's day.

In his book the *Friendship Factor*, the late Dr. Alan Loy McGinnis points out the qualities of good listeners.

"Good listeners listen with their eyes." It's hard to fake facial expressions. Glancing away while someone's talking is dismissive. Listening means leaning in and focusing our interest on the other person.

"Good listeners dispense advice sparingly." No one really cares what we would do if we were them because we're not them.

"Good listeners never break a confidence." There is a word for spreading around what someone tells us privately. *Gossip.*

"Good listeners complete the loop." Interrupting people breaks their chain of thought. We can be a link in the chain by asking a few clarifying questions and offering appropriate responses.

"Good listeners express gratitude." People are leery to open up for fear of ridicule. We can put their minds at ease by thanking them for trusting us and promising we will never use what they told us to hurt them.

Let those with ears to hear also listen.

Gossip

Pastor Mark Jeske

In the age of Facebook, Instagram, and Snapchat, how can you not talk about each other? People are pouring out an *immense* gusher of information about themselves because they *want* other people to know what they're doing.

There's a good way and a bad way to talk about friends. St. Paul gave his young pastoral advisee Timothy some insightful advice about how to manage his congregations: **"They get into the habit of being idle and going about from house to house. And not only do they become idlers, but also busybodies who talk nonsense, saying things they ought not to"** (1 Timothy 5:13). So when does sharing news become gossip?

- When it's not true.

- When it betrays a confidence that you hold in trust.

- When it digs up an old sin that has been repented of.

- When it damages someone's ability to get a job or keep a friend.

- When bad news is shared maliciously, for revenge or to tear someone down.

- When you enjoy someone else's misfortune.

Here's a much better way: **"Encourage one another and build each other up, just as in fact you are doing"** (1 Thessalonians 5: 11).

Mom makes a house a home
Pastor Mark Jeske

How life for women has changed!

My maternal grandmother never cut or colored her hair, never owned a pair of slacks, never was educated past seventh grade, and never operated a motor vehicle. My daughter and nieces are college educated and have traveled and lived internationally. And yet, in spite of all this social change, some eternal life rhythms will endure. It is still Mom who makes a house a home.

Mothers are God's special gift to family life. Women in general are wired for relationships, and her home is where little ones are nourished and raised and where family and friends gather. Men do some of the cooking and a lot more of the housework than they used to, but rarely have I been in a kitchen that didn't ultimately belong to the woman. Proverbs 31:15 celebrates the wonderful work that wonderful women do: **"She gets up while it is still night; she provides food for her family."** But it's more than just the food—it's the love and care that keeps the rest of us coming back.

Moms invest extra energy into special life moments like birthdays and anniversaries. They make sure that everyone feels important, their special days remembered. They are the card and gift givers. They are the cake bakers and present wrappers. They take time to decorate, put out nice tablecloths, cut some flowers, and have a centerpiece that fits the season.

Mom, remember when you thought nobody noticed or appreciated all you do? We did, and we do.

Mom is a disciple

Pastor Mark Jeske

The Spirit does his best work in Christian homes.

And among his chiefest and most valuable assistants are Christian mothers. My personal guess is that the vast majority of the people smiling back at me on Sunday morning were brought to faith through their parents' initiative and were first seriously discipled by their moms. Bible stories first heard snuggled in Mom's arms and lap are never forgotten. Little Christian songs sung around the house stay engraved in the heart forever.

It is Mom first who helps small children navigate the critically important relationship with Jesus. **"She speaks with wisdom, and faithful instruction is on her tongue"** (Proverbs 31:26). Little ones first hear God's words filtered through her heart and voice. Mom is their first counselor in problem solving with a Christian worldview.

The first prayers a child ever prays originate probably from Mom's lap. The last thing little ones in their jammies and cribs hear at bedtime is Mom's whispered prayer for them. It is from Mom first that small children learn how to live their faith—obeying the first time, sharing their toys, restraining their innate selfishness, learning how to say, "I'm sorry." "I need help." "Thank you."

Behavioral scientists are pretty sure that a child's educational patterns are set for life by age 5. I'm pretty sure that a child's spiritual attitudes at age 5 also will last a long, long time.

Give Mom the praise she deserves

Pastor Mark Jeske

I can readily understand why some women don't like reading Proverbs chapter 31. In some ways it describes an intimidating perfect wife and mother—*Superwoman*. A mere mortal woman will read that chapter and instead of being inspired by it will get depressed or feel worthless.

Proverbs chapter 31 is not intended to crush women with massive expectations and pressures. I suspect that God put that chapter there primarily to awaken appreciation in the eyes of their husbands and children. So much of what women do for their families is semi-invisible, humble, and non-remunerated. As a result it isn't seen, respected, or appreciated enough.

All you who are husbands or someone's child, pause for a moment right now and ponder the great value that your mother has brought into your life. Take a little stroll through Proverbs chapter 31 and recall all the ways in which your mom did those things for you. Give thanks to God for her. You might thank her too: **"Charm is deceptive, and beauty is fleeting; but a woman who fears the Lord is to be praised. Honor her for all that her hands have done, and let her works bring her praise at the city gate"** (Proverbs 31:30,31).

Do you suppose it was your mother who more than anyone else is responsible for your being a believer? Just think—she gave you your first earthly home, and she helped you find the Savior who gives you your heavenly home.

Raising the church

Pastor Matt Ewart

The Israelites were exiled from their land for a long time. When they finally returned to Jerusalem, there was a big mess to clean up. Among other things, they had to rebuild the temple that had been completely destroyed.

Now get this: It took over 7,000 days (about 20 years) for them to rebuild that temple. Every day mattered. Every brick counted. They weren't perfect by any means, and neither was the temple that they rebuilt. But their work was a testament to the fact that they trusted in God to see it through.

God does not call on Christians today to build a temple, but he does call on us to raise up the next generation. Now kids can be messy. Some are even destructive. At times it might feel like the room they're in is comparable to the ruined version of Jerusalem. But remember the big picture.

For each individual child, we have about 7,000 days until they reach adulthood. Maybe that child is your own. Maybe the child is one you teach in Sunday school. Maybe he or she is just a kid you see occasionally at church. Remember that every day matters. Every conversation counts. It isn't that you'll be a perfect role model or the child will end up perfect either. But every day we point to Jesus will stand as a testament to what God intended his church to be.

"Fathers, do not exasperate your children; instead, bring them up in the training and instruction of the Lord" (Ephesians 6:4).

Creation's curse

Pastor Mike Novotny

Your parents took a chance every Christmas. When they took your wish list to Toys "R" Us and went into debt for your seasonal high, they took the chance you would forget the connection between the gifts and the givers. In your holiday rush, would you remember their lasting love that led them to give these temporary toys?

God takes that same chance. In Romans, Paul laments, **"They . . . worshiped and served created things rather than the Creator"** (1:25). See the problem? The very creation the Creator created, the very gifts the Giver gave, were worshiped in his place. Instead of loving God and enjoying the gift, they just took the gift and forgot to love God.

We do that too. When our passion for sports consumes so much time that there is no quantity time for prayer. When the lake house pulls us away from worshiping with God's people instead of inspiring us to worship with God's people. When an addiction to cleanliness leads to grouchiness (which is far from godliness). We often love creation too much.

But there is hope. Instead of simply being offended, our Creator sent his Son into the creation. To search. To rescue. To redeem. Jesus not only forgave our "creationalotry," but he also sent his Spirit to open our eyes to a joy greater than all of creation can offer—the joy of seeing the face of a forgiving Father.

Doubt not

Pastor Matt Ewart

If I were to mention one of Jesus' disciples named Thomas, you might automatically attach a title to him. Many people today know him as Doubting Thomas.

He has that title because he was not with the other disciples when the resurrected Jesus appeared to them. When Thomas heard their story, he couldn't believe it. He resolutely stated that he would not believe Jesus was alive unless he experienced it for himself. And so the name Doubting Thomas was born.

As much as Thomas might have been wrong, he did have one thing going for him—one thing that you can learn from. When Thomas expressed his doubt, Jesus could address it. When Thomas shared what he was wrestling with, Jesus could guide him where he needed to go.

What doubts do you have about God? I want you to know that no matter how long you've been wrestling with a doubt, it's good to express it. Start by expressing it to God himself. Then maybe share your doubt with another person. You don't need to feel ashamed of your doubts.

It isn't doubt that destroys faith. It's unexpressed doubt. The Savior who washed away your sins does not want you to carry around the burden of doubt. He invites you to express it so he can address it.

"Then Jesus said to Thomas, 'Put your finger here; see my hands. Reach out your hand and put it into my side. Stop doubting and believe'" (John 20:27).

The object of God's kindness
Sarah Habben

An internet search for "random acts of kindness" came up with these:

1. Give up your seat for a pregnant or elderly person.

2. Don't interrupt when someone is explaining himself.

3. After a picnic, throw away your own trash—and someone else's.

Hmm. Sounds like Mom's 101 speech about being polite as opposed to acting like we were born in a barn. When did common courtesy get upgraded to acts of kindness? Maybe it's just a sad sign of how disconnected our society has become. We need a list to remind us to look up and notice another's needs.

If we truly want to understand this fruit of the Spirit, we need to look to *God's* kindness for parameters. Actually, according to St. Paul, we need to look to someone born in a barn: **"But when the kindness and love of God our Savior appeared, he saved us, not because of righteous things we had done, but because of his mercy"** (Titus 3:4,5).

If God's kindness toward us had a name, it would be Jesus. His kindness was no random act. It was carefully planned from the creation of the world. God's kindness was embodied in his Son, enacted on the cross, poured out on us in Baptism. We, who are experts at random malice and envy and hate, are nevertheless wrapped in God's loving-kindness . . . and it transforms us.

You are the object of God's kindness. Pass it on.

No one would find out
Linda Buxa

If you could do anything you wanted and *no one would find out*, what would you do? (Take a moment to think about it.)

Let's be honest, almost all of us first thought of a sin, didn't we? Get money illegally or immorally. Ruin a reputation. Take credit for someone else's work. Have an affair. Get even with someone. We focus on the "and no one would find out" portion of that daydream and think about what we could get away with.

We all have a part of us that enjoys darkness and wants to indulge in it. We are a lot like the people who lived in the time of Noah when God saw that every human heart was inclined to evil all the time. But that is who you *were*. Now, **"you were washed, you were sanctified, you were justified in the name of the Lord Jesus Christ and by the Spirit of our God"** (1 Corinthians 6:11).

Now you have the Father's approval, and this world's praise will mean less and less to you so **"be careful not to practice your righteousness in front of others to be seen by them"** (Matthew 6:1).

Teachers, coworkers, single parents, children, spouses, neighbors are all carrying some sort of burden, and you can be the one to bring joy. With a new heart and new eyes, let's ask ourselves again: If you could do anything you wanted and *no one would find out*, what would you do?

Using people

Pastor Mark Jeske

Does God have different expectations from different people? I think he does. His Word tells us that to whom much has been given, much will be expected. He expects more from believers, from leaders, from the wealthy, and from those with power. I think the reason for that is that their actions and attitudes have such huge impact on other people.

Can you imagine how heartsick God must have been to see human cruelty not only in far-flung parts of the world where his Word had never reached but also being demonstrated by the leadership of his chosen Israel? It made him sad; it also made him angry: **"Hear this, you who trample the needy and do away with the poor in the land . . . skimping on the measure, boosting the price and cheating with dishonest scales, buying the poor with silver and the needy for a pair of sandals, selling even the sweepings with the wheat. The LORD has sworn by himself, the Pride of Jacob: 'I will never forget anything they have done'"** (Amos 8:4-7).

The "Pride" of Jacob is a figure of speech for the One of whom Jacob was proud, i.e., God himself. His solemn oath was based on the gold standard for truth and integrity—his own reputation. Now—it's easy to pile on others for cheating in business and exploiting people who are vulnerable. When you are finished shaking your finger at the crooked merchants and corrupt politicians of the eighth century B.C., have a thought about how you will do business tomorrow.

Grow in faithfulness

Sarah Habben

A dad takes his daughters to the zoo, as promised. He is faithful to his word.

A couple celebrates their 50th anniversary. They have been faithful to their vows.

A congregation works hard to reach out to their community. They are faithful with the gospel.

More often than not, faithfulness comes at a price. The dad at the zoo gave up much-needed overtime. The husband chose to honor his marital vows despite his wife's past infidelity. The congregation sees no visible results despite all their faithful work.

Sometimes the price of faithfulness can seem too steep. Sometimes we may go through the motions of faithfulness with a deep frown. Sometimes we blame circumstances for making faithfulness impossible.

Now consider God. He makes some hefty promises. "I will supply all your needs. I will work evil for your good. I will forgive your sins. I will raise you from your grave." The price he paid to keep those promises? His Son's life. The attitude behind his faithfulness? Steadfast love. The circumstances that can prevent his faithfulness? Nothing in heaven or on earth or hidden in the human heart. Even **"if we are faithless, he remains faithful, for he cannot disown himself"** (2 Timothy 2:13).

God has declared his faithfulness. History proves it. It should be enough, but God does even more. To deepen our trust, he calls us his own forgiven people in Baptism and in Lord's Supper. We are convinced of his faithfulness. And out of such faith, *our* faithfulness grows.

An elder's wish for his children
Pastor Mark Jeske

Do you like being called a child?

Probably not, unless God is speaking. To be called a child usually implies that you are acting in an immature way. It's usually a put-down or rebuke. But when the speaker is older than you, way older, the term loses its sting and actually becomes kind of dear.

The apostle John appears to have been the last of the apostles to die. His short little letters to people in the congregations he oversaw are preserved for us in Scripture. He calls himself "the Elder," partly because of the authority he wielded and partly because he was, well, old. His letter ends with a powerful plea: **"Dear children, keep yourselves from idols"** (1 John 5:21). Of all the matters and issues in heaven and earth that they needed to pay attention to, he chose that one. Keep yourselves from idols.

An idol in American popular culture is a great thing—it means you're famous, have a huge social media following, and make lots of money. A spiritual idol in your heart is a deadly poison. Idols are anything you trust in, value, and love more than God. Idol obsession will inevitably choke out faith in our Savior Jesus and cause spiritual death.

Become aware of yours. Repent of your fascination with them. Fix your eyes on Jesus, the author of your salvation, and give him all your worship and trust. Give *him* your heart.

How angels say hello

Jason Nelson

People from different places say hello in different ways. The French say, *Bonjour!* Spanish speakers say, *¡Hola!* In Venice it's, *Caio!* And when angels meet people they typically say, *Fear not!* Angels' standard greeting goes beyond addressing the startling effect of their bedazzling appearance. Angels see that fear holds people back. Angels dial back our fears so we can unlock the potential of promising situations.

When Mary was promised she would be the mother of the Savior, she was troubled. **"The angel said to her, 'Do not be afraid, Mary, for you have found favor with God'"** (Luke 1:30 ESV).

Joseph was in a promising situation with Mary, but he was afraid to marry a pregnant girl. **"An angel of the Lord appeared to him in a dream, saying, 'Joseph, son of David, do not fear to take Mary as your wife, for that which is conceived in her is from the Holy Spirit'"** (Matthew 1:20 ESV).

Simple shepherds found themselves in the promising situation of being among the first to learn of the birth of the Savior. But they were terrified. **"The angel said to them, 'Fear not, for behold, I bring you good news of great joy that will be for all the people'"** (Luke 2:10 ESV).

What promising situations are you facing? If your reluctance is fading and you're not as afraid as you were, it could be that your angel is saying hello. **"The angel of the Lord encamps around those who fear him, and delivers them"** (Psalm 34:7 ESV).

Start from here

Linda Buxa

On June 6, 1944, strong currents carried U.S. military members more than a mile away from where they were supposed to land.

Instead of worrying about what went wrong, U.S. Brigadier General Theodore Roosevelt Jr., the son of former President Theodore Roosevelt, shouted, "We'll start the war from here!"

By the end of the day, they had met up with some of the other troops, advanced four miles, and suffered fewer casualties than if they had landed at their planned spot, which was more heavily protected.

You know what it's like to end up in a completely different spot than you had planned, don't you?

Maybe you wanted to be in a different spot financially. Sometimes your relationship status isn't where you thought it would be. No one dreams of having a child with a terminal illness, a stressful work situation, or a leader you didn't vote for. It would be easy to say, "This wasn't where I was supposed to be."

You're right. It isn't. But it's where you are. So what are you going to do about it?

God's mercies are new today. His faithfulness is great today. So start the battle from here. **"Finally, be strong in the Lord and in his mighty power. Therefore put on the full armor of God, so that when the day of evil comes, you may be able to stand your ground, and after you have done everything, to stand"** (Ephesians 6:10,13).

Who's with you?
Pastor Matt Ewart

Today you might face a challenge that you feel under qualified to handle. While sometimes we can shift tasks or responsibilities over to people who can handle them better, other times the issue will be one that only you can address.

It could be a relationship issue that needs to be worked out. It could be plans for the future. It could be a big project that's really weighing on you. Either way, you feel under qualified for the situation.

Moses felt the same way. God placed a task on him that left Moses feeling completely under qualified. When ordered to lead the Israelites out of Egypt, Moses said this: **"Who am I that I should go to Pharaoh and bring the Israelites out of Egypt?"** (Exodus 3:11).

When you feel under qualified to handle something and it's completely overwhelming you, you might ask the same thing Moses did. *"Who am I? How can I possibly take care of this? Why doesn't God pick someone else?"*

The good news is that God helps the overwhelmed by pointing to something better than themselves. He doesn't fix things by pointing out how talented you are or how great you are. How he encouraged Moses is how he encourages you too: **"God said, 'I will be with you'"** (Exodus 3:12).

When you feel overwhelmed and under qualified, remember that it isn't about who you are. It's about who's with you.

Do this in remembrance

Sarah Habben

"What are those people doing in the graveyard?" the child wonders, watching them insert small American flags near certain headstones.

"They are decorating the graves of soldiers to help us remember their sacrifice."

It's important to remember the cost of freedom and the value of peace.

"Do this . . . in remembrance of me," Jesus said the night before he sacrificed his life in a spiritual war that ended all spiritual wars (1 Corinthians 11:25). It was his last will and testament: that believers of all time would partake of the Lord's Supper. He wanted us to set aside a time, not annually but *often*, to remember his sacrifice—the price he paid for our freedom, our peace.

"What are they doing in the front of church?" the child wonders, watching the people around the altar.

"It's the Lord's Supper today. It's a way we remember Jesus, who died to save us. But more important, it's a way for Jesus to show that *he* remembers *us*. When we eat the bread and wine, we're also receiving Christ's body and blood. That heavenly food assures us that Jesus has not forgotten us in our sin—he has forgiven us."

Remember those who have died in service to our country. The blood they shed has helped to secure the freedom and peace you enjoy today. Whenever you take the Lord's Supper, remember your Savior's death. The blood he shed has secured your freedom from sin's bondage—and your eternal peace.

Designated survivor

Linda Buxa

During the State of the Union address, all the members of the House, Senate, Supreme Court, and Cabinets gather to hear the president recount the year and set forth a vision for the next.

Except one. The person chosen to be the "designated survivor" is secreted away. Should terrorism or an act of God occur, this chosen person will live to lead the country. (Though it's never happened in real life, there's a TV series that played out the what-if scenario.)

Because of our sin, we were all designated perishers. There was nothing we could do to save ourselves. That is why Jesus—*God with us*—came to be our designated Savior. Yet he wasn't hidden away in some secret place. He came to earth, faced our enemy, and took the punishment for us. He was the one who—even though everyone else was designated for Satan's terror—survived, overcame, and won. **"For Christ also suffered once for sins, the righteous for the unrighteous, to bring you to God. He was put to death in the body but made alive in the Spirit"** (1 Peter 3:18).

Now that he has suffered, he calls us by name and brings us to God. One by one he invites us to be designated eternal survivors too.

Gently, gently

Pastor Mark Jeske

You know, it's pretty easy to be disgusted with other people's moral failures. I can finger-point with the best of them, sitting in an easy chair with a cup of coffee and a newspaper and a scowl on my righteous face. Do you know what's a lot harder? Restoration.

That's right, restoration. Actually getting involved in the life of somebody who's broken. Sinful. Guilty. And you know what? That's God's work: **"Brothers and sisters, if someone is caught in a sin, you who live by the Spirit should restore that person gently. But watch yourselves, or you also may be tempted"** (Galatians 6:1). It is much easier to hang out only with the nice people who still have their lives together. It's much more labor-intensive to be a friend to someone who's still drinking, still cheating, still avoiding church, still racking up credit card bills for dumb purchases. But it's God's work.

Jesus came to our world not to pin medals on the achievers but to rescue the fools, people like you and me. How he smiles when we show that same compassion to people around us that he first showed to us. Sinful rebels are likely to listen to rebukes of their sin and promises of Christ's forgiveness only from people who have staying power, who have earned the right to listen and earned the right to speak.

It's God's work. Don't good shepherds temporarily leave the 99 and seek the one lost one?

june

The name of the LORD is a fortified tower;
the righteous run to it and are safe.

Proverbs 18:10

Creation is calling

Pastor Mike Novotny

When my toes inched closer to the 1,000-foot drop, no one had to tell me to be impressed with the Grand Canyon. There was something awe-inspiring and breathtaking and glorious about the view, no matter which direction I looked. No wonder over four million visitors stop by the canyon each year.

Ever wonder why we are moved by moments like that? Why do tropical sunsets and towering mountains and the belly laughs of little kids move us so profoundly? Why do we reach for our cameras when green trees burst into blazing oranges and reds? Why do we automatically sigh in relaxation when the lake is calm and the sun is warm? Why does this world so often leave us silently mouthing, "Wow . . ."?

The apostle Paul could answer all those questions with one word—*God*. In Romans, he states, **"God's invisible qualities—his eternal power and divine nature—have been clearly seen, being understood from what has been made"** (1:20). In other words, you can see the God you can't see. How? By understanding what has been made. By connecting this created world to the Creator. By looking around in wonder and then looking up to worship a wonderful God.

The next time this life moves you to stop and stare, stop and see God. Look down into the magnificent canyons, across the coffee shop table at your laughing friends, into the bright eyes of a newborn after a nap, and finally up to the invisible face of God, which might not be that invisible after all.

Creation is from God

Pastor Mike Novotny

If you ever want to see the ugliest dinosaur ever, go to my mom's house. For some odd reason (that only mothers would understand), my mom has kept my fifth-grade art class project—a fire-baked clay dinosaur. Take one look at my pink Uglysaurus and you will realize something about my nature. Art ain't my thing!

Contrast my art with God's art. A starry night glowing with a thousand distant dots of light. The complexity of conception and the growth of a soon-to-be-born child. The taste buds on your tongue and the synapses inside your skull. There (and in a billion other places) you will see pure genius and unfathomable power. Perhaps that is why Paul wrote, **"God's invisible qualities—his eternal power and divine nature—have been clearly seen, being understood from what has been made"** (Romans 1:20). Eternal power. God had the brainpower to think up everything you see. God had the muscle power to turn his creativity into actual creation. What can you say besides, "God is amazing!"?

So often in life we feel weak. Impotent. Powerless. Maybe a word of encouragement is all around us, right here in creation. Creation is preaching a message about its Creator. He is wise. Kind. Brilliant. Powerful. Limitless. Combine those qualities with his reckless love for us found on the cross, and you have a God who can strengthen trembling hearts and weak knees. You have a Creator worth worshiping.

Creation is like God
Pastor Mike Novotny

Two years back, Tojo made me sushi. Hidekazu Tojo is one of the greatest sushi masters in the world. For our 12-year anniversary, my wife and I went to his restaurant in Vancouver. Simply put, this 4′9″ man created the best food I have tasted in my life. On the walk back to our hotel, my bride and I looked at each other and smiled, "This!"

"This!" is theological slang in our family. It means "this is like God." God is incredible like "this!" God is exciting like "this!" God is memorable like "this!" God is thrilling like "this!" You get the point. "This!" just might be the most used vocabulary word in our house!

The idea comes, once again, from the apostle Paul. He wrote, **"God's invisible qualities—his eternal power and divine nature—have been clearly seen, being understood from what has been made"** (Romans 1:20). God's qualities, what God himself is like, is understood from our experiences here on earth. The reason we enjoy this is because God is enjoyable. Being in his presence will not be categorically different than this. Rather, it will be like this but (1) a billion times better and (2) never, ever, ever ending. If that thought does not get you excited about heaven, I have no clue what will!

So don't wait around for Sunday to worship your Creator. When your favorite song stirs your heart or when a loved one holds your hand or when Tojo brings out another plate, smile and say, "My God is like this . . . but better!"

You can't out give God

Sarah Habben

I love studying Christian stewardship. I'm reminded that God isn't a bean counter, balancing some heavenly checkbook to see who is pulling their weight. Yes, he wants generous and cheerful givers . . . but he practically bounces with anticipation over all the ways *he* will out give *us*. **"Test me in this,"** God says, **"and see if I will not throw open the floodgates of heaven and pour out so much blessing that there will not be room enough to store it"** (Malachi 3:10).

Yet, too often we cock an eyebrow at his promises and tighten our grip on our treasures.

We're not alone. In the book of Haggai, God had to urge his people three times, "Build my house!" They were so busy with their jobs and home renovations that God's house remained in ruins. And yet, despite all their striving, their wages were never enough and drought threatened their livelihood. "Think carefully about your ways," said God. "You are in want because you've failed to put me first."

If God had stopped there, his people would have built his church with bricks of fear and guilt. But he followed his chastisement with a word of hope. **"I am with you"** (Haggai 1:13). God's house was to be built with bricks of trust based on God's promises—none of which have ever crumbled to dust.

God is still with us, enabling us to give. He doesn't guarantee to match our giving dollar for dollar. No—he's more generous than that. He *out gives* us . . . starting with the gift of his Son.

Choose gentleness

Sarah Habben

When I was little, I would try to squeeze Dad's fingers hard enough to make him react. My body would go rigid with effort long before Dad felt any discomfort. I wasn't being gentle; I just didn't have the power to cause him pain. "Now do it to me, Dad!" Dad would give my fingers a quick, tight squeeze. It was obvious that he had the power to hurt but was choosing not to.

Gentleness is not feebleness. It's strength under control. And it's a fruit of the Spirit for all those whom God calls to a Christian life. So how are we doing? Parents—are you disciplining gently? Spouses—is there gentleness in your speech? Employers—are you practicing gentle leadership? Friends—do you listen gently? Or are we each using whatever power we have to put the squeeze on others?

Jesus shows us that meekness has its basis in love, not weakness. **"Come to me, all you who are weary and burdened, and I will give you rest. . . . Learn from me, for I am gentle and humble in heart"** (Matthew 11:28,29).

Learn from Jesus. If you are burdened by the memory of your reckless words, come to Jesus' cross where those words have been erased. If you are losing your struggle with anger, remember your baptismal waters where your sinful nature was drowned. If you falter in your walk of faith, come to Jesus and be restored by his sweet word of forgiveness; be empowered to choose gentleness.

A loving perspective

Pastor Matt Ewart

Lately the political and racial tensions in our country have been extremely high. Issues that once divided groups now fracture actual relationships. Perhaps you have some relationships that are severed or troubled because of these issues.

On this side of heaven, you will not agree with everybody on everything. That's okay. But God does provide people a way to navigate when differences arise. Christians in the first century were divided over some big issues. Here's what Paul said to them: **"Do not cause anyone to stumble, whether Jews, Greeks or the church of God—even as I try to please everyone in every way"** (1 Corinthians 10:32,33).

To "please" everybody means you know what's important to them. You know what moves their hearts and what hurts their hearts. And while you might disagree with them over what the problem is, you at least prioritize people before politics.

To put it in other words, it is impossible to love someone whose perspective you refuse to understand. Is there a person today whose perspective you need to know more about? Go out of your way to learn what makes his or her heart work.

After all, that was how God approached you. Not only was your view of things different; your view was wrong. Regardless, he pursued you in love. He knew what made you hurt. He knew what stole your hope. He entered this world to see things from your perspective and to fill what was missing.

Shrinking mountains
Jason Nelson

"Mount Everest, you beat me the first time, but I'll beat you the next time because you've grown all you are going to grow . . . but I'm still growing!"—Edmund Hillary

Sometimes life is a walk in the park. Sometimes. And sometimes we stand at the foot of a rugged obstacle and crane our necks, wondering how in the world we are going to overcome it because there's no way around it. Serious illness is a big ol' mountain. Losing a job is a big ol' mountain. A cheating spouse is a big ol' mountain. The death of a loved one is a big ol' mountain. How will we ever get over it?

God says you'll get over it because he's going to shrink that mountain: **"I will go before you and will level the mountains"** (Isaiah 45:2). God says he's going to use the passing of time, his healing power, and some new opportunities to flatten it. He says he's going to shrink that mountain. Don't think he can't do it. **"I am the Lord, and there is no other. I form the light and create darkness, I bring prosperity and create disaster; I, the Lord, do all these things"** (verses 6,7).

God says he's going to shrink that mountain because he's going to make you grow. He's going to make you bigger than the mountain. Don't think he can't do it. **"I am the Lord, and there is no other; apart from me there is no God. I will strengthen you"** (verse 5).

I think I'm making progress

Linda Buxa

Pablo Casals is considered one of the greatest cellists of all time. When he was well beyond what many people would consider retirement age, he was asked why he continued to practice for hours a day. His reply? "I think I'm making progress."

What would it look like if we embraced Pablo Casals' way of thinking—about our faith?

"We continually ask God to fill you with the knowledge of his will through all the wisdom and understanding that the Spirit gives, so that you may live a life worthy of the Lord and please him in every way: bearing fruit in every good work, growing in the knowledge of God, being strengthened with all power according to his glorious might so that you may have great endurance and patience, and giving joyful thanks to the Father, who has qualified you to share in the inheritance of his holy people in the kingdom of light" (Colossians 1:9-12).

For people who believe in Jesus, we have one goal: heaven. And if we're on earth, we haven't reached it yet. So we look for ways to know God better so we can grow more, serve more, trust more, pray more, share our hope more, thank more, forgive more.

Practice doesn't make perfect. Jesus does. But your practice will give you more opportunities to let others know about the One who has made them perfect too.

Are we secure or vulnerable?

Pastor Mark Jeske

How are you at dealing with ambiguity in life? Does it drive you crazy? Are you a black/white person, all or nothing?

You know, the more you read your Bible, the more you get comfortable with paradox. We live in two worlds simultaneously. Our salvation is both inclusive and exclusive, by grace and yet through faith. We are both dying and immortal, sinners and saints, dirty and pure. It is important that you embrace both of these seemingly contradictory truths, for if you accept only one, your spiritual life will be unhealthy and unbalanced.

Here's an example from Scripture: **"We know that we are children of God, and that the whole world is under the control of the evil one"** (1 John 5:19). Perhaps your first reaction to that passage is, "Well, God, which is it? Can I live in complete security as your child, or is this world under Satan's control?" The answer is yes. Satan is still the **"ruler of the kingdom of the air, the spirit who is now at work in those who are disobedient"** (Ephesians 2:2). Respect his sinister power and murderous intent.

Find your security not in your own ingenuity or strength but in the great victory that Jesus won over sin, death, and Satan. Confess your sins to him, receive his mercy and forgiveness, and fill up on the Word to strengthen your mind and will. Soon will come the time of perfect peace and joy in heaven.

In the meantime, prepare yourself for war.

Follow me
Pastor Matt Ewart

When Jesus said, "Follow me," his first disciples had to walk away from other things first. Some walked away from their fishing businesses. Others walked away from their tax-collecting booths. To this day, following Jesus requires people to walk away from something or someone.

Even though there's nothing in this world that can compare to Jesus, that doesn't make this next sentence any less true:

Some days it's just plain hard to follow Jesus.

Nobody knew that better than his first disciples. For the first part of Jesus' public ministry, he was very popular with the crowds, but there came one specific day when everything changed. Jesus was no longer the popular guy to follow, and many ended up deserting him. As droves of followers stopped following, Jesus turned to the Twelve and asked them straightforwardly, **"You do not want to leave too, do you?"** (John 6:67).

There will come days for you when following Jesus is not the popular thing to do. Days when you don't want to leave something else in order to follow him. When those days come, remember that every temptation to unfollow Jesus is an invitation to follow something else.

Peter understood that. When tempted to unfollow Jesus, Peter asked a question that provided extraordinary clarity in a time of fogginess: **"Lord, to whom shall we go? You have the words of eternal life"** (John 6:68).

There are many things you can follow, but only One will take you where you want to go.

The Spirit was there—hovering

Pastor Mark Jeske

The late Rodney Dangerfield built an entire comedy career riffing off his lowly status in the world. Yanking on his necktie, twisting his neck, rolling his bugged-out eyes, he claimed he got no respect from anybody. People laughed at his self-mocking humor, but they also identified with him. Who of us has not felt invisible, unnoticed, and unappreciated?

The Spirit of the Lord is one-third of the mighty Trinity, and yet you'd hardly know it from the scant and inadequate attention he gets from many Christians (guilty). He gets some props on Pentecost Sunday, but then the silence descends again.

In fact, the Spirit of the Lord has been present everywhere and always throughout human history. He is the first person of the Trinity to be mentioned by name in Scripture: **"In the beginning God created the heavens and the earth. Now the earth was formless and empty, darkness was over the surface of the deep, and the Spirit of God was hovering over the waters"** (Genesis 1:1,2). His hovering was not the dithering indecision of someone who didn't know what to do. It was just a brief pause, amping up strength, finalizing ideas, brimming with vision and passion for the six explosive days of creative activity about to happen.

The Spirit still hovers, still creating, still tracking every last bit of human activity, with the passionate goal of enjoying his relationship with believers forever.

Notice him. Appreciate him. Give him a little respect.

Displaying a treasure

Linda Buxa

A few years ago, my husband traveled to Japan for work and I went along. While there, some friends and I went shopping for pearls.

As the salesman showed us different types, he explained that pink pearls are often sought out for being the most beautiful, but they don't actually work against the background of my Caucasian skin tone. He then put them against black velvet. There, you could see just how beautiful these pearls really were.

It took the right background to show off the true beauty of these treasures.

First John 4:10 tells us how God displayed the true beauty of the treasure of his love: **"This is love: not that we loved God, but that he loved us and sent his Son as an atoning sacrifice for our sins."**

To appreciate how beautiful God's love is, we see it placed on top of his sacrifice. The cross shows how serious he was about sin needing to be punished and how committed he was to us.

And in a twist, the cross shows us that not only is God's love a treasure, but he thinks we are a beautiful treasure too. **"The kingdom of heaven is like treasure hidden in a field. When a man found it, he hid it again, and then in his joy went and sold all he had and bought that field"** (Matthew 13:44). That's the way God works. He knew we were hidden, and he sacrificed everything he had—his Son—to get us back.

Stuck in ancestry

Jason Nelson

I think the most important line in Tim McGraw's lovely song "Humble and Kind" is this: "Visit Grandpa every chance that you can." Grandpa isn't going to be around forever, and he knows it. He's feeling a little sentimental these days. His love for his children and grandchildren is inflated by what he sees in them and what he hopes for himself through them . . . to be remembered. Someday he will just figure into the family's ancestry. His genetic material will continue in people he didn't conceive and will never meet because he was written out of the story and was never mentioned again.

It is just a fact. **"Your sons will take the place of your father"** (Psalm 45:16 GW). God sustains families and his kingdom through generation continuity. Eventually, all the attention turns to those next in line. Grandpa will be forgotten until someone bumps into him on Ancestry.com. But God allows Grandpa's faith in Jesus, his Christian values, and maybe a few of his corny jokes to live on in the descendants doing the research because Grandpa taught his sons and daughters and they in turn did the same.

Being remembered is part of the afterlife. So is the satisfaction of having shaped future generations. Christ is known today because Grandpa and others like him kept a promise. **"I will cause your name to be remembered throughout every generation. That is why the nations will give thanks to you forever and ever"** (verse 17 GW).

A parent's prayer for wisdom
Sarah Habben

Dear Jesus, did you create children just to teach adults wisdom? Because it takes a boatload of wisdom to raise them. And sometimes, Lord, I just seem to come up dry. That's why I'm glad you've told me exactly what heavenly wisdom entails . . . and it's more "heart" than "smarts."

"The wisdom that comes from heaven is first of all pure; then peace-loving, considerate, submissive, full of mercy and good fruit, impartial and sincere" (James 3:17).

Heavenly wisdom is holy. (I sometimes act holier-than-thou.) When I correct my children, drain me of self-righteousness.

Heavenly wisdom is peace-loving. (I sometimes add fuel to the fire.) When tempers flare, help me patiently bear my children's anger and bridle my own.

Heavenly wisdom is considerate. (I like to be correct at any cost.) When I speak with my children, make me more concerned with being *kind* than being *right*.

Heavenly wisdom is submissive. (I prefer to be on the receiving end of submission.) Help me to submit to your will so that I'm not rude or overbearing.

Heavenly wisdom is full of mercy. (I sometimes fixate on my kids' mistakes and overlook their strengths.) Help me show them the same patient mercy you've shown me.

Heavenly wisdom is sincere. (Sometimes I throw advice at my kids without really listening.) Give me a heart that cares, deeply, about my children's concerns.

Lord, I don't need all the answers, but please give me a wise heart. Amen.

A parent's prayer of repentance

Sarah Habben

Dear Jesus, I must have disappointed you today. I woke up grumpy and stressed. To my tired eyes, all the opportunities you gave me to thankfully serve looked instead like burdensome obligations.

My kids, for one. I confess that I did my best to make them feel responsible for my bad morning. (If I didn't have to pack their lunches! If they had done their homework the night before! If they didn't hog the bathroom!) I charged around the house like a cantankerous rhino. I snagged my favorite pants in the process. It took a leap of logic, Lord, but I blamed a kid for that one too.

The day spiraled down from there. I was a rude driver, an impatient employee, a resentful housewife. And when my kids came home, they gave me what I deserved.

A big hug. Wait. What?

Yup, a hug. And it melted me. Their unconditional love drew an apology from my heart; a resolve to do better, to start over, to honor their mercy.

Thank you for these children, Lord. Thank you for the way you used them to demonstrate *your* love. A love that is undeserved and wholly merciful. A love that chooses to forget my sins. A love that draws repentance from my stubborn heart. A love that inspires me to serve with thanks and joy. Amen.

"The LORD is compassionate and gracious. . . . He does not treat us as our sins deserve or repay us according to our iniquities" (Psalm 103:8,10).

A prayer for patience

Sarah Habben

Dear Jesus, you know how you once fed five thousand men with a boy's meal and many of them became more concerned with their stomachs than their souls? That must have tested your patience.

And you know how your disciples kept arguing about which of them would be the greatest in heaven, even when your entire ministry had been a demonstration of humble *service*? Still, you never lost your cool.

And you know how the priests (who should have recognized you as the promised Savior, the Lamb of God who takes away the sin of the world) were the very ones who rejected you and pinned you to a cross? Still you prayed over them, "Father, forgive."

Lord, I am guilty of all those sins and more. I'm more concerned with my stomach than my soul. I'm reluctant to serve. I'm slow to confess my faith. I reject your will. I hold grudges. I lose control of my tongue and temper.

And yet you show me mercy.

Lord, thank you for your immense patience in my life. Let it put a smile on my face as I show patience to others. My children. My spouse. My coworkers. My government. Lead me to witness patiently of your mercy, so that others might come to believe. Amen.

"I was shown mercy so that in me, the worst of sinners, Christ Jesus might display his immense patience as an example for those who would believe in him and receive eternal life" (1 Timothy 1:16).

The Spirit was there—inspiring

Pastor Mark Jeske

The fallout from Adam and Eve's first rebellion was devastating—they had poisoned themselves; lost their innocence and divine image; lost their home in paradise; and lost their daily, easy communication with God.

The early chapters of the book of Genesis tell how quickly their descendants lost all knowledge of God. The world now essentially needed to be re-evangelized to rekindle the saving faith that they had lost. The only way that such faith can be created is through the Word of God. And it is to the Holy Spirit that we owe our gratitude for taking on himself the great task of bringing the Word through prophetic speaking and writing: **"Prophecy never had its origin in the human will, but prophets, though human, spoke from God as they were carried along by the Holy Spirit"** (2 Peter 1:21).

You might say that the prophetic and apostolic Word is "inSpired," "in-Spirited," for the Holy Spirit both provided and edited the content. Only through the Word will we ever have any kind of certainty about who God is, what he has done, and how we fit into his plans. Only through the Word can unbelievers be transformed into believers. Only through the Word can we have a glimmer of how to live in such a way as to please him and fulfill the mission for which we were born.

When you read and hear the Bible, you can have 100 percent confidence that you are hearing God himself speaking to you.

Church jargon: Hallelujah

Pastor Mark Jeske

Thanks to the magnificent Baroque composer George Frideric Händel and his famous chorus, all the world has heard the word *hallelujah*. Rufus Wainwright and Bruno Mars earnestly sing the word in their very secular songs. It is unfortunately also perceived and sometimes ridiculed as Christian jargon. To make fun of evangelical Christians, all you have to do is adopt a slightly Southern accent, slap your thigh, and yelp "HăllaLOOyah!"

It is in fact a magnificent word of praise, sent heavenward for many thousands of years. *Hallel* is a Hebrew imperative commanding praise, *Hallelu* makes it plural so that everybody is included, and *Jah* is the abbreviation of *Jahveh*, God's personal and proper name in the Old Testament. It is found throughout the psalms, and the throne scenes in Revelation chapter 19 echo the cry.

Praising God is one of the main reasons for which you were created. It is like breathing for a Christian: **"Praise the Lord. How good it is to sing praises to our God, how pleasant and fitting to praise him!"** (Psalm 147:1). Praise acknowledges our smallness and his bigness; praise gives tribute to the brilliant Designer and Engineer of the universe; praise shows Christ that you appreciate his extremely expensive Calvary gift, all the more precious because it's free; praise shows the Spirit that though you can't see him, you know he's at work in your world.

When you say it, mean it.

Fathers are needed to bring strength and discipline

Pastor Mark Jeske

Every child cherishes his or her mother's tender heart and the emotional bond that comes with it. But children do well also to appreciate their fathers' strength, both physical and inner strength. That inner strength comes from a lesser emotional vulnerability that gives them the ability to insist on the right thing to do even when it's hard or unpleasant.

A good dad accepts his role as the last word in discipline. He needs to back up Mom's words. A child who has never learned how to obey orders will never do well in school and is probably unemployable. Children who have not first learned to respect their parents may never learn to respect other people, and they may not really like themselves either.

Children who have not learned respect and obedience for their earthly fathers may really struggle with the concept of a heavenly Father: **"Moreover, we have all had human fathers who disciplined us and we respected them for it. How much more should we submit to the Father of spirits and live!"** (Hebrews 12:9). Good dads show their kids how to do the hard jobs first and save the easy ones for last . . . how to keep their word . . . how to finish a job . . . how to defer pleasures and save money . . . how to accept responsibility.

When we dads do our job, we model the important structure and stability that our heavenly Father brings to our lives.

Fathers are needed for leadership

Pastor Mark Jeske

It takes no brains to figure out the woman's *unique* role in the home, i.e., what she alone is gifted for. Husbands and wives alike can be breadwinners, maintenance engineers, house cleaners, and cooks. But it is she alone who gives birth; she alone can nurse.

So is there anything unique to what the man brings? Machines have helped equalize the physical strength gap. Scripture has an important teaching about how God designed the home to work: **"The husband is the head of the wife as Christ is the head of the church, his body, of which he is the Savior"** (Ephesians 5:23). To the wife has been given management of childbearing, nurture, and sexuality. To the husband God gave the task and role of leadership.

He is called the head. But not corporate head, i.e., the one who gives orders and controls things. He is to be head as Christ is head of the church, his body. In other words, it's something almost organic, whereby he carries out his role for the good of the whole family. Somebody has to have a tie-breaking vote when there isn't total agreement. Someone makes the final call on who will take turns yielding today.

Christian husbands accept responsibility for everyone's well-being. As chief servants, they go first for the dirtiest and most dangerous jobs. They also have a head, Jesus Christ, from whom they take instruction and to whom they know they are accountable.

Look carefully

Linda Buxa

I was in the garage attic bringing down sleds and shovels for the impending winter when I took a wrong step. A very wrong step.

I missed the beam and stepped right through the insulation and Sheetrock. I started falling to the floor below. Suddenly, I jolted to a stop; my right arm was stuck in a truss, and I was hanging by one arm while my feet dangled below. Thankfully, the pull-down ladder was right next to my feet, and I was able to crawl out. Over a year later, even though I still have some muscle damage, I'm grateful I didn't fall to the floor and shatter bones—or worse.

What happened in seconds has given me a graphic visual for Ephesians 5:15,16: **"Look carefully then how you walk, not as unwise but as wise, making the best use of the time, because the days are evil"** (ESV).

Christians, look carefully then how you walk through this life. Careless financial decisions leave you bankrupt. Poor relationship choices fill you with regret. Reckless words result in deep wounds. Abuse—whether substance, physical, or emotional—results in generations of baggage.

Look carefully, then. Be wise. Make the best use of your time. This is not your time of folly. This is your time of grace. It starts now.

(Just a reminder that if you've been living as the unwise, Jesus has forgiveness for you. His mercies are new every morning. Thanks to the cross, you don't have to carry guilt or shame. It is finished!)

Glass half full

Pastor Mark Jeske

Doesn't Jesus love all people equally? Didn't the Lamb of God take away the sins of the world? Didn't Christ utterly crush Satan and end his power over us all?

Yes he did. Objectively speaking, God in Christ reconciled the *world* to himself (see 2 Corinthians 5:19). But subjectively people still need to know about it and believe it to have it. We are saved by grace *through faith*, and that means that many of the world's people will forfeit the fabulous inheritance that was bought for them. Even Jesus Christ, the greatest gospel messenger ever, didn't win them all. He suffered and died in the midst of the very people who should have been his most passionate followers.

Does that sound like failure? God doesn't see it that way, and neither did the apostle John. Writing to leaders in an early Christian congregation, he celebrated a glass half full: **"It has given me great joy to find some of your children walking in the truth, just as the Father commanded us"** (2 John 1:4). Just *some* of your children? Yes. And John rejoiced over every one.

You and I can keep our eyes and hearts on what's in our congregational glass rather than becoming bitter about what's not. We can let God take care of the winnowing out and the judging. Let's spend our energy proclaiming the gospel everywhere we can, rejoicing at each one of the Spirit's conversion successes, and encouraging those who walk in the truth.

Breaking free
Pastor Matt Ewart

After God freed the Israelites from horrible slavery conditions and rescued them from Egypt, you'd think that they would be happy to be free. But on more than one occasion, they actually wanted to go back. They didn't like the uncertainty of where their next meal would come from. It terrified them that they didn't know how their canteens would get filled up again. It was hard for them to adapt to a new way of life. But here's the thing that they had to learn:

Where they came from was not as good as where God was taking them.

You'd think that we too would be happy and content, but that isn't always the case. Today like every day, you will actually want to go back to the darkness. Sin's deceitfulness promises you a familiar way to live your life, and it promises you comforts and satisfaction. You will want to go back time and time again.

So when tempted to forfeit what God has won for you, remember that the power of Jesus, who conquered death, is alive in you right now. And though the road ahead of you will be difficult, just remember:

Where you come from is not as good as where God is taking you.

"For we know that our old self was crucified with him so that the body ruled by sin might be done away with, that we should no longer be slaves to sin" (Romans 6:6).

Get in the game
Linda Buxa

My daughter had too many fouls too early in the game, so she was pulled and someone else went in. At halftime, the coach walked up to her and said (in his most gentle coach voice, of course), "You are useless to me on the bench!"

Sometimes, isn't that what God says to us?

"What good is it, my brothers and sisters, if someone claims to have faith but has no deeds? Can such faith save them? Suppose a brother or a sister is without clothes and daily food. If one of you says to them, 'Go in peace; keep warm and well fed,' but does nothing about their physical needs, what good is it? In the same way, faith by itself, if it is not accompanied by action, is dead" (James 2:14-17).

If you have faith, but aren't loving, serving, praying, and holding others accountable, God is telling you, "You are useless to me on the bench!"

That could sound like a guilt trip, if it weren't coming from your amazing, merciful God who is telling you, "You are so useful and valuable to me that I want you—need you—to be active on this faith team."

He doesn't ask you to do this on your own, though. He's given you a coach, the Holy Spirit, to teach you, guide you, encourage you, cheer for you, and maybe even let you struggle a bit so you can become better.

It's time to get off the bench and get in the game.

The Spirit was there—gathering

Pastor Mark Jeske

In life's games and sports, it is assumed that everybody starts even, that the outcome is to be based on the participant's skill and effort. In spiritual things, alas, we start in a deep hole, like starting a football game behind 1,000 to 0 at opening kickoff. We are born disconnected from God, born infidels, doomed, and damned.

But the Spirit loves us too much to let us go. His holy mission is nothing less than to reconnect all of God's lost children with their loving Father and Savior Jesus. Through words and washing of pure grace, the Spirit brings us back to life and changes our status from God's enemies to his children.

More—he connects us to other believers, amplifying the wonderful experience of being saved. We become part of a giant faith network that is meant to work together for the common good: **"We were all baptized by one Spirit so as to form one body—whether Jews or Gentiles, slave or free—and we were all given the one Spirit to drink"** (1 Corinthians 12:13). Your economic status, your social class, your language or nationality or race all do not matter. All are loved; all believers become part of this bond, this spiritual body, the body of Christ.

The New Testament epistles frequently use the word *church* as a synonym for that wonderful fellowship of faith. *Church* in its best and purest meaning is not the *building* where local congregations meet for worship, nor the local *corporation*. It's the *people*.

People connected to people by the Holy Spirit.

God's goodness

Sarah Habben

I recently read an article titled, "Are You a Good Person?" In the article, Life Coach Karen says, "You have to put yourself in the center of your life and then you'll enjoy doing things for other people. Serving others at your own expense will only make you resentful." Dr. Hanson, a neuropsychologist, agrees: "Goodness is seeking the happiness and welfare of *oneself* and others. People are good when their own core needs are met."

So, phew, don't expect goodness from me before I've had my morning coffee.

It won't surprise you that this "me first" version of goodness doesn't match God's guidelines. **"He has shown you, O mortal, what is good. And what does the LORD require of you? To act justly and to love mercy and to walk humbly with your God"** (Micah 6:8).

Where's the part about seeking my own happiness? God's requirements just highlight the ways I fall short of goodness! It's a list that leaves me with one prayer: *O give thanks to the Lord for HE is good.* With my welfare in mind, the good God sent his Son to save me. With no resentment, the good Savior credited his perfect life to me. With quiet humility, the good Spirit works in me so that I conform to God's will.

I can be good God's way because my "core need" has been met: I'm forgiven. I can be good God's way because *Jesus* is the center of my life.

With the Spirit's help, I can even be good before my morning coffee.

A word of affirmation
Pastor Matt Ewart

Mark Twain once said, "I can live for two months on a good compliment."

It has been said that there are five basic ways to communicate love to someone, and giving them words of affirmation is one of them. To some extent we all need encouraging words to know that we matter to others. We could all use a good compliment every once in a while.

In fact, if you think back to the most influential person in your childhood, chances are that you remember a compliment they paid you. Maybe they acknowledged a gift in you. Maybe they highlighted a talent that you didn't think was there. Words matter.

So my question for you today is this: Whose compliment would mean the world to you?

That's fine, but keep in mind that guidance and your identity from God weigh much more. His encouragements outweigh those of your best friend. What he says about you is true, and the promises he attaches to you cannot be broken.

If Mark Twain said he can live for two months on a good compliment, what God says to you through Isaiah can give you life and hope forever.

"I took you from the ends of the earth, from its farthest corners I called you. I said, 'You are my servant'; I have chosen you and have not rejected you. So do not fear, for I am with you; do not be dismayed, for I am your God" (Isaiah 41:9,10).

june 28

Skipping ahead to the end
Linda Buxa

When sports get intense, I get up from the couch and move to the kitchen. I sometimes cover my eyes when movies get scary or sad. And then there are books. I jump ahead a few pages to see how things resolve; then I go back to find out what details I missed. That way I can read without being anxious. Can you relate at all?

If we get worked up about inconsequential things, how is it we can work our way through real life? As adults, we can't escape to the kitchen or cover our eyes when we face financial struggles, relationship problems, and health issues. But we can jump ahead to the end.

That's why I love Easter. When Jesus defeated death, he guaranteed how our stories end.

"I know that my redeemer lives, and that in the end he will stand on the earth. And after my skin has been destroyed, yet in my flesh I will see God; I myself will see him with my own eyes—I, and not another. How my heart yearns within me!" (Job 19:25-27).

We can get through all the concerns that weigh on our hearts, all because we know the end. On the day God calls us home, where there is no more mourning or crying or pain, we will see Jesus—our Redeemer—face-to-face.

How my heart yearns within me.

When all the choices are bad

Jason Nelson

Those of us shaped by Western civilization are programmed for binary operations. We think in terms of win or lose, good guys or bad guys, Coke or Pepsi, the Packers or the Bears. But life in a broken world isn't so cut and dried. Our lives aren't simplistic, and our choices can be very complicated. I don't want to trivialize difficult situations by offering any more examples. But if your life has been like mine in any way, you have had to make tough decisions when all of the choices were bad.

King David faced only bad choices with his rebel son Absalom. David gave orders to put down the rebellion but still go easy on his son. Absalom was killed by a defiant military commander. David discovered he couldn't have it both ways. He was left no choice but to grieve, **"O my son Absalom! My son, my son Absalom! If only I had died instead of you"** (2 Samuel 18:33).

God faced only bad choices with us. It was either condemn to hell the rebel people he created to love or punish his only begotten Son in our place. How difficult that had to be for him. He announced from heaven at Jesus' baptism, **"This is my Son, whom I love; with him I am well pleased"** (Matthew 3:17). A short time later Jesus was hanging on a cross and dying instead of us.

May your conscience serve you well when all of the choices are bad, and may your soul find peace.

Feeling trapped

Pastor Matt Ewart

On their way out of Egypt, the Israelites were confronted with something that made them panic. The Egyptian army behind them was bad enough, but it was the Red Sea in front of them that sank their hope. The sea left them nowhere to run. Because of the sea, they were trapped.

Or so they thought.

Sometimes in life you find yourself in a similar place. Sometimes you just feel trapped. Maybe you're feeling trapped right now by something that has developed in your life and you don't know how things will turn out. Everyone's circumstances are a little bit different, but there is one thing we all have in common. There's one thing that traps us all.

As if the hardships that chase us down aren't bad enough; in front of us we all face the certainty of death. Hardships we can navigate around, but death leaves us nowhere to run. Because of death, we are trapped.

Or so we thought.

What the Israelites experienced as they walked through the Red Sea on dry ground was a small foreshadow of what Christ would do when he entered death. He conquered it. He made a way through it. So whether it's a hardship of life or the fear of death, Jesus can take the thing that makes you panic and turn it into the avenue of your deliverance.

"In your unfailing love you will lead the people you have redeemed. In your strength you will guide them to your holy dwelling" (Exodus 15:13).

july

Now the Lord is the Spirit, and where
the Spirit of the Lord is, there is freedom.
2 Corinthians 3:17

God bless our native land

Pastor Mark Jeske

In the first week of July, you will probably hear me humming my favorite hymn to God on behalf of our country. The tune is so beloved around the world that quite a few countries have adopted it as a quasi national anthem. The British use the tune for "God Save the Queen."

Massachusetts native Charles T. Brooks wrote a little poem that is the perfect twin to this marvelous tune. But really you could sing his lovely prayer no matter where on earth your citizenship resides:

God bless our native land; firm may she ever stand through storm and night.
When the wild tempests rave, Ruler of wind and wave, Do thou our country save by thy great might.

God's guiding and protective hand are usually not immediately visible. But the pages of Scripture leave us absolutely no doubt that the Lord of history guides and shapes the great flow of historical events. He lifts up nations and kings to be useful for his agenda, and he knocks them down when he can no longer stand their behaviors.

May God forgive our many sins; may he use our unique position in today's world to bring his saving gospel far and wide; may his rich blessings inspire us to be a blessing to others.

For her our prayers shall rise to God, above the skies; on him we wait.
Thou who art ever nigh, guarding with watchful eye, To thee aloud we cry, God save the state!

Barking dogs

Pastor Jon Enter

"Just because I'm tied up to the porch doesn't mean I can't bark at cars when they drive by!" That's what a to-be husband told me in premarriage class in front of his future wife. He saw no problem flirting with women after being married. It didn't bother him to degrade women by objectifying them.

Last time I got a haircut, an attractive woman walked past the front of the barbershop. The guy cutting hair next to me literally barked at her. Everyone laughed.

Really, is it funny?

Men have a problem. Women too easily become objects to them. Women have a problem. Men.

Okay, it's not that simple. Women struggle too with impure thoughts and ungodly actions. Male or female, married or single, what do you do when your God-given libido is ticking and tickling you to do something God says breaks his heart?

Cut it off at the source—your mind. **"Among you there must not be even a hint of sexual immorality"** (Ephesians 5:3). Before words come out of your mouth, before actions come out of your body, they start as a temptation in your mind. Confess it. Not even a hint of something sexually wrong can ever find safety between your ears. If it does, it grows into detestable words and actions.

Immediately as that thought hits you, confess it to Christ. "Forgive me! Help me! Make me pure in mind so I'm pure in action!" Stop the starting point of sin; stop the action.

july 3

You always have help

Pastor Jeremy Mattek

I once saw a story about a mom who had accidentally locked her infant son inside her car along with her keys and phone on a hot summer day. She borrowed a stranger's phone and dialed 911.

"Ma'am," the emergency dispatcher said, "how's your son right now?" "He's doing okay," she replied. "Ma'am," the dispatcher said again, "we won't send anyone unless the child is actually in some kind of distress." And then the dispatcher hung up. The woman thought she knew where to find help. Instead, she found disappointment.

That's a painful feeling. But it happens often.

And every time someone disappoints you, that person gives you reason to believe he or she won't be there for you again. Room for doubt is created, which is a painful companion in your time of need.

Consider Jesus. As he hung on the cross, he had many needs. The need of relief from pain. The need of nourishment. The need of just one person who would be there for him. But no one was. No one came. Not because someone who promised to be there for him wasn't, but because God was keeping a promise to be there for you through anything. Even as he watched his only Son writhe in pain, he considered your need for comfort, hope, companionship, and forgiveness most important.

At the cross of Jesus, we see how true it is that God is determined to be our **"ever-present help in trouble"** (Psalm 46:1).

Love your country

Pastor Mark Jeske

Politics in the United States has always been rancorous, sometimes worse at times than others. In 1856 Representative Preston Brooks gave Senator Charles Sumner a vicious beating with a cane in the Senate chamber. These days there aren't any actual physical attacks between lawmakers in the Capitol, but the bitterness of recent elections knows no limits. There seems to be a lot more polarization than reconciliation.

Political parties can't move people when they are happy. It is in their interest to stoke grievances and get people upset enough to blog and tweet, march and demonstrate. The media cannot resist all this mass of negative energy. Sometimes there are social evils that need people in motion. But wise citizens are careful with their anger and husband it carefully. The din of politics must not leave us with ungrateful hearts to the Lord who has richly blessed us, sometimes because of our work and sometimes in spite of it.

God invited his captive Israelites to pray for their Babylonian enslavers: **"Seek the peace and prosperity of the city to which I have carried you into exile. Pray to the Lord for it, because if it prospers, you too will prosper"** (Jeremiah 29:7). We are not experiencing anything remotely like the Babylonian captivity. Don't let Satan steal your joy in citizenship. Don't let the snarls of political punching and rhetoric and maneuvering give you a bitter heart.

Love your country. Pray for your country.

Going without knowing

Jason Nelson

"By faith Abraham, when called to go to a place he would later receive as his inheritance, obeyed and went, even though he did not know where he was going" (Hebrews 11:8).

My name is Abraham. I was born in Ur of the Chaldeans near the Euphrates River. You would call this place Iraq. I don't remember much from when I was a kid except that my family moved around a lot. We were nomads. I'm embarrassed to tell you we worshiped idols. We even had little statues we packed up and carried along with us. Then one day God, the true one, came to me and said, "Abraham, I am your shield and great reward, and I want you to pick up and move." I thought, "Now what?"

God said he would make me into a great nation and that my descendants would be as many as the stars in the sky. He said that from me would come somebody so special that he and I would be a blessing to every nation on earth. Well, it all sounded pretty good. But I didn't even want to tell my family and friends. I knew what they were going to say: "Abraham, c'mon now. You're thinking like a camel. Where is this place? What's going to happen to you there?" All I could say was, "I don't know. But I'm going."

So what's your name? Where does God have you headed in life? Not exactly sure? Not a problem. I found out that faith is going without knowing.

Is tithing God's law?

Pastor Mark Jeske

One of the characteristics of the human management of the church over the centuries is the disappointing tendency for leaders to create extra rules for the faithful (as though the Bible's God-given laws were not enough). We leaders mean well, of course. We want to straighten you out, shape you up, make you more productive, get you moving in the right direction, and protect you from the devil and your own worst instincts.

In Old Covenant times, God designed a religious life for the Israelites that was based on the assumption that they needed his heavy hand of control and discipline, like minor children. One example was in their money management—tithing (the bringing of 10 percent of one's income as an offering to the Lord) was an explicit requirement.

In New Covenant times, God has decided to treat us as adult children (not that we always deserve such high trust). *There is no mandatory tithe*: **"Each of you should give what you have decided in your heart to give, not reluctantly or under compulsion, for God loves a cheerful giver"** (2 Corinthians 9:7). As you make your spending decisions week to week and month to month, reflect on God's generosity in giving you all you have, including your income. Reflect on how your gifts are a splendid part of your worship life and give God glory in your decisions. Rejoice in all the good things that come from your congregation's ministries.

Give freely, from your heart, the percentage that you have chosen. Enjoy every gift!

Believe in yourself
Linda Buxa

"Jesus stood and said in a loud voice, 'Let anyone who is thirsty come to me and drink. Whoever believes in me, as Scripture has said, rivers of living water will flow from within them. By this he meant the Spirit'" (John 7:37-39).

I was watching the Disney Channel with my kids and a motivational commercial came on about being yourself and finding your talents. That was decent until the moral at the end had one kid encouraging all the other kids to "believe in yourself."

Now, I'm a rose-colored glasses, glass-is-half-full kind of person, yet I don't love that we have come to accept "believe in yourself" as a truth; when in reality it's a lie. Telling me to believe in myself only embarrasses me. I know my weaknesses, my flaws, my insecurities. Sure, I can clean up and put on a good front, but on my own, I will ultimately let myself—and you—down. I don't have a self-created, unending well of self-control, love, joy, peace, or patience.

But I know the One who does—and I hear about him in the Bible. When I'm searching for truth and hope, I don't turn on the TV, but I turn to the Scriptures, which **"are written that you may believe that Jesus is the Messiah, the Son of God, and that by believing you may have life in his name"** (John 20:31).

My sister is living like an unbeliever
Pastor Mark Jeske

It is the curse of the age in which we live that the majority of people believe that there is no absolute truth, that everything is relative, that people are free to decide on their own sense of right and wrong. Nobody can tell anybody else what to do. Nobody is allowed to judge anyone else.

You would expect those philosophies from unbelievers. What a shock it is when you hear those ideas and see an unchristian lifestyle from someone who was brought up in the faith. It's a big deal. God's holy law is binding upon every human being; all are accountable to him, whether they know it or not, whether they believe it or not.

The way people think and talk and live matters to God: **"The acts of the flesh are obvious: sexual immorality, impurity and debauchery; idolatry and witchcraft; hatred, discord, jealousy, fits of rage, selfish ambition, dissensions, factions and envy; drunkenness, orgies, and the like. I warn you, as I did before, that those who live like this will not inherit the kingdom of God"** (Galatians 5:19-21). What to do when someone you love is flirting with spiritual suicide?

Never give up. Earn the right to speak by listening first. Love unconditionally. Keep your panic down and your voice soft. Don't nag, but do speak God's words of law to awaken the conscience you know is still there. Assure her of God's boundless mercy. Pray for her. And then watch patiently for signs of spiritual life again.

Nothing works out for me
Pastor Mark Jeske

Do you have any friends who are always saying things like: "Just my luck." "I always get the short straw." "If there's a line that isn't moving, I'm in it." "I just can't get a break." Or do your friends hear *you* saying those things? Were you just joking, or do you harbor a secret fear that you are doomed to a life of frustration and disappointment?

Scripture's good news for God's people helps us see that those negative voices in the back of our mind were planted there by the deceiver, who wants you to think and feel like a loser. In fact you are a winner, because you are connected to Christ, the ultimate winner.

Little Israel had absorbed all manner of disasters and disciplines, but none of those bad experiences could take away the central fact that the Lord delights in his believers and has a happy outcome for each one: **"Sing, Daughter Zion; shout aloud, Israel! Be glad and rejoice with all your heart, Daughter Jerusalem! The Lord has taken away your punishment, he has turned back your enemy. The Lord, the King of Israel, is with you; never again will you fear any harm"** (Zephaniah 3:14,15). The gospel makes optimists of us all. Let your mind dwell on Christ's mighty works on your behalf. Let your mind resonate with the Spirit's words and presence in your life.

And practice some new self-talk: "I wonder what amazing thing God is going to do for me today?"

Spiritual preparation
Pastor Mark Jeske

Farming just has to be the occupation most connected to reality. You can't rewrite the rules of agriculture and expect a harvest. There are fixed times and methods for plowing, planting, watering, fertilizing, and waiting; and then finally comes the happy time for gathering in.

The prophet Hosea used agricultural metaphors to describe how important it is for believers to tend to their relationship with their God. Just as in farming, there are important times and attitudes to keep that relationship healthy: **"Sow righteousness for yourselves, reap the fruit of unfailing love, and break up your unplowed ground; for it is time to seek the Lord, until he comes and showers his righteousness on you"** (Hosea 10:12).

Breaking up the unplowed ground refers to repentance—honestly admitting your sinful failings. Sowing righteousness refers to opening your ears and heart to the Word of God and letting its powerful seed take root and flourish within. Trusting in his unfailing love gives you confidence that your sin is forgiven, that Satan's power is checked, and that you still have a place in God's family. Seeking the Lord refers to earnest prayer, offering your worship and praise and laying out your needs and dreams in full confidence of his favor. And just as farmers then have to wait, we too will joyfully anticipate God's showers of righteousness and blessing. Watch for them.

It's time to seek the Lord.

God wants you to live

Pastor Jeremy Mattek

In Numbers 21:5 the Israelites asked Moses, **"Why did you bring us up out of Egypt?"** It was a strange question because the Israelites had been praying that God would bring them out of slavery in Egypt. But after their prayer was answered, it wasn't long before they found something new about which to complain.

Most surveys and polls today indicate that a good chunk of the world's population feels the same way. Everyone's unhappy about something. And like the Israelites, we are often pretty quick to identify what we *think* needs to change in order to feel better. And those moments usually reveal something very important about us.

Israel's cries for comfort and satisfaction in the desert revealed that they wanted to feel comfortable and satisfied more than they wanted God.

And when the venomous snakes God sent caused them to see their sin, they cried out for help and saw exactly what God wanted more than anything. He wanted them to live. He told Moses to put a snake on a pole so that **"anyone who is bitten can look at it and live"** (Numbers 21:8).

God has graciously given us a place to which we can also look and live—no matter the desert, no matter the sin. We look to Jesus' cross for something that can satisfy any soul, no matter how thirsty it is.

We find the forgiveness of every sin and the promise that God will let nothing in all creation keep us from being comfortable and happy forever in heaven.

Letting others help
Linda Buxa

"Carry each other's burdens, and in this way you will fulfill the law of Christ" (Galatians 6:2).

One of the best parts of believing in Jesus is that you get to be part of an enormous extended family. As you look around and see your brothers and sisters who may be hurting, struggling, and needing help, you get to pitch in. This is your opportunity to demonstrate the love, kindness, peace, patience, and compassion that the Holy Spirit has given you.

But the part I often conveniently forget, overlook, and avoid is that others in my spiritual family have been given the command to help *me* carry *my* burden. And maybe that's a humbling realization for you too. When we bottle up our struggles and temptations, we rob others of the joy that comes from serving, and we miss out on the blessings that come from being supported.

God places other believers in your life so you can be a blessing to them—and so they can be a blessing to you. Thanks to the people around us who love Jesus, we are surrounded by people ready and willing to help. It's time for us to let them.

If you don't have a Christian community around you, find one and get involved. You'll get to see God's love in action.

Be bright
Jason Nelson

There are some dark corners in the world. You can find them if you go looking for them, but please don't go looking. Cryptic headlines come out of sinister websites disguised to look like news agencies. Shady political operatives plant rumors about opponents. Some CEOs are willing to keep investors in the dark in order to keep their money. Secret militias conduct maneuvers in remote places. Not to mention the dark thoughts in the nooks and crannies of our own minds.

The dark side communicates with code words intended to rally like-minded people to join in the pursuit of their kind of pure: pure culture, pure race, pure politics, pure religion, pure profit, or a combination of the above. Some insist the dark way is the only way to get there. That's devil talk. Nothing is darker than implying evil is necessary for a "good" cause. **"The way of wicked people is like deep darkness"** (Proverbs 4:19 GW).

"The light of righteous people beams brightly" (Proverbs 13:9 GW). This world doesn't need less clarity, less transparency. It needs light. We are the bright side. When we are enlightened by the gospel and good learning, we can be enlightening to others and flip the switch when everything is dark. Jesus' radiance is reflected in our openness. We are beacons when we are plainspoken with truth, straightforward about God's will, and generous with his love. I promise you it will make a difference. The evidence is in. Light dispels darkness every time.

God's love really is unconditional

Pastor Mark Jeske

Christianity is the only faith that dares to stake you to all the benefits up front.

Every other religion that has sprung from the mind of man makes demands on people first. They have to perform in some way—meditate, sacrifice, prove worthy, achieve various levels of moral perfection, participate in religious rituals—and then they will be rewarded. The Christian Scriptures tell a different story, that the human race is too warped with sin ever to please God or fulfill his laws as a condition of acceptance. So God did it for them.

Jesus came to earth and took a human body into his deity. He lived a perfect life for us the imperfect, accepted the condemnation that hung over our heads, suffered the death we deserve, was buried and rose again, all to give us what we could never achieve on our own. **"Now to the one who works, wages are not credited as a gift but as an obligation. However, to the one who does not work but trusts God who *justifies the ungodly*, their faith is credited as righteousness"** (Romans 4:4,5).

Your life with God begins with the staggering news that he has already justified you in Christ Jesus. You don't have to perform for him to get him to like you. He already likes you. In fact, his love for you is unconditional. That love inspires you and me to believe Scripture's promises, and our faith is credited to us as righteousness in our account with God.

Wow.

My best friend is getting divorced

Pastor Mark Jeske

I haven't experienced divorce personally, but watching its effect on friends of mine tells me that it must be like amputation without anesthesia. Both husband and wife may be equally at fault, but even when one or the other has committed some major marriage-wrecking acts, the "innocent" partner knows that he or she contributed to the breakdown too.

What do you say to someone you love whose marriage has been destroyed? First, just be there. With the loss of a spouse, your friendship now is twice as important. When Job was going through his string of personal losses, he really, really needed his friends. They, however, were more interested in accusing and blaming: **"Anyone who withholds kindness from a friend forsakes the fear of the Almighty. But my brothers are as undependable as intermittent streams"** (Job 6:14,15).

Listen to your wounded friend. Be slow to criticize. Gently help him take responsibility for things that were his fault and find the right ways to make amends where possible. Help her work on forgiveness and finding inner peace through Jesus' love for her. Staying close to Jesus is a must—don't let her skip church to avoid having to tell her story over and over. Be there for the long haul—these wounds will heal, but slowly. "Family" times like Christmas will be the worst. Perhaps you can set another place at your table on those days.

Learn from these hard experiences and take better care of your own spouse.

Lasting change
Pastor Jon Enter

What change has your soul been screaming at you to make in your life? What's stopping you?

In 1997 Dennis Rodman kicked a cameraman in the groin at a NBA Bulls basketball game. He was fined $20,000 and an 11-game suspension without pay. Rodman argued he was the victim, having to pay a hefty penalty only because he is rich. He focused on anything other than his actions and admitted no fault.

If you want change in your life, lasting change, real change, wow-my-life-feels-and-is-better change, then open your heart fully to God. Confess it all, everything. Without excuse. Without exception. Without fear. For God loves you, hears you, and answers your prayer, just as he did for King David after his string of selfish sins. David confessed, **"Against you, you only have I sinned and done what is evil in your sight. . . . Wash away all my iniquity and cleanse me from my sin"** (Psalm 51:4,2). After David opened up his heart, trusting God's grace, David heard the sweetest sounding words any broken sinner can hear: **"The LORD has taken away your sin"** (2 Samuel 12:13).

May David's confession be your confession. Speak his words as yours. But slowly. With heartfelt contrition over your past. "Against you, you only have I sinned and done what is evil in your sight. Wash away all my iniquity and cleanse me from my sin." And God has! With peace in your heart, hear God's words of forgiveness, "The LORD has taken away your sin."

Good company

Jason Nelson

Every time I go to church, I look around at my sisters and brothers and thank God for the privilege of being in such good company. I know none of them is perfect, and by now they know I'm not either. We know a lot about each other. And we love each other anyway.

There have been serious challenges in the lives of these good people. They have suffered suicides of family members, the tragic loss of spouses, out of wedlock pregnancies, relentless battles with mental illness, poor health, and physical disabilities. Some made youthful mistakes and still have lapses in judgment. Faith has skipped a generation in some of our families, and now grandparents are bringing grandchildren to church. We are always happy to see each other and have welcomed many newcomers. There is a well-padded seat for everyone. And we never ever get tired of hearing about all the different ways that Jesus loves us.

This is a Psalm 98 kind of place. We sing new songs because the Lord really has done marvelous things with this church. This is a Psalm 150 kind of place. Many talented people participate in the worship service in different ways. This is a Psalm 46 kind of place. It is a refuge when we are weak and weary and a source of strength to help us get through the drudgeries of life. This is a Psalm 122 kind of place. I really like going to this house of the Lord and taking other people with me.

Is there still a Sabbath day?

Pastor Mark Jeske

People who have been trained in basic Bible studies have read the Ten Commandments. This short list is a strikingly useful summary of God's will for the way in which he wants to be treated and the ways in which he wants us to treat other people. But when you read the commandment about remembering the Sabbath day, what goes through your mind?

In Old Covenant times, God set aside every Saturday for the believers to worship, remember the original creation week and his day of resting, and to appreciate the wonderful relationship that they enjoyed with their heavenly Father. They were absolutely forbidden to work on Saturdays. Under the New Covenant brought about by Christ: **"Do not let anyone judge you by what you eat or drink, or with regard to a religious festival, a New Moon celebration or a Sabbath day. These are a shadow of the things that were to come; the reality, however, is found in Christ"** (Colossians 2:16,17).

Thus today there is no Sabbath *day*. Although Sunday is sometimes called the Sabbath, in fact it is not. It is a great day to worship God, remembering Christ's Sunday resurrection and the Spirit's Sunday Pentecost coming. But you may do work on any day of the week without sinning. What does remain is God's exhortation for believers to prize above all things their happy relationship, their peace and rest, with God through Christ Jesus.

"There remains, then, a Sabbath-rest for the people of God" (Hebrews 4:9).

What's in your wallet?

Pastor Mark Jeske

Jesus' Sermon on the Mount (Matthew 5-7) is full of challenges to the conventional religious thinking of the time. He upended traditional notions about oath taking, divorce, revenge, almsgiving, and prayer. He also confronted the Pharisees' core conviction that their wealth proved that they had the favor of God resting on them: **"Do not store up for yourselves treasures on earth, where moths and vermin destroy, and where thieves break in and steal"** (Matthew 6:19).

Jesus was not criticizing saving money or building up your family's wealth. His words do not imply guilt for people who invest in mutual funds, have an IRA, a pension, CDs, or savings accounts. Scripture in various other places encourages thrift, avoidance of debt, and wealth accumulation. Jesus' words have at least three benefits: First, they relieve poor people from the fear that God is punishing them. Second, they remind all believers of money's power to corrupt and addict. Third, they remind us all that life on this earth is short and that eternity is long.

According to Jesus, as helpful as it is to get rid of debt and build up a cash reserve, it is far more important to accumulate treasure in heaven. What did he mean by that? Just this: to value and prize your relationship with God as your most important possession, far more valuable than money, and to make sure that no false god will hinder your entering into the Paradise he has prepared for you.

An answer for everything

Jason Nelson

I don't enjoy speculating about hypotheticals. I don't care how many angels can dance on the head of a pin. I want to move past splitting hairs to prove I'm a little more right than the next guy. There's too much muddy water in the river of life already. I'm trying to retrain myself to respond like Christians did in the early centuries, because they had an answer for everything.

If you ask me where God came from or how old everything is, I'm just going to say: *I believe in God, the Father almighty, maker of heaven and earth.*

If you ask me how God could get a lady pregnant and do all that stuff with Jesus, I will say: *I believe in Jesus Christ, his only Son, our Lord, who was conceived by the Holy Spirit, born of the virgin Mary, suffered under Pontius Pilate, was crucified, died, and was buried. He descended into hell. The third day he rose again from the dead. He ascended into heaven and is seated at the right hand of God the Father almighty. From there he will come to judge the living and the dead.*

If you ask me about the pathways to heaven, I'm going to say: *I believe in the Holy Spirit, the holy Christian Church, the communion of saints, the forgiveness of sins, the resurrection of the body, and the life everlasting.*

And then I'm going to ask you to say, *Amen.*

Let it go

Pastor Mark Jeske

If anybody had a right to hold a grudge, it was Joseph. His older brothers bitterly resented what they perceived as his smart mouth and his favored status with their father. So they jumped him, sold him to a caravan of slave traders heading for Egypt, and told his father that a wild animal had killed him.

Joseph suffered the indignity of being resold, of working as a slave, and then being thrown into prison on unjust charges. As he sat in his cell, his soul could have been consumed with rage toward his cruel brothers. Instead, he waited for God to help him. And help him God did—raising him up ultimately as the pharaoh's chief assistant.

He had a chance to exact his own revenge on his brothers when they came to Egypt for food during a famine. He said this instead: **"'Don't be afraid. Am I in the place of God? You intended to harm me, but God intended it for good to accomplish what is now being done, the saving of many lives. So then, don't be afraid. I will provide for you and your children.' And he reassured them and spoke kindly to them"** (Genesis 50:19-21).

When God asks you to forgive someone who has hurt you, it's not because the hurt was nothing. It is in spite of the fact that the hurt was big. Forgive anyway, just as in Christ God has forgiven you. Let the spirit of Christ, and of Joseph, live in your heart and words today.

Stand firm!

Linda Buxa

Taking on a preschooler who has made up his or her mind is a formidable task, isn't it? He would rather wait 15 minutes until his classmate is finished with the red scissors than acquiesce and use the blue one. She would rather sit at the dinner table for two hours than eat the one green bean on her plate—even though eating it would mean she could get back to playing with her toys. Thousands of books have been sold that offer advice on how to parent strong-willed kiddos. That's because stubborn kids aren't exactly cute.

A stubborn faith, well, that's something to hope for, because we believe in a stubborn Savior. From the moment Jesus came to earth, he would not get distracted by Satan's offers or by humans' shortsighted pleas. On the cross, he refused the temptation to come down and save himself. Instead, stubbornly, **"for the joy set before him he endured the cross, scorning its shame, and sat down at the right hand of the throne of God"** (Hebrews 12:2).

Because of his victory, we now get to fight our spiritual battles with his power. We patiently wait for his rewards, even when the world is trying to distract us. We fix our eyes on him, because he fixed his eyes on us. Even when it's hard, we read the one book that matters most, the Bible, because it gives us the truth on how to be stubborn. **"Be on your guard; stand firm in the faith; be courageous; be strong"** (1 Corinthians 16:13). Preschooler strong.

I think my coworker is an atheist
Pastor Mark Jeske

Probably a *lot* of your coworkers are atheists or agnostics, or at least want no connection to any Christian denomination. The Pew Research Center's research shows that 25 percent of Americans identify as "nones," as in "none of the above."

We live in a post-Christian age. There was a time when society "expected" people to go to church, or at least maintain a church relationship. Not anymore. But don't be shocked. Scripture said it would be like this: **"Above all, you must understand that in the last days scoffers will come, scoffing and following their own evil desires. They will say, 'Where is this "coming" he promised? Ever since our ancestors died, everything goes on as it has since the beginning of creation'"** (2 Peter 3:3,4).

Jesus himself told us that the love of most would grow cold. Revelation predicts that Satan will get so confident of his growing power that he will plot the final battle of Armageddon. He and all his followers have already been judged and will be crushed.

But in the meantime, you and I are God's medics in the war zone. The way we talk about our faith and the integrity with which we act will be watched. Never give up on people, since we don't know where the Spirit's words will take root. Always be ready to speak God's words of accountability and mercy and the wonderful forgiveness and immortality that we have in Jesus Christ.

The rest is up to God.

Slept out by 3 A.M.

Jason Nelson

Sleep deprivation is an epidemic. The Centers for Disease Control and Prevention say it's a public health problem. People admit that tiredness affects their concentration, memory, driving, and performance at work. It must be worse globally because many in the world have mortar shells banging off their bedroom walls or are trying to sleep in cramped spaces piled one person on top of another.

We lie awake because our thoughts are spinning like the wheel of a hamster with a full thermos of coffee. Jesus gives us an invitation we can recite when we are slept out by 3 A.M. or even earlier. **"Come to me, all you who are weary and burdened, and I will give you rest"** (Matthew 11:28).

Our minds run out of curious ways to piece things together in dreams; then our thoughts rush at us one after another. Another night of being slept out too early. We need to fall back to sleep. Take a deep breath, exhale slowly, and say it softly: *"Come to me all you who are weary and burdened."*

And then we think about the consequences. We have to turn it off. We have to go to work. We have to take care of our families. We have to hit on all cylinders and make important decisions. We can't be zombies. We have to get some rest. Say it again even softer: *"Come to me. I will give you rest. There is nothing you can do about anything from a dark room at 3 A.M. But I can."*

Unnecessary lies
Pastor Jon Enter

I was sitting in an airport restaurant exhausted, hungry, eager to get home to hug my family. A high-powered businessman with a suit and an expensive haircut sat next to me at another small table. He pulled out his phone and called his wife. "Ahh," I thought, "he's a good husband checking in with her." They talked for a few minutes. Suddenly he said, "Hey, I gotta go. My food is here." Their conversation quickly ended. He hadn't even ordered! I thought something drastically different of him after that.

Why did he lie? He didn't have to. Why do you lie? You don't have to. But it happens all too often. Big lies. Small lies. Unnecessary lies. Because of sin within, the default setting on our brains is BAIL YOURSELF OUT BY LYING. **"The Lord detests lying lips, but he delights in people who are trustworthy"** (Proverbs 12:22).

There's a strangle hold on your heart, making it hard to be honest with others. But there is one place to be fully, faithfully honest all the time. With God. God who knows your heart, your hurt, your helplessness. He knows your need before you even ask. There's no need to lie before the One who already knows. So be honest with him right now. What is your greatest need? He will hear and answer. When you are trustworthy with Christ, he will change your heart to be trustworthy with others.

You have God's attention

Pastor Jeremy Mattek

I recently attended the funeral of a young man. The church was overflowing with people. Most of their attention was directed to the young man's mother. There were countless hugs and many words of encouragement and comfort.

I happened to see the mother two weeks later and asked how she was doing. "I feel lonely," she said. But she wasn't talking about missing her son. After the funeral, not one of the hundreds of friends who had attended had even called to see how she was doing. Her need for comfort was ongoing. And two weeks later, she didn't have it.

Mothers who've lost their sons aren't the only ones to feel alone in their pain. You and I often struggle too. Whatever the cause, loneliness and anxiety are far too common experiences for everyone.

Even Jesus knows how it feels to be alone. As he hung on his cross, his enemies laughed, his disciples ran away, and not even his Father in heaven responded to his cries for help. Jesus died alone. But he did so willingly, showing us exactly how far he is willing to go to put our needs ahead of his own, even if our greatest need was to be forgiven of the sins that killed him.

Though we aren't always faithful in coming first to Jesus for rescue in our misery, he is always faithful in providing it whenever we call on him. **"Call on me in the day of trouble,"** Jesus said, and **"I will deliver you"** (Psalm 50:15).

Count the stars

Pastor Mark Jeske

It was hard enough to bear the burden of infertility. Maybe more than 10 percent of couples struggle with it today. But two millennia before Christ your children were your old-age pension. Abraham had even more pressure—he was living in Canaan as a stranger in a strange land. He was related to no one. Worse—years ago God had promised him a child, and each year he and Sarah got older, the more remote that promise seemed. Was God just playing him? Or did God lack the power to do what he said?

God's plans were still firm, but the time had not yet come. He had some powerful encouragement for his man Abraham as he waited and a visual sign to keep his faith strong. He spoke directly to him: **"'Look up at the sky and count the stars—if indeed you can count them.' Then he said to him, 'So shall your offspring be.' Abram believed the Lord, and he credited it to him as righteousness"** (Genesis 15:5,6). Imagine how brilliant the night sky would have looked in a place with no humidity, air pollution, or streetlights.

All was well. Abraham believed God's reaffirmed promise. His faith was credited to him as righteousness before God. And God did keep his promise—Isaac the miracle boy *was* born to two old people (ages 89 and 99).

When you are struggling in your faith, take a little walk outside and look up. Let those same stars remind you that God always keeps his word.

Marry a believer
Pastor Mark Jeske

Isaac, the second patriarch of the promise, and his wife, Rebekah, had twin boys, Esau and Jacob, who neither looked alike nor acted alike. Esau had always been a headstrong young man. Though the firstborn ahead of his twin brother, Jacob, he thought so little of his "birthright" family position that he traded it away for a bowl of stew (Genesis 25:27-34).

He compounded his spiritual carelessness: **"When Esau was forty years old, he married Judith daughter of Beeri the Hittite, and also Basemath daughter of Elon the Hittite. They were a source of grief to Isaac and Rebekah"** (Genesis 26:34,35). Not only has polygamy always been a bad idea and brought misery to every household that tried it, Esau's choice of two Canaanite women was particularly poor. The Canaanites had their own religious beliefs completely at odds with what Esau had learned from his father, Isaac, and grandfather Abraham. How could Esau's two pagan wives not have pulled him farther away from worship of the true God?

How important is it to you to date people you know are Christians? How important is it to have a Christian spouse? You know, one of the main jobs of a Christian spouse is to provide a lifelong buddy system to keep one's spouse on the path that leads to heaven. Christians who marry unbelievers may assume that they will lead the unbeliever to Christ. It is sadly just as likely that the unbeliever will drag the believer away from Christ.

I feel so wounded

Pastor Mark Jeske

Every day brings its own disappointments and frustrations: car trouble, argument with your spouse, disagreeable boss, nagging headache. But those are just little nicks. Life's heaviest burdens come from the devastating blows whose hurt stays with us for decades: a father who told us we were stupid and would never amount to anything, a perfectionist mother who could never say "good job," humiliations from bullies, betrayal by a best friend, a felony record whose dark cloud never goes away.

In Christ the healing from those deep wounds begins right now. Through faith in Christ you receive good news that you have great value to the Son of God himself, that your own moral failings are forgiven, and that you will be given daily strength to survive and overcome. Through Christ you will grow in your own ability to forgive those who have wounded you, and in that way those open wounds can turn into scars. The memory is still there, but the pain is diminished.

The ultimate relief will come in heaven. After the spiritual warfare and conflict of this life, you will be invited into the Paradise of the blessed, even better than the Garden of Eden, where you will experience complete wholeness for the first time ever. **"On each side of the river stood the tree of life, bearing twelve crops of fruit, yielding its fruit every month. And the leaves of the tree are for the *healing* of the nations"** (Revelation 22:2).

They're for the healing of *you*.

Love one another
Linda Buxa

"By this everyone will know that you are my disciples, if you love one another" (John 13:35).

My kids are normal, which means that at home they will intentionally bicker, pick on, and annoy each other. Once, however, when we lived in California, my oldest one marched up to a schoolmate and let him know, "No one picks on my little brother but me!"

Adorable, right? I mean, she absolutely knew it was her job to protect her siblings—until they got home and it was a free-for-all.

God calls the church a family. I realize that we are prone to do the same thing—and it's not as cute for us as it is for little kids. I'll defend my Christian brothers and sisters in public, but in private I am quick to look for flaws. Maybe you can relate. The place where we should love each other deeply is actually the place where we judge each other harshly. Have you seen their clothes? They don't pay attention to their kids. Their worship style is wrong. Why can't she get her life together?

The apostle Paul had an important message for people who lived two thousand years ago, and it is still relevant. **"The entire law is fulfilled in keeping this one command: 'Love your neighbor as yourself.' If you bite and devour each other, watch out or you will be destroyed by each other"** (Galatians 5:14,15).

Our options are (1) love one another and let the world know we are his disciples. Or (2) bicker until we destroy each other.

I prefer option 1.

Waiting on God
Pastor Jon Enter

Is your life off the charts awesome? No pain. No problems. No failures. Like someone should write a book about you because all you do is win, win, win. If that's not you, what's lacking in your life? What are you waiting on God to do, to heal, to fix?

Waiting on God is hard, especially as God could make it all better with a flick of his little finger. He spoke and the mountains were born. He waved his hands and the oceans went just so deep. He has almighty power that he uses as he pleases.

If you're still waiting on God's blessings, is there something not right in your life? Maybe. But remember God's consequences to sin are immediate and obvious. If you've had blessing removed as a consequence to sin, that's God working in love. That's God making a sinful life an uncomfortable life so you repent and then rejoice in his forgiveness.

But there are times when God delays. He holds back blessings as a test to see where your focus is: self or Savior. That's not unfair or unloving. It's God being a good Father, testing you so you grow in trust and gain strength for an upcoming attack of the evil one.

"I waited patiently for the Lord; he turned to me and heard my cry" (Psalm 40:1). Are you waiting patiently, trustingly, faithfully? God will not let you down. On his timetable, he brings blessings. Get ready. They're coming! Until then, wait patiently.

august

May all who love you be like the sun
when it rises in its strength.

Judges 5:31

Pay your debts

Pastor Mark Jeske

You know, it's one thing to drag your feet on debt repayment if you are absolutely broke. It's another thing entirely when you have all or part of the money but make no move to repay. It's bad if you're that disorganized—being a good steward of your God-given assets is part of the Christian life. It's bad if you're unaware of the hidden costs of debt—while you dawdle, interest charges are slowly eating up your money. It's bad if you borrowed from a friend or relative and delay repayment, because now you're taking advantage of someone who was kind to you.

Pay your debts: **"Do not say to your neighbor, 'Come back tomorrow and I'll give it to you'—when you already have it with you"** (Proverbs 3:28). Strategic indebtedness—to buy a house, for instance—is good debt. Debts that pile up because you're not keeping track is actually sinful. You are wasting resources that came from God himself, and you are sending a message to God that you're not a good manager.

Listen to Jesus' parables about the bags of gold and minas (Matthew 25 and Luke 19). The king looks at how his servants managed their assets (which they are managing on his behalf) and takes their performance into consideration when he is deciding how to apportion the next round.

If you put the time and energy into managing your financial resources, you are inviting God to trust you with even more.

Think: whom are you worshiping?

Pastor Mark Jeske

Until we see the triumphant Lord Jesus returning on the clouds, our worship is by faith and not by sight. What is there of God to *see* when you go to church? Just symbols—maybe a cross to remind us of Jesus, a dove for the Spirit, interlocking triangles for the Trinity.

The majesty of who it is we worship must come from the Word through the eyes of faith. Here is what St. John was allowed to see in his exile: **"Grace and peace to you from him who is, and who was, and who is to come, and from the seven spirits before his throne, and from Jesus Christ, who is the faithful witness, the firstborn from the dead, and the ruler of the kings of the earth. To him who loves us and has freed us from our sins by his blood . . . to him be glory and power for ever and ever!"** (Revelation 1:4-6).

The resurrected Lord Jesus is immortal and eternal, and we shall be too—he the "firstborn" and we to follow. He is greater than any and all rulers of the earth—they will all fall to their knees before him. His was the blood shed for the forgiveness of our sins, and his is the glory, both the glory that radiates from his beautiful face but also the glory that comes from our mouths, giving him the worship he deserves.

Worthy is the Lamb who was slain to receive power and riches and wisdom and strength and honor and glory and blessing!

Encourage each other
Linda Buxa

"Encourage one another and build each other up, just as in fact you are doing" (1 Thessalonians 5:11).

When we lived in California, my daughter played water polo—and I was clueless. Imagine soccer, basketball, and wrestling combined in the water. Because I couldn't see under the water, I had no idea why the refs were calling fouls. And, honestly, because you only see heads and swim caps, I couldn't always find my own daughter in the pool. So because I couldn't nitpick, I yelled, "Go!" or "Good job!" or "Yea!"

Wouldn't it be nice if we all stepped back a bit to simply cheer on our spiritual family too? We can't always see what happened in the past or what is going on in their lives, so I bet they need a lot less nitpicking and far more encouraging. What if we found a way to cheer, "Go!" or "Good job!" or "Yea!" The world is already doing a good job of telling us all the ways that we come up short, that we don't make enough money, that we aren't beautiful or handsome or in shape enough, that we aren't valuable.

So let's be the ones who encourage others, pick them up, dust them off, give them grace, and encourage them to do their best. Then let's look forward to the day, thanks to Jesus, when we will hear God say, **"Well done, good and faithful servant!"** (Matthew 25:21).

You'll be home one day
Pastor Jeremy Mattek

Sometimes my father took me camping while I was growing up. On one trip, we had finished setting up the tent just in time for dinner, which is when we were attacked by a couple dozen seagulls dive-bombing our hotdogs. Later that evening, a thunderstorm rolled in and revealed two things: we hadn't tied down the tent as securely as we had imagined, and the tent wasn't as waterproof as the packaging had promised. By midnight, our camping trip was done, and we were back home again resting comfortably in our beds.

We laugh about that trip now. But at the time, while seagulls were swooping at our heads and our tent was falling apart, it was hard to laugh about anything. Just like it sometimes is in our lives.

In 2 Corinthians chapter 5, Paul compares our bodies to a tent. And like the tent on our camping trip, they're not entirely immune to destruction. We get sick. We suffer injuries. We get attacked by diseases that dive-bomb us without our permission. And then, of course, every funeral is a reminder that one day death will roll in like a thunderstorm and completely overwhelm our fragile bodies.

But like Paul says, our bodies are simply tents. And as long as we're in them, we're never really at home. But one day, we'll be at home in heaven. Through Jesus, our heavenly Father forgave the sinfulness that causes our destruction and gave us the right to look forward to our eventual arrival at an eternal house in heaven, where we will finally rest comfortably.

Are Christians supposed to fast?

Pastor Mark Jeske

People deny themselves food for all kinds of reasons: to lose weight, to purge what they believe are toxins in their bodies, or as a form of political protest (e.g., a hunger strike). Fasting in certain situations was a mandated behavior in Old Testament times, but it is not a law for believers who live under the New Covenant (i.e., the era in which we now live).

But fasting is a discipline that is an option for New Testament Christians: **"While they were worshiping the Lord and fasting, the Holy Spirit said, 'Set apart for me Barnabas and Saul for the work to which I have called them.' So after they had fasted and prayed, they placed their hands on them and sent them off"** (Acts 13:2,3). Temporary cessation of eating can focus your attention on an important spiritual goal and give you good practice at developing willpower (instead of caving every time you smell bacon). It is not a necessary precondition for prayer, but it does send a message to God how serious you are about your prayer requests, and the time you save in food preparation and consumption is now available to you for Bible study.

Christians often practice some sort of self-denial during the season of Lent (the seven weeks before Easter). It is optional, not mandatory, and over the centuries has brought benefit to believers' lives. If some sort of self-denial helps you think more about Jesus and appreciate his saving work more, go for it.

Live in peace; die without fear

Pastor Mark Jeske

The great gospel message of Jesus Christ sets us free in many ways: free from the guilt of our sins, free from God's righteous condemnation, free from identity confusion, free to serve God and other people. The gospel enables us to reframe our entire worldview from God's point of view: **"The righteous perish, and no one takes it to heart; the devout are taken away, and no one understands that the righteous are taken away to be spared from evil. Those who walk uprightly enter into peace; they find rest as they lie in death"** (Isaiah 57:1,2).

Since we know that we are immortal, we are freed from the terrible pressure to get it all now. We don't have to feel cheated about whatever material possessions and experiences we never got, because we are serene in our confidence that we have an eternity of joy before us. Those who die in the Lord aren't losing out on more years on the earth; they are entering the real life that Jesus Christ bought for them.

The removal of those terrible fear pressures enables us to enjoy our lives much more fully. We can bear misfortunes with patience; we can celebrate the good fortunes of others without a shred of envy or resentment; we can find joy in little acts of service, smiling inwardly to know that God sees them even if nobody ever thanks us.

We can live in peace. We can die without fear.

All of me

Jason Nelson

This time Peter got it right. Other times he was way off with his outbursts. But this time his dialogue with Jesus was spot on. Peter showed amazing insight into the way God made us and how Jesus totally changes us. **"'Lord, are you going to wash my feet?' . . . Jesus answered, 'Unless I wash you, you have no part with me.' 'Then, Lord,' Simon Peter replied, 'not just my feet but my hands and my head as well!'"** (John 13:6,8,9).

Peter didn't like the idea of Jesus only being his podiatrist. He wanted Jesus to be his general practitioner. Peter wanted Jesus to treat all of his symptoms and put the healing on all of his systems.

We are not compartmentalized beings. Our thoughts, feelings, actions, and beliefs don't launch from separate silos. God designed us to be vertically integrated from the top down. The fireworks in our brains drive everything.

When the Holy Spirit renewed our minds by giving us faith in Jesus, he washed everything about us. He enables us to think like we've never thought before, feel like we've never felt before, do what we couldn't do before, and believe what we didn't believe before. He enables each of us to **"love the Lord your God with all your heart and with all your soul and with all your mind and with all your strength"** (Mark 12:30). So we can echo Peter: "Lord, it's all of me or nothing at all."

Stories don't save

Pastor Jon Enter

I was at the funeral of a former member who had stopped attending church. Her husband told this story at the funeral. It was about a time they had gone out for dinner: "'Well?' she asked, leaving the restaurant. 'Yup!' I said in reply. 'Yesssss!' she celebrated." The husband explained, "That meant the liquor bill was more than the food bill." Everyone laughed. I didn't. I felt sad at the lack of peace they had in Jesus.

Have you been to a funeral for someone with no apparent relationship with Jesus? There's no hope. No peace. No comfort. There's emptiness. Anger. An unending feeling of loss. So people tell stories. Stories about how great a person he was. How generous she was. About a big liquor bill.

"Do not grieve like the rest of mankind, who have no hope" (1 Thessalonians 4:13). There is something incredibly beautiful that happens at a Christian funeral. The same hurting hearts gather. The same reason for no hope and no peace is there because on our own we are comfortless. But we are not alone. We are not on our own. We have Christ! We have Jesus who conquered death, who shattered the devil's eternal grip on our souls. We have someone, the One, who brings peace even in death as Jesus destroyed the power of death forever. For you. For your loved ones. For all who trust in him as their almighty Savior from sin.

How does this peace change the way you live?

august 9

Terror and comfort
Pastor Mark Jeske

What is your understanding of what happened in the transition from the Old Covenant to the New Covenant? What changes did Jesus Christ actually bring about in the way God and his believers interact? It is a false comfort to say, "We are free in Christ" and by that mean that we are free from God's Law. The detailed instructions for civic life in the Israelite theocracy are indeed gone, as are all the ceremonial laws spelling out rules for sacrifices, kosher foods, and mandated religious observances.

Jesus teaches us how to think about God's Law: **"Do not think that I have come to abolish the Law or the Prophets; I have not come to abolish them but to fulfill them"** (Matthew 5:17). The ceremonial religious laws all pointed to Christ and became superfluous when he came to earth. He didn't abolish them; he *fulfilled* them.

But there still remain God's moral laws, as summarized by the Ten Commandments. These are still very much in force, and this is a terrifying reality. God still expects and demands moral perfection from his earthly creatures and threatens punishments to disobeyers. But Jesus came also to fulfill God's moral law in our place. His perfect obedience is now accounted to us by faith in him. Through Christ alone your terror of accountability to a level of perfection you could never achieve is replaced by comfort.

Christ came not only to *die* for you. He came to *live* for you too.

You need the Spirit to get it

Pastor Mark Jeske

In many ways marriage is way harder than it looks. Just think of the odds stacked against you—you have to live your life tied to another sinner till death parts you, and your spouse is stuck with you alone till the grave claims one or the other. The marriage bond is lifelong—no going back, no do-overs, no side relationships, no secret boyfriends, no mistresses. You have to find a way not to let decades of hurts and disappointments blow the bond apart.

You might have expected the easy and frequent divorce in pagan cultures, but you would find it also in Israel at Jesus' time. Jesus' words about the lifelong commitment in marriage shocked not only the Pharisees but his own followers too: **"The disciples said to him, 'If this is the situation between a husband and wife, it is better not to marry.' Jesus replied, 'Not everyone can accept this word, but only those to whom it has been given'"** (Matthew 19:10,11), i.e., you need the wisdom and power of the Holy Spirit to get it, to grasp the value of lifelong commitment.

The Spirit not only teaches you God's original design but also reveals the secrets of how lifelong marriage can be a joy instead of a slog. We can choose to show compassion, kindness, humility, gentleness, and patience. We can choose to go first in service to our spouse, and we will then enjoy the surprise of finding that all our needs are being met in return.

Don't give up
Pastor Jeremy Mattek

In 1972 NASA launched a satellite named Pioneer 10. Its mission was to reach Jupiter and beam gathered information back to Earth. But after about a year of traveling through space, it reached its destination. And kept going.

By 1997 Pioneer 10 was more than 6 billion miles from the sun and was still sending radio signals and awesome pictures to NASA. It became known as "The Little Satellite That Could." NASA designed it to last three years, but it didn't quit.

Sometimes, however, we quit. Or at least we're tempted to—when the kids aren't listening or when we invest time in something that didn't turn out. Maybe a relationship has gotten beyond frustrating. The feeling of wanting to give up can come from anything.

Even Jesus was familiar with painful situations. I don't think anyone would have blamed him if he had given up when he felt the pain of the whip or nails. But he didn't. And one reason he didn't was because he knew the pain was temporary, which doesn't mean that the pain wasn't real or concerning. It was. Just like yours is. It's just that Jesus was more concerned about something that was more meaningful to him—you.

He carried his temporary cross so that your tired head could one day wear a crown of glory, so that your tired body would have a reason to keep going. **"Therefore, we do not lose heart,"** it says in 2 Corinthians, **"for our light and momentary troubles are achieving for us an eternal glory"** (4:16,17).

Blessed are you

Linda Buxa

In Acts chapter 17, some Jewish people were mad! The news that the Messiah had come and had died and had risen was being shared. So they formed a riot and dragged a group of believers in front of the city's officials and made all sorts of false claims about them: **"'They are all defying Caesar's decrees, saying that there is another king, one called Jesus.' When they heard this, the crowd and the city officials were thrown into turmoil. Then they made Jason and the others post bond and let them go"** (verses 7-9).

You know what? We love the part when being a Christian brings us peace. But for thousands of years, we see over and over again that peace with God does not necessarily mean peace with others. Speaking the truth in love gets people angry. Caring more about people's eternal destinations than their earthly status makes them defensive. You may lose friends or your family relationships may suffer because you are part of God's family.

Your God knows life here is hard, so he wants to encourage you: **"Blessed are you when people insult you, persecute you and falsely say all kinds of evil against you because of me. Rejoice and be glad, because great is your reward in heaven, for in the same way they persecuted the prophets who were before you"** (Matthew 5:11,12).

It isn't always going to be easy. Hang in there. Your reward is coming. Your Jesus is coming back.

Elevator talk
Pastor Jon Enter

Have you tried talking to someone in an elevator? Awkward! Why is it we become impaired socially and verbally as soon as we step into that vertical box of silence? The quietness is so unnerving that you want to say something, but you don't know where to start so . . . you hope . . . the doors will open and the situation will be over.

That's a great description of how you may feel when someone puts you on the spot to say something spiritually significant to calm his or her hurting heart. Because of your brokenness and your own hurt, you wonder what gives you the right and the responsibility to help others when you need help yourself.

The answer: Jesus. Jesus calls on you to calm other people's hearts as he calms and comforts yours. And as you do, as you proclaim his peace, God applies it to your heart too. Don't worry. The Spirit will guide you through the awkwardness, through the I-don't-know-what-to-say moments. **"The Spirit helps us in our weakness. We do not know what we ought to pray for, but the Spirit himself intercedes for us"** (Romans 8:26).

All you have to do is pray and point. Say a prayer: "Lord, please help me; I don't know what to say." And then say something. Start talking, and you'll be amazed at what the Spirit pours out of your heart of faith. Simply point that person to Jesus. God will handle the rest. He always does.

Son of God, eternal Savior

Pastor Mark Jeske

Human life was broken by Adam and Eve's rebellion, and that means that human beings will be broken too. There have always been people who struggle to survive; there are now, and there always will be. But there have always been those with a surplus of earthly goods, and the Creator watches to see what they will do with that economic power. In his view they have been blessed to be a blessing.

He loves to see a spirit of sharing and mercy: **"The generous will themselves be blessed, for they share their food with the poor"** (Proverbs 22:9). The generous also build houses to help others, volunteer to clean up neighborhoods, provide shelters for battered women and children, provide safe places for the elderly and frail, and care about the education of the poor.

Rev. Somerset Lowry wrote a lot of hymns, but "Son of God, Eternal Savior" is the best known. It is an eloquent poem of praise to Christ for his sacrificial life and death and calls on Christians to imitate his servant-spirit. The final stanza is inspirational:

As you, Lord, have lived for others,
so may we for others live.
Freely have your gifts been granted;
freely may your servants give.
Yours the gold and yours the silver,
yours the wealth of land and sea;
We but stewards of your bounty
held in solemn trust will be.

It's okay to be human
Jason Nelson

An old mistrust persists even among Christians. Worthwhile pursuits are demonized because they produce new information or new ways of doing things. Biases linger against science, against higher education, against psychology, against research, against concern for the planet, even against receiving medical attention. Folks are suspicious of such endeavors because they are . . . well . . . human. I guess they are viewed as attempts to dethrone God. But that's shortsighted and unfair to some fine people.

Let's acknowledge original sin and the problem of human depravity. That stains everything. But God dealt with it by becoming human. **"The Word became flesh and blood, and moved into the neighborhood. We saw the glory with our own eyes, the one-of-a-kind glory, like Father, like Son, generous inside and out, true from start to finish"** (John 1:14 MSG).

Let's also remember: **"Every desirable and beneficial gift comes out of heaven. The gifts are rivers of light cascading down from the Father of Light. There is nothing deceitful in God, nothing two-faced, nothing fickle. He brought us to life using the true Word, showing us off as the crown of all his creatures"** (James 1:17,18 MSG).

We don't need to be wary of progress. We all benefit from it. God created people to bring it on. The world never was flat, and God is still God. He condemns sin, but he doesn't condemn being human. At just the right time, he was too.

My son says he's lost his faith

Pastor Mark Jeske

I don't think there could be a more crushing realization for a Christian parent than to realize that a son or daughter has lost his or her faith and wants nothing to do with God. We would rather that our children would suffer injury or illness than reject their Savior. What to do when that happens?

Don't give in to panic, bitterness, defensiveness, blaming, or fear. No nagging, guilt, or pressure. Once they've been in the faith, our children must choose to embrace scriptural beliefs for themselves. You cannot believe for them, and they will bitterly resent it if you try to bully them.

Be patient. They may be testing you. They may be trying on various personas to see how they feel. Time and the hardness of life on earth may break down some of that bravado. You aren't alone—remember Jesus' parable? **"When** [the son] **came to his senses, he said, 'How many of my father's hired servants have food to spare, and here I am starving to death! I will set out and go back to my father and say to him: Father, I have sinned against heaven and against you'"** (Luke 15:17,18). Listen more than you talk. Love always. Never give up. No amount of brave agnostic talk can get rid of inner guilt. Emphasize God's mercy, that his arms are always open, that you're never too far gone. Don't stop praying.

And keep believing in the gospel's power.

Getting even

Pastor Mark Jeske

The most powerful force for social change during the civil rights movement in the 1950s and 1960s was not anger and violence. Though minorities in America had every reason to boil with rage, it was not rage that changed things. In fact, the outbursts of racial rioting, looting, shooting, and arson in the 1960s only dealt terrible setbacks to racial reconciliation.

The real power for change came from the moral leadership of people like Dr. Martin Luther King Jr., whose strategy of nonviolence triumphed because it is God's strategy: **"If you suffer for doing good and you endure it, this is commendable before God. To this you were called, because Christ suffered for you, leaving you an example, that you should follow in his steps"** (1 Peter 2:20,21).

How are you at the Christian skill of absorbing injustice? Do you believe in patience and persuasion, or do you harbor revenge fantasies in your mind? Do you subscribe to the "don't get mad, get even" philosophy? When injured in some way, do you feel compelled to "teach them a lesson"? As Christians we can leave the judging completely to God. He will get it done, all of it, at his time, and in the most perfect and appropriate way.

Here's a prayer and promise you and I can make to God today:

Dear Lord, I am not going to continue a cycle of hate and retaliation. It stops with me. Please help me. Amen.

The church's one foundation

Pastor Mark Jeske

The vast story of God's interactions with the people of the world he created has a lot of moving parts. Perhaps some people get overly caught up in various details of the long story of the Israelites or the long history of the growth of the Christian church.

Every now and again it's a good thing to get back to the heart and core of it all. Among all the stories and teachings and history, one thing matters most of all: **"I resolved to know nothing while I was with you except Jesus Christ and him crucified"** (1 Corinthians 2:2). Those were Paul's words about his own ministry, and they are a good guide still for how leaders in the church prioritize their time and energy. As important as our works of love, worship, and service are, far more important still are the great works and words of Jesus Christ for us.

A Church of England pastor named Samuel J. Stone wrote a beautiful poem about the absolute centrality of Jesus Christ to our faith lives. If you think of the church as a grand building, it must be built on Christ to last:

The Church's one foundation is Jesus Christ, her Lord;
She is his new creation by water and the Word.
From heaven he came and sought her to be his holy bride;
With his own blood he bought her, and for her life he died.

We're in a track meet
Pastor Mark Jeske

We all have a dreamy fantasy that everybody should live into his or her 90s, enjoy great health, and then gently fall asleep and pass into eternity without any drama or illness. We're always shocked when people, Christians even (!), die "out of order."

People's life spans stubbornly resist our desire that everyone should have a consistent number of years on this earth. Elderly people sometimes sigh with longing for heaven, unable to understand why they're living so long in such frail circumstances. Mourners at the funeral of a child can't stop tormenting themselves with the feeling that the child has been cheated.

If you are a little familiar with Scripture, you have heard our lives in Christ referred to as "running our race": **"Let us run with perseverance the race marked out for us, fixing our eyes on Jesus, the pioneer and perfecter of faith"** (Hebrews 12:1,2). You know, a track meet is actually a pretty good metaphor for our lives on this earth. Have you ever attended or competed in one? There are running events of all lengths—sprints like the 100 meters and the long distance endurance contests of five thousand and ten thousand meters.

Some of us serve the Lord by running a long-distance race. Others are chosen for a sprint, with a life measured in only a few years or even months.

It's all good. In Christ we will have an eternity to talk about it.

Called out to go all out

Jason Nelson

The Latin word for *church* is *ecclesia*. It means those who are "called out." Christians are sheltering out of place because we are in the world but not of the world. Sometimes we sit in church like it's heaven's waiting room, hoping the Great Physician will call us in soon so we can finally get some relief. But what if the called out went all out? What if we held nothing back while we are still here?

What if we were the first to admit we've made mistakes and continue to cause confusion about what it means to be a Christian?

What if we stopped competing with one another and we all went out with the gospel to outflank the devil's influence?

What if we fostered creativity and uncorked the talents of people we've held in reserve?

What if we went out expecting to find people as they are, invited them to come in that way, and helped them grow in God's grace?

What if we showed people who aren't sure about much how Jesus went all in for us?

What if we all went out and had some fun?

What if we flooded this place with the steady drip, drip of messages like these Grace Moments devotions?

What if we always emphasized the clear teachings of the Bible? God says, **"I can guarantee that on this rock I will build my church. And the gates of hell will not overpower it"** (Matthew 16:18 GW).

Happy Senior Citizens Day!

Linda Buxa

"Even to your old age and gray hairs I am he, I am he who will sustain you. I have made you and I will carry you; I will sustain you and I will rescue you" (Isaiah 46:4).

Senior citizens, today must seem like a welcome break from the routine of feeling undervalued. After all, society today isn't very kind to our older friends, is it? All the ads for anything fun show healthy, vibrant young adults. Any ads with senior citizens? Well, apparently you all need some form of medication or life insurance.

God has a completely different idea though. He tells you that your age, wisdom, and life experience make you valuable to your spiritual family. You have lived lives that prove how God sustains you. You faithfully pray not only for your earthly family but also for others. You display a trust in God that comes not from an easy life but from seeing how God has refined you because of life's storms.

Plus, you still have work to do. **"Even when I am old and gray, do not forsake me, my God, till I declare your power to the next generation, your mighty acts to all who are to come"** (Psalm 71:18). You share the good news of God's salvation with the next generation. Your offerings and volunteering help churches and ministries keep proclaiming his good news. You might not be able to move from your bed, but your prayers can move mountains.

We need you. We love you!

There's no need to remember what God has forgiven

Pastor Jeremy Mattek

In a teen Bible class, a student asked me, "At funerals, why do people only say good things about the person who died?" I asked her, "What would you want people to say about you if you had died?" She thought about it and said, "I wouldn't want them to tell the truth."

Would you want the people who know you best, who've seen you at your worst, to share the truth as they remember you? This student knew the truth, that when it comes to remembering our lives, it feels better to be selective and to forget certain things.

But there's no pretending in front of God. The Bible tells us that he pays such close attention to us that he knows the exact number of hairs on our heads. In other words, no matter what we'd like to hide, he knows the truth.

But God is selective about what he chooses to remember. I **"will remember their sins no more,"** he says in Jeremiah 31:34. But he doesn't just choose to not think about the whole truth. He chooses to remember what Jesus' sacrifice means for me and you. It means the records of our wrongs have been erased so that not even God remembers them.

And if God doesn't remember your sins, then why should you? Why should you beat yourself up about past mistakes when God only celebrates your perfect status in Christ through faith?

When the truth of your sin is hard to forget, recall the truth of what God chooses to remember.

She's only sleeping

Pastor Mark Jeske

My wife has an aunt she never met, mainly because that aunt died as a child, died on Christmas Day, died in her father's arms. Could there be a more devastating blow to any human being? When you think of all the disasters that continually rain down on humanity, is not this the worst, that you must bury your own child?

A man named Jairus knew just how that felt. His 12-year-old daughter had fallen ill and then died. He and his stricken family were shell-shocked with grief, relieved only slightly when Jesus came to their house. The mourners were already setting up quite a racket, and Jesus wanted them out of the house so he could do some ministry: **"He said, 'Go away. The girl is not dead but asleep.' But they laughed at him"** (Matthew 9:24). Only Jesus could say something so outrageous, so seemingly heartless, to a grieving family. But it was the truth.

Jesus took the little girl's cold, stiff hand and spoke words of life to her. Immediately her warmth returned, along with all the other signs of life from respiration to heartbeat to brain activity. She got up by herself. She was alive again!

This amazing story has sustained many grieving Christian families who have had to bear the death of a child. But children can be believers too. Through the washing of Baptism and the power of the Word, they can believe too.

And that means in death they're only sleeping.

Playing in the cracks

Jason Nelson

Where I went to college, every student had to take piano lessons. It was a requirement. Aptitude had nothing to do with it. Eventually, I was counseled out of the program. My instructor said, "Nelson, there are white keys and there are black keys, but you play in the cracks." Ouch.

Actually, it was a relief. I was miserable. My stubby fingers were not suited to playing piano. The bongos maybe. But not piano. Everything suffers when there is a mismatch between the tasks at hand and the talents of the person trying to perform them. There are two ways to deal with it. We can work hard at developing the skills needed, or we can move on. That same instructor asked me what year I was in college. I told him I was a junior. He said if I had five more years, maybe I could play a song, so I moved on. I eventually discovered I was better suited for a different kind of keyboard.

"There are different kinds of gifts, but the same Spirit distributes them" (1 Corinthians 12:4). It would be nice if the Holy Spirit tattooed a bar code on our foreheads so our parents and teachers could scan it and tell us what we would be good at. But unless you are a prodigy, it may take a while for you to discover your gifts. Please keep trying, because you have God's assurance they are there.

Astral taxonomy

Pastor Mark Jeske

How many stars exist? Astronomers in my youth didn't know—must be millions of them, we were told. By 1980 the estimate had mushroomed to 100 billion, i.e., 100 billion *galaxies*. The launching of the Hubble telescope in 1990 was a further eye-opener for all sky gazers—chatter among astronomers today estimates that there could be over two trillion *galaxies*. Our own personal galaxy, the Milky Way, is believed to have 100 billion stars. Multiplying those two numbers together yields a lot of zeros, and it's still just educated guessing.

The One who made each and every star, however, has no trouble keeping track of his spectacular creations: **"He determines the number of the stars and calls them each by name"** (Psalm 147:4). Isn't that astounding? Each of the trillions of giant burning gas balls in the universe is important enough to the Creator to be noticed *and named*. Wow! What a spectacular display of the absolutely unlimited energy at the command of the God of the universe . . . billions and trillions of stars blazing away in the outer reaches, far too far away for anyone on the earth ever to see.

Go outside on the next clear night and find a place to look upward without street or highway lights. Marvel at the stars God lets you see and marvel at the trillions more you can't. Let the night sky reinforce your conviction that he is incredibly intelligent, kind to us, and powerful beyond any limit.

Why is evil unpunished?

Pastor Jon Enter

Why do bad people get away with bad things and get ahead in life? It seems unfair, unfaithful of God.

Here you are working your hardest to avoid temptation and doing right when you see others doing wrong, and they get the promotion, get the girl, get the attention, get ahead. Why doesn't God just smack them with well-deserved divine judgment? "What happened to Carl?" "Oh, you didn't hear? He lost his temper, and God struck him with a lightning bolt; fried him up crisp!"

Thank the Lord he doesn't respond to sin with instantaneous lethal force. None of us would've made it through childhood. God delays his punishment for a time to lead people into the mercy of his Son, and he is patient with us. **"The Lord is not slow in keeping his promise, as some understand slowness. Instead he is patient with you, not wanting anyone to perish, but everyone to come to repentance"** (2 Peter 3:9).

Rather than crying out to God against those who do evil: "That's not fair! Why is evil unpunished? God, get 'em! Punish them!" Let's cry out to God *for* those stuck in evil who do not know the mercy of Christ as we do: "Go get 'em, God! Draw them into your mercy! Change their lives from evil like you did for me. Draw them into your grace."

Pray for those who are held captive to evil before their time of grace and God's delay of punishment runs out.

"A penny saved is a penny earned"

Pastor Mark Jeske

American patriot Benjamin Franklin was known to be a thrifty guy. His *Poor Richard's Almanac* (PRA) was widely read in the colonies and contained many a nugget of wisdom. He is credited with saying, "A penny saved is a penny earned," but that phrase has actually never been found in any PRA edition. It's not in the Bible either. It goes back at least another century in England as anonymous wisdom that popped up in several books.

But though the wording may not be biblical, the concept certainly is. All of us struggle with learning how to restrain our spending and consumption. Solomon had been watching human behavior for a long time and knew how weak we are: **"The wise store up choice food and olive oil, but fools gulp theirs down"** (Proverbs 21:20).

Buying stuff is just so sweet, isn't it? For some people it gets addictive, giving them a dopamine release in their brains just like drugs. Shopping makes them feel good about themselves, and so they repeat the experience over and over, loading up their credit card balance. Building a financial reserve is hard work, takes discipline, and depends on self-control. **"Whoever gathers money little by little makes it grow"** (Proverbs 13:11). You can gather it by choosing not to spend it just as well as by making it.

Saying no to yourself now allows you to say a bigger yes later.

It's not a crutch
Jason Nelson

I learned something important from an agnostic philosophy professor I had in graduate school. He was a believer but gave up on God when his brother was killed in a car crash. Afterward, he felt Nietzsche's declaration, "God is dead," was more apropos than Jesus' declaration, **"I am the resurrection and the life"** (John 11:25). He challenged Christianity as something weak people use as a crutch. He helped me realize that my faith in Jesus is *not* a crutch.

He peddled nihilism, extreme skepticism, as the only realistic philosophy of life. I tried to present the counterpoints of Christianity. Jesus is not a crutch. He is not the fairy godbrother of uneducated dopes. The cross is not a rabbit's foot. Heaven is not some Neverland we escape to because we can't handle reality.

One evening he kind of ticked me off. So I asked him, "Doc, if we take your philosophy to its inevitable conclusion, will the world be a better place?" He thought about it and said, "No." I said, "I rest my case."

Several months later I got a letter from him because he wanted to continue the discussion. He raised hard questions. I wrote him back with honest and hopeful answers from a Christian perspective. As God ordained, I ran into him years later in an airport. We greeted each other and exchanged pleasantries. When I was called for boarding, we shook hands and I said, "By the way, it's still not a crutch."

What to say at a funeral #1

Pastor Mark Jeske

The night of the visitation before my father's funeral, there were three things I dreaded hearing, though I knew I would hear them over and over for three hours: "I'm so *sorry* to hear about your father's passing." "I'm so *sad* for your loss." "You have my *condolences* (i.e., I'm grieving along with you)." Those things might be appropriate when a complete unbeliever has died. But when a Christian passes, those words may not actually help a grieving family, and they might make their grief worse.

There's a better way. Remember what Jesus said when he came to visit Mary and Martha as they were grieving for their brother, Lazarus. He didn't say how sad or sorry he was or offer condolences. He celebrated Lazarus' place in God's family and spoke of him *as still alive* (which in fact he was). He told Martha, **"I am the resurrection and the life. The one who believes in me will live, even though they die; and whoever lives by believing in me will never die"** (John 11:25,26). When the body of a Christian dies, the soul is carried to heaven and *keeps on living with God in heaven*. Seriously! Christians never die!

Here's what I longed to hear that long night of visitation: "We celebrate your dad's homecoming with you." "We rejoice with you that he finished his race well." "How reassuring it must feel to know that your dad is safe with Jesus now and forever."

What to say at a funeral #2
Pastor Mark Jeske

People grope for things to say at a wake. Our brains strain to make sense of death, the senseless invader. I think that's one reason why people still buy cards to send or leave—others came up with some beautiful words to say, and you can rent their expressions when your own mind is a muddle. When people finally make it up to the front where the close family is standing, they struggle to be stoic and tough: "Well, I guess it was her time." "We all gotta go sometime." "God must have decided he lived long enough." "She doesn't have to suffer anymore." May I offer the opinion that there's not a lot of support and comfort in any of those phrases?

If we really mean what we say about *celebrating* a Christian's life, no matter how long or short it may have been, then let's talk about the person's significance. The writer to the Hebrews spent an entire chapter reviewing a long list of the great heroes of faith and concluded, **"We are *surrounded* by such a great cloud of witnesses"** (Hebrews 12:1). The companionship, example, guidance, encouragement, love, mutual service, emotional bonding, and personal growth that we received from the departed must have meant a lot to get you away from your TV and easy chair that night and bring you to the church or funeral home.

How about these words instead: "What a gift he was in my life." "I so appreciate her!"

What to say at a funeral #3

Pastor Mark Jeske

It's happened to me more than once in my pastor days. I've been encouraging the family during the funeral visitation and trying to build a positive spirit in the room. As the service is about to begin, a well-meaning funeral director comes to the front, asks everyone to be seated, and says that there will be one *final* procession in front of the casket, "so that you can say your goodbyes" and "bid your farewells *one last time*." Arrgh! Everybody starts crying again.

Those words only amp up the fear of death in people's minds. So does the word *bereaved*. It hammers home the sad idea that you've *lost* something, that something valuable has been *taken* away from you. When you decide on a retirement financial plan and write that first check to fund your investments, you don't think of yourself as "bereaved" of a significant amount of money. You have every intention of seeing that money again. With interest!

We haven't *lost* our loved ones in Christ. If you lose something, you don't know where it is. We know exactly where our loved ones are—safe in Jesus' arms. We have only "invested" them and expect to get them back with interest. **"We believe that Jesus died and rose again, and so we believe that God will bring with Jesus those who have fallen asleep in him"** (1 Thessalonians 4:14).

Don't pass by the casket saying your last goodbyes. Smile and say, "See you soon."

september

These commandments that I give you today are to be on your hearts. Impress them on your children. Talk about them when you sit at home and when you walk along the road, when you lie down and when you get up.

Deuteronomy 6:6,7

The whole change thing

Jason Nelson

My son is perpetually remodeling his home. One morning he was demolishing a wall and his four-year-old asked what he was doing. My son said, "I'm changing things." After a thoughtful pause, my grandson told his dad, "I don't like change" and stormed off. Five seconds later he returned and announced that his two-year-old brother doesn't like change either.

I was employed to help people deal with the whole change thing: understanding it, managing it, and making it. No one ever hired me to help them resist it. We come by that naturally, especially when our sense of familiarity and stability is threatened. It's hard to see how demolition can result in renovation. But that is standard construction practice and the way God works in our hearts. Change is a spiritual necessity.

"Don't you know that all of us who were baptized into Christ Jesus were baptized into his death? We were therefore buried with him through baptism into death in order that, just as Christ was raised from the dead through the glory of the Father, we too may live a new life" (Romans 6:3,4). We are baptized because we need to change. And we need to change 365 days every year.

We change every time we remember whose name is in the water of Baptism: the Father, Son, and Holy Spirit. We change when in that name we push down awful impulses we must demolish. We change when we build a new life in that name.

Watch your mouth

Pastor Mark Jeske

World War II posters exhorted the folks back home to a great variety of support tasks, such as conserving energy, self-denial in consuming materials needed for the war effort, and buying war bonds. They also urged U.S. citizens to guard military information very carefully: "Loose lips sink ships!" "Keep it to yourself—the enemy is listening." "Zip it—careless talk costs lives."

We're still in wartime, you know—spiritual warfare. The enemy loves loud and loose talkers because he knows how much damage they can do. We can leak out secrets about other people that seriously damage their reputations . . . lose our tempers and say cruel and harsh things we don't really mean but which will live forever in other people's memories . . . blurt out hurtful racist or sexist insults and thus keep racial and gender tensions inflamed . . . tell inappropriate jokes . . . or ridicule elected officials. St. James rightly says that the tongue **"is a fire, a world of evil among the parts of the body"** (3:6).

Have you ever said things you regret? You can't unspeak words that have cleared your teeth, but you can prevent further damage: **"Set a guard over my mouth, LORD; keep watch over the door of my lips"** (Psalm 141:3). Here are some filters to use when you feel your tongue stirring: Is it true? Is it fair? Is it motivated by anger, envy, or resentment? Will it hurt someone? Will it honor God?

Please join me in watching our mouths today.

Reprogrammed past

Pastor Jon Enter

Quick. What makes you feel guilty? What past sin suddenly, quickly crumbles your heart into feelings of worthlessness? For some spiritually dumb reason—let's call it what it is—we let the devil convince us we are better Christians for living in guilt over the past. As if that appeases God. Wrong! False! Liar! God does not work by guilt; he works by grace.

Guilty means "liable for punishment." To feel guilty over a sin you've already confessed to Jesus' cross of mercy, to feel guilty over a sin Jesus already paid for by his merciful love screams out, "Jesus, your sacrifice wasn't enough! I need to beat myself up to feel closer to God!" You'd never verbalize that to the Almighty. But guilt places a block between you and the release of Jesus' grace.

"I will forgive their wickedness and will remember their sins no more" (Hebrews 8:12). If God forgets your past—no matter how horrible your wrongs were—why don't you? It's because the devil thrusts your past indiscretions in your face constantly and continually to make you feel guilty. Don't let him! Live by grace, not by guilt. When the memory of your past attacks you, from your heart of faith proclaim, "The only thing that counts about my past is Christ died on a cross and took away my sins." You'll see an incredible change in your life from guilt to grace, focusing not on your failure but on God's great victory!

You are free

Pastor Jeremy Mattek

In June 1865, Major General Gordon Granger landed at Galveston, Texas, and announced that the American Civil War had ended and all slaves were now free. This happened more than two years after President Abraham Lincoln signed the Emancipation Proclamation in 1863. Not knowing of the Proclamation, countless people were still living in slavery.

Sadly, the same type of thing still happens. The U.S. no longer condones slavery. But people feel enslaved every day . . . to alcohol, to pornography, to feelings of bitterness and anger. To be enslaved means that you no longer feel in control. And when what controls you is sin, when you feel chained to the same sinful choices again and again, the discouragement and guilt that result can make you feel as though you're living in slavery.

But sin's slavery is one from which you've already been set free. Not by your ability to overcome the addiction or stay away from the temptation. But by the declaration of Jesus, who died on a cross to take the punishment for your sin so that you could live every day knowing that you are forgiven.

"Stand firm, then," the Bible says in Galatians 5:1, **"and do not let yourselves be burdened again by a yoke of slavery."** Remember that you've been set free—the next time temptation creeps in, the next time you're overwhelmed with guilt or you feel weak.

Remember that **"it is for freedom that Christ has set us free."**

When will the end come?

Pastor Mark Jeske

Predicting the precise date of the end of the world has been a fool's errand for self-appointed prophets for centuries, no, for millennia. God just isn't saying. He wants all believers to be ready at any time. In his last days of teaching during Holy Week, Jesus himself sketched out a fairly elaborate scenario of the future that awaited his apostles and the church they would build, but of the date he said nothing.

But he did say this: **"The gospel must first be preached to all nations"** (Mark 13:10). Jesus is not only the Lamb of God who took away the sins of the whole world; he is also the Giver of the Spirit who would energize the believers to fan out and bring the gospel far and wide in person.

It may seem today as though vast swaths of humanity are more closed off to the gospel than ever. Think of the broad Islamic belt where overt Christian worship and witness are forbidden by governmental authority, or the millions of people in East Asia whose governments sought and still seek to outlaw Christianity as a vestige of hated colonialism.

Waves of revolutions in communication technology can now bring the gospel behind walls and man-made barriers, across deserts and oceans, and in this way accelerate God's desire that the gospel reach all nations. Books, radio, television, international satellites, and the internet are now found everywhere on the globe.

Be ready! Jesus' prediction may be close to fulfillment.

He's working
Linda Buxa

"'What no eye has seen, what no ear has heard, and what no human mind has conceived'—the things God has prepared for those who love him—these are the things God has revealed to us by his Spirit" (1 Corinthians 2:9,10).

On the morning of April 29, 2011, President Obama gave permission for Navy Seals to raid Osama bin Laden's compound the next day. That evening, President Obama and his national security team attended the White House Correspondents' Dinner. Video footage shows they betrayed none of the weight that was on their minds—even as a comedian joked about the United States' seeming inability to find the world's most wanted man. The next morning, the administration filled the White House situation room, waiting for the Navy Seals to accomplish their mission successfully.

Honest citizens will admit that while they may have an opinion on current events, they don't have all the information. Honest citizens of God's kingdom admit the same. While we think God has lost sight of our enemies, he knows exactly how the battle will turn out. As we wonder how in the world our troubles are going to do anything positive in our lives, God sees how they will draw us closer to him and bring him glory. While we sit there eating dinner one night, we can't even conceive that in the morning he is going to accomplish his mission successfully.

So let's be patient. He's working.

Massive payout
Pastor Mark Jeske

In theory people are excited by the promises of Christianity because of what they will gain from it, right? I imagine that some people are disappointed when what they first encounter is the *cost* of following Jesus. They need to quit cheating people in their business lives. They need to quit cheating on their spouses. They need to quit cheating God in their money management.

Or imagine the cost of leaving one's home to live in a country not your own to be a missionary. Exotic, exciting mad adventure? Maybe. But it's just as likely to be a long grind of language study, endless frustrations at navigating a culture very different from your own, the constant mental pressure of being an outsider who doesn't belong there, and dealing with government agencies that don't think they owe you anything.

Jesus knows all of these costs and asks you to bear them anyway. He says he will more than compensate you for anything you have ever given up for him: **"Everyone who has left houses or brothers or sisters or father or mother or wife or children or fields for my sake will receive a hundred times as much and will inherit eternal life"** (Matthew 19:29). Earthly rewards are not why we choose to make sacrifices for Jesus. We do it because we love him and want to share the gospel.

But it's nice to know that Jesus has some treats in our future.

Show me
Pastor Mark Jeske

The original sin of Adam and Eve cost them everything, including being driven from the Garden of Eden, where they had enjoyed deeply personal interaction with God. After the fall, our relationship with God is more indirect. He speaks to us, but through the Bible, not audible speech. We speak to him, but indirectly, leaving messages on his voice mail, as it were, through our prayers. We do not have the luxury of immediacy of speech and instant response; we do not have the luxury of the sight of his face. We must live by faith until Jesus returns.

Living by faith to many religious people is a heavy, heavy burden. They desperately want something to see. They want to *touch* the divine. They want God to reveal himself fully and demonstrate his power before all so that, as they think, it won't be so hard to believe. In short, they want signs from heaven: **"'Teacher, we want to see a sign from you.' He answered, 'A wicked and adulterous generation asks for a sign! But none will be given it except the sign of the prophet Jonah. For as Jonah was three days and three nights in the belly of a huge fish, so the Son of Man will be three days and three nights in the heart of the earth'"** (Matthew 12:38-40).

Let the powerful message of Jesus' resurrection leave your heart content and satisfy your spirit until he returns for you in his glory.

Greed

Pastor Mark Jeske

Just about everybody has an allergy these days. The vulnerability lies within us and is set off by various things—pollen, dust, cat dander, dairy, peanuts, and gluten to name a few. Alas, seeds of far worse damage also lie within us, the seeds of deadly sins.

Sins like materialism. It's not so hard to see it in other people, but it's much harder to see in your own heart and life. Jesus warned his disciples about the siren song of money lust: **"He said to them, 'Watch out! Be on your guard against all kinds of greed; life does not consist in an abundance of possessions'"** (Luke 12:15).

Is it good to be ambitious? Sure. Is it okay to build your family's wealth? Yes. Is it good to be a saver? Of course. So how can you tell if you are getting greed sickness? *One*: do you see all you have as gifts from God, to be used for his agenda? *Two*: do you set aside a noble percentage of your income as a gift for the Lord (who gave you everything in the first place)? *Three*: do you measure the success of your life by the amount of wealth (or lack thereof) you've been able to amass? *Four*: have you ever cheated someone else, like a customer or your company, to enrich yourself?

What's the antidote? Take inventory of your life. Place at the very top of your list the forgiveness of your sins that you have through Jesus Christ your Savior.

Timing that trade

Jason Nelson

Stock traders have a saying, "The end of the world only comes once, so you have to time that trade carefully." Stock traders know it's very difficult to time the market. So when there's a fear-driven sell-off, the smart money starts buying.

It is impossible to time the end of the world. But some attempt to decipher Bible books like Daniel and Revelation to predict the final judgment and be among the few to come out ahead. They want to peg every troubling current event on a prophetic timeline to the apocalypse. I understand that people want to see God at work in a world that seems random and out of control.

"But the exact day and hour? No one knows that, not even heaven's angels, not even the Son. Only the Father knows" (Matthew 24:36 MSG). Jesus can't even time that trade, and he knows about everything. What does that say to us about the appropriateness of obsessing over it?

This is my personal theology about the end of the world. It's going to happen when it's going to happen. Nothing I can do about it. Not going to worry about when or how. I just want to let this little gospel light of mine shine today and forward to tomorrow. Then I'll be ready when it comes. So far it's working for me. So if you're convinced the end is near, can I have all your stuff?

Be kind to other Christians

Pastor Mark Jeske

Are you stressed out by how many different denominations there are in Christendom? To some believers, it is a terrible sign of weakness that there is such disunity in the visible Christian church. To others, it is a comfort to know that the marketplace of ideas is at work. People can flow to where their needs are met. If they feel neglected or abused by one group, they have legs and feet. They can walk. Just as the marketplace of ideas and services makes businesses better, the diversity in the church world can push congregations and denominations to up their game.

One terrible feature of this diversity, however, is the frequent incivility between people of different Christian "tribes." Guarding turf and scoring doctrinal points sadly can become more important than seeing God's big picture: **"'Teacher,' said John, 'we saw someone driving out demons in your name and we told him to stop, because he was not one of us.' 'Do not stop him,' Jesus said. 'For no one who does a miracle in my name can in the next moment say anything bad about me, for whoever is not against us is for us'"** (Mark 9:38-40).

Doctrinal fences do matter. But no smug, sarcastic, or condescending words should ever come out of our mouths when speaking of other Christians. We can make our doctrinal points, but be just as eager to see what other Christians can teach us about how to deliver the message to a constantly changing culture.

Faithful struggles

Pastor Jon Enter

I should be farther along the pathway of faith than I am. I fail. Way too often. As a dedicated believer, I really should be better than this. I shouldn't wrestle as much. Then I look around at all the happy, shiny believers; they seem so much better at this faith thing than I am.

I am quite confident that you feel similar. When we sin, we plead for God's good mercy, which he graciously gives. Thank you, Lord! Why aren't we better since we're forgiven and released from that sin? We strive and struggle to live the righteous life God demands, but then we fail again. When will God get fed up with our struggling and be done with us?

He won't! God's love overpowers and overtakes our sins. **"No temptation has overtaken you except what is common to mankind. And God is faithful; he will not let you be tempted beyond what you can bear. But when you are tempted, he will also provide a way out so that you can endure it"** (1 Corinthians 10:13). Every time we confess our wrongs, Jesus' grace washes us completely clean, making us shiny and holy again to fight against the darkness of temptation.

When you look around, see God's shining forgiveness in yourself—not just in others. Joyfully realize your struggle against sin isn't a failure of faith; it shows the Holy Spirit active in your faith. Your struggle against sin is strong faith in action.

Tapped in

Jason Nelson

When I was assigned this batch of devotions, our editor asked if I wanted to keep writing or if I was feeling "tapped out." I really appreciated that she asked me to continue to serve this ministry and yet was sensitive to the fact that the well can run dry for writers. Her question really got me thinking.

How do we avoid becoming tapped out? Forgive me, but I think it's by staying "tapped in." Every day something new happens in our nation, in our families, and in our personal lives. Nothing stays the same. All of us who want to communicate the gospel of Jesus to others need to stay tapped in. We need to stay tapped in to what's going on in big worlds and little ones. And we need to stay tapped in to the breadth of what the Bible says and the depth of God's love so we can show people that his Word is meaningful in every situation.

That is essentially how God told Isaiah to do it. **"Take a large scroll and write on it with an ordinary pen"** (Isaiah 8:1). There was a lot going on in Isaiah's day. There was a lot to say about God's judgment and salvation. Isaiah was going to need a big piece of paper. And he used everyday language to help people understand that God's instruction applies to everything and God's grace creates every dawn.

"This too shall pass"
Pastor Mark Jeske

One disadvantage of Hollywood movies and historical novels based on Bible stories is that most viewers and readers can't tell for sure what is biblical and what comes from scriptwriters. In the *Passion of the Christ*, for instance, the writers have Jesus the carpenter inventing modern tall chairs and tables at a time when people were used to reclining around a low table. Cute thought, but—not in the Bible.

There are some very popular proverbial phrases in English that many people assume come from Scripture but in fact do not. One of my favorites is "this too shall pass." Its origin is probably from tales of medieval Persian poets, in one of which it was inscribed on a ring, "guaranteed to make a happy man sad and a sad man happy." It is a comfort to know that times of stress and misery will not last.

The wording may not be biblical, but the concept is. Human life as we know it is changing constantly and soon enough will come to a halt on the day of judgment. In all this chaos and change, however, our Lord Jesus wants us to be sure of one important constant: **"Heaven and earth will pass away, but my words will never pass away"** (Matthew 24:35). Jesus' words assure us of his love for us, his incredible gift of forgiveness, and the promise of immortality with him.

Life in heaven is forever.

Servants, not lords

Pastor Mark Jeske

Is it hard for you to go back and forth between the business world and your Jesus world? From Monday to Friday you are in the middle of people grasping and shoving for power and money. The end justifies the means. The strong dominate the weak. The fast beat the slow. The big eat the small. The wealthy are envied and the poor are ignored.

The kingdom of God operates with very different principles. Jesus challenged his listeners to decide for whom they were working and who was their audience: **"You know that the rulers of the Gentiles lord it over them, and their high officials exercise authority over them. Not so with you. Instead, whoever wants to become great among you must be your servant, and whoever wants to be first must be your slave—just as the Son of Man did not come to be served, but to serve, and to give his life as a ransom for many"** (Matthew 20:25-28). Is it God whose approval you crave most of all?

Serving others is easier in Christian environments, like your church and your home. But you can live like this in your workplace too—putting your customers' interests above your own, always telling the truth, respecting your boss, accepting responsibility for things that were truly your fault, and going the extra mile to meet people's needs.

God's sneaky surprise is that it is those who act like servants who will be lifted up.

God is close

Pastor Jeremy Mattek

When our family got a new dog, she didn't sleep at all the first night. She spent the night and many nights barking, howling, and whining. We contacted her previous owners to see if they had any suggestions and discovered that they also had another dog and the two of them had slept in the same kennel together, snuggling against one another.

Our dog's restlessness made sense. She was lonely, so she barked, howled, and whined in the hope that she would find some way to make that pain go away.

People feel lonely too. And they sometimes bark for attention. Others howl in self-pity, hoping someone feels sorry for them. Some whine and complain when they're missing something important. These are all different ways of saying they're discontented. They believe something they need is far away from them.

Jesus believed that too. But as he hung alone on his cross, he didn't bark for attention, howl in self-pity, or try to scratch his way out of his current situation. He didn't do any of those things because he believed that the one thing he needed was already in his possession.

It was you. You were his when he cried, **"It is finished"** (John 19:30) and died alone, knowing your sins had been forgiven. And what we have as a result is the promise that we'll never have to feel as alone as he did.

At the cross, we see God himself snuggling the warmth of his love close to our hearts so that we never have to feel alone or discontented ever again.

The rescue swimmer
Linda Buxa

"In your righteousness, rescue me and deliver me; turn your ear to me and save me" (Psalm 71:2).

In the Coast Guard, the rescue swimmers' motto is this: "So Others May Live." Jumping out of the safety of a helicopter—so others may live. Swimming in water so dangerous that they could drown too or in water so cold they could get hypothermia—so others may live. Being punched by the very people you are trying to save (because they are so disoriented) that they see you not as a hero, but as a threat—so others may live. Training as an EMT, so that after you rescue people, you can administer life-saving treatment—so others may live.

Your Savior Jesus' motto was also, "So Others May Live." He gave up the glory of heaven, where he was ruling with the Father, to come to earth as not only God but also completely human—so you may live. He "swam" into our mess with us, being tempted in every single way that we are—so you may live. He took beatings from—and was killed by—the very people he was coming to save (because they were so disoriented by sin) because they saw him not as the promised Savior but as a threat to their social standing, comfort, and traditions—so you may live. And not only did he come to take the Father's wrath for your sin, but he came to give you life-giving treatment (the good news that you are at peace with God)—so you may live forever.

Wild things

Jason Nelson

Aldo Leopold wrote, "There are some who can live without wild things, and some who cannot. I am one who cannot" (*A Sand County Almanac*). I feel bad for those who can live without wild things. They are missing something of God. Jesus taught spiritual truths referring to figs, lilies, birds, and mountains. His resurrection is the first *fruit* of all who fall asleep in him. Eden was a perfectly natural place. Everything God made is organic. And everything man makes draws on something God made.

Francis of Assisi had deep appreciation for God's creation. His love for nature is legendary. He said he couldn't live without wild things: "Creatures minister to our needs every day; without them we could not live and through them the human race greatly offends the Creator every time we fail to appreciate so great a blessing" (*The Legend of Perugia*).

Renaissance learning added to Luther's respect for God's creation. He said, "We are at the dawn of a new era, for we are beginning to recover the knowledge of the external world that we had lost through the fall of Adam. We now observe creatures properly. . . . But by the grace of God we already recognize in the most delicate flower the wonders of divine goodness and omnipotence" (*Table Talk*).

The Bible agrees: **"For since the creation of the world God's invisible qualities—his eternal power and divine nature—have been clearly seen, being understood from what has been made"** (Romans 1:20).

Never ~~not~~ be afraid

Linda Buxa

In the movie the *Croods*, the father's motto is: Never not be afraid. So he keeps the family huddled together in a cave to keep them safe. When the cave is destroyed, the family has no choice but to leave, a terrifying thought.

I get that. I'd like to be a lot like that father. Wouldn't it be great to huddle? After all, this world is not at all like the Father planned it to be. Between technology addiction, the heroin epidemic, binge drinking, and online predators, it seems terrifying to consider the possibility that we let our kids out into this world.

It would also be so easy to huddle with your spiritual family. The people in your church are nice and safe, while "the world" seems out to get you. (Which, admittedly, is true.)

Should you be concerned about the temptations of this world? Absolutely. Should you be consumed by them? Not at all. After all, **"the Spirit you received does not make you slaves, so that you live in fear again; rather, the Spirit you received brought about your adoption to sonship. And by him we cry, 'Abba Father'"** (Romans 8:15).

This means that the God who made the world, who is actively involved in this world, the God who keeps every promise to you is your Father, your protector. And your *Abba*, your Daddy, tells you it will be fine: **"Do not fear, for I am with you; do not be dismayed, for I am your God. I will strengthen you and help you; I will uphold you with my righteous right hand"** (Isaiah 41:10).

Faith of a child

Pastor Mark Jeske

Have you ever noticed how often Jesus' teachings present *paradoxes*, i.e., statements that seem upside down? He said that the last would be first, that the vile sinners on the margins of society would get to heaven before the church leaders, and that the greatest achievers in God's eyes were those who made themselves servants. He taught frugality and lived that way and yet welcomed an extravagant display of worship from a woman who dumped some extremely expensive perfume on his feet.

Another of these wondrous gospel ironies is that the trained and learned religious scholars of his time could not make heads or tails out of his teachings, but little children got it. Jesus mused once, **"I praise you, Father, Lord of heaven and earth, because you have hidden these things from the wise and learned, and revealed them to little children. Yes, Father, for this is what you were pleased to do"** (Matthew 11:25,26).

It's hard for the "nice" people of society to see themselves as lost and broken sinners; it's hard for scholars to see themselves as ignorant and needing illumination; it's hard for the rich and powerful to think that they are really small and weak. Children have no problems with any of those concepts. They know they're naughty; they know they're ignorant; they know they're weak. Maybe that's why they embraced their Savior more quickly than the elders.

Is your faith like that of a child?

Your life is in God's hands

Pastor Jeremy Mattek

I'm not much of an artist. If you put a paintbrush in my hands, I would likely produce a sloppy mess. But if you put that same paintbrush in the hands of Picasso, you would see a masterpiece.

When God called Moses to lead Israel out of Egypt (Exodus 3), Moses recognized immediately that his hands were far too small to carry out successfully such a great responsibility. **"Who am I?"** Moses asked God (verse 11). So God reminded Moses that he was asking the wrong question. The right question? "Who is *God*?"

Each time Moses pointed out his own weakness, God pointed him back to God. Israel's hope was in God's hands. Moses was, in a sense, the paintbrush—the tool used by the artist to create a masterpiece.

Just like you.

There are times when our hands feel too small to carry all the burdens of life. We know the mistakes we've made. There are many times we're tempted to cry out in frustration, "Who am I?" But as it was for Moses, that's the wrong question.

Our hope should never be in the strength of our hands, but in the strength of our God's. Like Moses, we have the right to carry out our next task with confidence; because we know exactly whose hands our lives are in. They are in God's hands, who has watched over and loved his people, who has promised to be with us, and who gives us strength for the journey by taking out of our hands burdens he never intended for us to carry.

God did this to me

Pastor Mark Jeske

When events in our lives turn bad, it's natural to look for the cause(s). We blame others; we beat ourselves up; and sometimes we assume that since God is the Lord of the universe, it must have been he who brought down disaster on our heads.

A woman named Naomi once lost most of what mattered to her: she lost her home as famine drove her little family into exile, her husband died, and then both of her sons died. Her daughters-in-law tried to cheer her up, but she would have none of it: **"No, my daughters. It is more bitter for me than for you, because the LORD hand has turned against me! Don't call me Naomi** (i.e., "pleasant"). . . . **Call me Mara** (i.e., "bitter"). . . . **I went away full, but the LORD has brought me back empty. . . . The LORD has afflicted me; the Almighty has brought misfortune upon me"** (Ruth 1:13,20,21).

The poor woman added a fourth disaster to her life, i.e., assuming that her God had turned against her. Now—with divine revelation we can see that sometimes God does indeed send hardships into people's lives. But without that clear scriptural analysis, we should never assume that God is the first cause of our pain. In fact, Scripture also tells us that God watches from heaven with a hurting heart at the evils our human rebellion has brought.

His mercy sets limits to our suffering. His mercy finds a way to turn evil into good.

A Moabite finds the true God

Pastor Mark Jeske

It is interesting to see how God used Naomi's life, cratered with the disasters of losing her home, husband, and sons, as a platform for doing some wonderful new things. A famine had driven Naomi's family to live in the nearby country of Moab. Although the Moabites had distant kinship with the Israelites, they had strayed far from Israel's God. In their culture, Baal, the storm god, and Chemosh, whose priests encouraged child sacrifice, were the chief deities.

Naomi's Moabite daughter-in-law Ruth had been raised in that religious culture. But Naomi had made such a powerful impact on the young woman that Ruth chose to throw in her lot with her now-widowed mother-in-law. Even though it could seriously hurt her chances of remarriage, she vowed to stay close to Naomi and, even more important, to the God whom Naomi worshiped: **"Ruth replied, 'Don't urge me to leave you or to turn back from you. Where you go I will go, and where you stay I will stay. Your people will be my people and your God my God'"** (Ruth 1:16).

Think how hard it must have been for Ruth to challenge all of the religious beliefs she had been taught as a child. Think how other Moabite Baal and Chemosh worshipers would have pressured her not to abandon her national faith. But she did it anyway, turning to the God of Israel, whose mercy, Word, and Spirit changed her life forever.

The Holy Spirit is still creating new believers in unlikely places.

A self-sacrificing love

Pastor Mark Jeske

Life is hard for widows in the 21st century. Life was even harder for widows in the 12th century B.C. There was no social security, survivor's benefits, Medicare, or Medicaid. In a dog-eat-dog world, Ruth did a remarkable thing—she accepted the obligation to find a way to provide for her older mother-in-law, Naomi. A Moabite now living in Israel, Ruth was an alien and had to find work at the very bottom of the ladder—gleaning scraps of grain at harvesttime.

The owner of the fields where she toiled, a man from Judah named Boaz, took note of her extraordinary example: **"I've been told all about what you have done for your mother-in-law since the death of your husband—how you left your father and mother and your homeland and came to live with a people you did not know before"** (Ruth 2:11).

It is in the crucible of hardship that character is refined and developed. The Spirit of the Lord led Ruth to make sacrifices on behalf of Naomi, and Naomi brought value to Ruth's life by teaching her about the Lord. Even in their day-to-day struggle to survive, the Lord was slowly bringing things together for the good of those who loved him. May Ruth be a hero to you in your times of struggle. May her story inspire you to be willing to love, sacrifice, serve, and wait for the Lord.

And may the Lord bless your faithful service as he did Ruth's.

A Gentile joins the ancestry of the Jewish Savior

Pastor Mark Jeske

It was God's majestic plan to provide a Savior for a sin-cursed world by using the family of Abraham and Sarah as his platform. Their descendants, the Israelites, were tasked with preserving the faith and cultivating an attitude of readiness for the coming of the Messiah. Scripture meticulously documents with detailed genealogies how God scrupulously kept his promise. Christ was born a Jew.

But extraordinarily enough, there were several non-Israelite women who contributed their blood to the Savior's line. In this way even in Old Testament times, God planted the seed of the idea that the Messiah was really for all people of the world. One of those chosen "outsiders" was Ruth the Moabite. She became married to Boaz, the owner of the Bethlehem fields where she had been gleaning.

Their marriage was blessed with a son: **"Then Naomi took the child in her arms and cared for him. The women living there said, 'Naomi has a son!' And they named him Obed** [i.e., "one who serves"]**. He was the father of Jesse, the father of David"** (Ruth 4:16,17). What an amazing outcome to what had been a miserable story. Widow Naomi gained a wonderful son-in-law and a grandson, Ruth would no longer have to scrounge for grain scraps, Boaz gained a wife of phenomenal heart and integrity, and the future King David had a great-grandmother of whom he could be proud.

Ruth was originally a Moabite. Christ is for all.

True repentance
Pastor Jon Enter

My daughters know they aren't supposed to jump on the couch. They've been told. They know. So why do they continue to turn the sofa into their own personal trampoline? Maybe you can relate to my enthusiastically energetic girls. Did you leap around the living room as a child, avoiding the floor that was made magically of lava? How fun!

Until you got caught. I caught one of my daughters jumping on the couch last week. She burst into tears. She knew she was wrong. Her words of repentance to her upset father were truly remorseful. I said to her what your Father says to you when you confess your sins to him. "True repentance is twofold. Daddy, I'm sorry. And, Daddy, I don't want to do that again." If you lack that second heartfelt desire, then you aren't repentant. You are sorry you got caught.

When Jesus saved an adulterous woman from being stoned, forgiving her of that life of sin, Jesus said to her, **"Go now and leave your life of sin"** (John 8:11). In other words, don't be sorry you got caught only, but in the peace of forgiveness, work to never fall into that sinful trap again.

If you are struggling in faithfulness, what active, intentional steps can you take to avoid the triggers causing that sin? Without removing those triggers, you set yourself up to fall again. What needs to change so you follow Christ's command to leave your life of sin?

Safe in his arms

Pastor Mark Jeske

We live in the paradox of needing to plan for a long life but to be mentally prepared to die today. I hope that tension doesn't drive you crazy. You probably know people whose sudden death surprised everybody. Perhaps that will be your manner of exit. Or not—your life might be a very long haul yet.

Are you weary? Have you had some spiritual breakdowns? Are there stretches of your life where you wandered away from the Lord? Are you afraid of the road ahead because you are painfully aware of your weaknesses? What a comfort it is to realize that the Lord is committed to a successful journey for you: **"To him who is able to keep you from stumbling and to present you before his glorious presence without fault and with great joy—to the only God our Savior be glory, majesty, power and authority, through Jesus Christ our Lord, before all ages, now and forevermore! Amen"** (Jude 1:24,25).

We will fall, but he will catch us. We will grow weak, but he will give us strength enough for each day. We will get lost, but the Shepherd will seek us out. We will be assaulted, but our Champion will fight for us. Jude tells us these things not so that we can get lazy and careless, but to give us encouragement and peace in our souls. He will bring us home, faultless and joyful, safe in his arms.

To the only God our Savior be glory!

The check always bounces

Jason Nelson

If you decide to sell your soul, don't take a check.

The intrigue of swapping moral character for something we think would make us happy goes back to the Dark Ages and tales of a German astrologer named Faust. The story has been told and retold many times through the centuries. But the gist is the same. The devil or his representatives are always willing to write us a check so we can have influence, wealth, or some other kind of ecstasy, but we will pay a greater price in the end. His check always bounces, and you lose your soul. The rush of euphoria is for a limited time only, and then the suffering goes on forever.

That was the basic deal Satan offered Jesus (Matthew 4), and it is his standing offer to us. It is the only deal he makes. **"When he lies, he speaks his native language, for he is a liar and the father of lies"** (John 8:44). Engaging in any enterprise that pays you well to do something wrong is making a deal with the devil.

I wonder what deal the devil made with the people who sit in call centers and go phishing for personal information from the unsuspecting so they can steal identities and empty bank accounts. They almost got mine. Whatever they get paid is not enough because it's a Faustian bargain. That is a business of lies from the father of lies. Their checks are going to bounce.

God will work your hardships into his good plans

Pastor Mark Jeske

Joseph must have felt as though his life was spinning out of control. One day he was a beloved son of a wealthy Bedouin, and the next day he was bound and trudging in a slave caravan to Egypt. For all he knew he would never see his family again. He must have felt abandoned, not just by his brothers but by God too.

God let his situation deteriorate even further, and when his man was at the very bottom, imprisoned for a crime he did not commit, God lifted him up. Now a vice-pharaoh, Joseph was perceptive enough to look back at his life and see that God had never left him at all, that God's good plans were unfolding even when Joseph couldn't see *anything* good happening for him. He realized that his hardships became a platform for God to do something extraordinary. He told his stunned brothers: **"So then, it was not you who sent me here, but God. He made me father to Pharaoh, lord of his entire household and ruler of all Egypt"** (Genesis 45:8).

Your God loves you dearly, and he will make everything in your life come together for your good sooner or later, one way or another. As you grow older, may you find Joseph's serenity and confidence in your loving Father. May you rejoice at what you see and trust what you can't.

In Christ not a one of your hardships is wasted.

Your burden is lifted

Pastor Jeremy Mattek

A talk show host once announced to his audience that he had recently purchased $15 million of hospital debt in Texas. These were debts various families owed the hospital for medical services. But now, instead of owing the hospital the money, they owed this talk show host. But he didn't purchase these debts so he could collect on them. He purchased them so he could forgive them. He contacted each of these families and told them they no longer owed anything. He set them free from an incredibly heavy burden.

Our hearts can carry some heavy burdens too. And often those burdens come from a large debt we also owe—a debt of sin. Maybe there's one particular sin you've struggled with. Maybe you feel overwhelmed by how easily you give into many different sins. Whatever the sins that burden your heart, you can know this: you can't just pretend the debt doesn't exist.

Thankfully, you don't need to pretend in order to be released from its heavy burden. In the life and death of Jesus, we find someone who took the entire debt of our sins graciously into his possession for the sole purpose of forgiving it. God invites you to confess freely what you and he both know to be true, so that you can be set free by the One who is faithful to his promise to forgive you of everything:

"If we confess our sins, he is faithful and just and will forgive us" (1 John 1:9).

october

Therefore, since we have been justified through faith,
we have peace with God through our Lord Jesus Christ.
Romans 5:1

I've made some messes, Lord

Pastor Mark Jeske

A guilty conscience is not always a good thing. Guilt can paralyze you. It can make you want to avoid and evade God, put off praying, and find other things to do on Sunday morning.

Sometimes, though, you just get tired of making excuses, blaming somebody else, or minimizing the evil you've done. Sometimes you just can't stand carrying that load any longer and want to be rid of it. It's time to come home to your heavenly Father and be honest about the messes you've made: **"Do not remember the sins of my youth and my rebellious ways; according to your love remember me, for you, Lord, are good"** (Psalm 25:7).

Notice the attitude of the person praying: 1) humble tone; 2) confession of personal responsibility; 3) appeal not to one's own worthiness but to the Lord's love; 4) trusting that God's goodness and mercy will have the last word over his anger and judgment. These are the great gifts of Christ our Savior, and they are given for free. Forgiveness from God has double power. First, it relieves the pressure and dread. Second, it strengthens your spirit with the Spirit. You have new incentive to clean up some of your messes and repair damage. You kind of like being around God again, and as always, when you are touched by his Word, your life gets better.

Don't put it off. Come home.

Slow miracles

Pastor Mark Jeske

People's favorite Bible stories usually involve God's immediate and overwhelming power-rescues. We love how he dazzles and comforts us when he shows his mastery over the universe by stilling a storm with a word, preserving Shadrach in a fiery furnace, or incinerating Elijah's sacrifice on Mt. Carmel with a fireball straight from heaven.

Sometimes God prefers to act all at once. But sometimes his miracles and interventions in human history are slow, so slow you can't see them happening. When God takes his time answering your prayers, it's not because he's punishing you or because he doesn't care about your struggles or because he's gone deaf. There are reasons for his timetable.

To the Israelites Moses counseled patience. Even though they were instructed by the Lord to begin the conquest of Canaan, it was going to take a long time: **"The Lord your God will drive out those nations before you, little by little. You will not be allowed to eliminate them all at once, or the wild animals will multiply around you"** (Deuteronomy 7:22).

God has never stopped doing miracles. We want his help turning around a wayward child, and his divine therapy is invisible to us but nonetheless real. We pray for financial relief but can't see the big changes that God has set in motion. We pray for liberation from a personal addiction but don't see change.

Don't panic because of what you can't see. Remember: "Little by little."

Time to confess

Linda Buxa

One of the upsides to having siblings is you can put the blame on someone else—especially when they aren't around.

Broken dishes? Not me. Mud in the house? Not me. Wet towel on the floor? Not mine.

That might have worked for a while, until your parents did some digging. Then you learned the hard way that it is better to fess up than to cover up.

Consequences only get worse as we get older, don't they? King David tried to cover up his adultery by murdering the woman's husband (not a good idea), and then he kept quiet. **"When I kept silent, my bones wasted away through my groaning all day long. Then I acknowledged my sin to you and did not cover up my iniquity. I said, 'I will confess my transgressions to the Lord.' And you forgave the guilt of my sin"** (Psalm 32:3,5).

When David tried to hide his sins, the guilt and weight of them made him sick. When he admitted to God what he had done, he heard the sweet words of forgiveness. God already knew David's sins, the same way he knows yours. Carrying guilt makes you feel anxious, alone, hopeless, and worthless. It makes you want to hide from God, the one whose voice speaks forgiveness. Sometimes it takes a while, but when you confess them, you say, "Here, God, they're yours. Jesus already paid for them, so I don't have to carry them around anymore. Thank you for taking them away."

And he forgives the guilt of your sin.

Notice your blessings too

Pastor Mark Jeske

One of the personal characteristics that I really don't like about myself is how quickly I notice pains and troubles and problems (about which I then grumble) and how slowly I notice blessings, help, and opportunities for praise.

I am one with the Israelites during their wilderness march. They complained constantly (see the Bible's book of Numbers). And it wasn't as if their hardships were imaginary. To the contrary! Their journey was hard on everybody. Camping for decades with several million other people in close proximity sounds like no fun to me. I would probably have failed some of God's tests too, like panicking when there was no water.

Moses led the people well. He reminded them of the horrible slavery and genocide that they had escaped in Egypt. He celebrated their steady, miraculous manna food supply. And he reminded them gently: **"Your clothes did not wear out and your feet did not swell during these forty years"** (Deuteronomy 8:4). His hearers probably looked at their clothes and their friends' clothes and said, "By George, now that you mention it, I *am* still wearing the same tunic and cloak from 40 years ago. And hey—so are you!"

Notice your blessings too. Did you escape a major car repair this year? Were you spared an expensive hospital stay? Are your children all alive? Do you have a telephone? Does a machine wash your clothes?

Does God still love you? Does heaven await?

Asking for what needs to be

Jason Nelson

"There is a time for everything, and a season for every activity under the heavens" (Ecclesiastes 3:1).

Autumn is a favorite season for many folks living in the northern temperate zone between the tropics and the tundra. It's a crisp and colorful transition away from mowing, tanning, boating, and running out the door without a parka. Autumn is a nice time to appreciate what used to be and thank God that we enjoyed a lot of sunshine. And it is a nice time to ask God to give us what needs to be, a change in the seasons.

Seasonality is God's rhythm. He engineered it into our world and our lives. **"God made two great lights— the greater light to govern the day and the lesser light to govern the night"** (Genesis 1:16). We live each day according to the rhythm of lots of light fading into not much light. We plan a year's worth of activities based on the comfort of being outside or inside. A lifetime flies by as we turn the calendar from one season to the next. When we've had just about enough of what used to be, God gives us what needs to be.

The rhythm is so strong that we can all feel it at the same time. And we can join together in asking God to give us what needs to be.

Lord, give us a time to heal, a time to build, a time to laugh, a time to dance, a time to mend, and a time for peace. Amen.

Too much stuff

Pastor Jared Oldenburg

I ran across a book by Marie Kondo called the *Life-Changing Magic of Tidying Up*. Her premise is that we simply have too much stuff. The research seems to back up her conclusion. The average home in America has 300,000 items. If you were to move, that averages to over 10,000 lbs.

There are really two issues at play here. The first is that we have seemingly countless ways to get more and more and more. At the same time, we don't have great means to get rid of our stuff. That's a physical thing; that's a systems thing.

The real issue is a personal thing and could be boiled down to our view that what we have is insufficient. Have you ever compared your stuff with other people? Do you entertain the idea that you need more to be happy? If you're anywhere near average, you don't just have some stuff; you have *a lot* of stuff.

Jesus himself gives us this warning: **"Watch out! Be on your guard against all kinds of greed; life does not consist in an abundance of possessions"** (Luke 12:15).

What's the big deal? There's more to life than your things. The cure is not to just get rid of all your stuff. Gollum in *Lord of the Rings* only had one item, and I wouldn't say he had a healthy relationship with his Precious. The real goal is to change your heart. Empty out your greedy heart that longs for more and instead ask the Lord to fill it with contentment with the things that he has already given you.

Memorizing hymns

Pastor Mark Jeske

People who are clever at writing advertising jingles can make a lot of money. Know why? Jingles work. When short phrases are set to singable and memorable tunes, they stick like glue in people's minds. I can still remember some from 55 years ago.

God revealed to Moses that his time on earth was short and that it was time for his farewell address to the Israelite people. Moses' final words ran to 34 chapters. The Lord wanted the 31st particularly memorable—he had Moses write it in verse and set it to music: **"Now write down this song and teach it to the Israelites and have them sing it, so that it may be a witness for me against them"** (Deuteronomy 31:19). Music has always been a powerful vehicle for bringing God's Word to a human heart and lodging it fast.

Still in my brain from childhood are also dozens of hymn stanzas. I am grateful to my parents and Christian teachers for helping me get those great words and tunes inside me, and I invite you to keep it going by learning important Christian hymns and songs and teaching them to your children and grandchildren.

I once visited the sickbed of a frail saint whose life was almost over. Together we sang, "Be near me, Lord Jesus; I ask you to stay close by me forever and love me, I pray. Bless all the dear children in your tender care, and take us to heaven to live with you there."

We were both crying at the end.

Work out
Pastor Mark Jeske

Who can understand it? People of our country are more obese and out of shape than ever, and yet the fitness industry is booming. You can work out your core with Pilates, step aerobics, ab crunches, yoga, Tai Chi, stationary bikes, and aerobic dance. You can walk until your Fitbit says you can sit down again. The really fit can run half marathons or do triathlons.

Did you know that your faith needs exercise too? Satan will see to it that you will be presented with every incentive to build a life without God. He will steal what he can steal and persuade you to neglect or throw your spiritual treasures away. The second-last book in the New Testament is a fiery little letter urging Christians to prepare for the assaults of the evil one: **"Dear friends, build yourselves up in your most holy faith and pray in the Holy Spirit"** (Jude 1:20).

What does your spiritual workout look like? Well, you're doing one right now. By reading devotional materials like these Grace Moments, you are redirecting your thoughts to God and his Word. Your time in the Bible pours strength into your spirit and armors you against the arrows of Satan's lies. Worship time reconnects you with your Savior, reinspires your heart, and clarifies your thinking. Church time also bonds you with other workout warriors who will encourage and love you.

You can even read your Bible while you're walking on the treadmill.

Contend for the faith

Sarah Habben

"To those who have been called, who are loved in God the Father and kept for Jesus Christ: Mercy, peace and love be yours in abundance. Dear friends . . . I felt compelled to write and urge you to contend for the faith that was once for all entrusted to God's holy people" (Jude 1:1-3).

Why did Jude have to urge his readers to "contend for the faith"? Because they were in danger of embracing a lie: *It doesn't matter how you live, because you're forgiven.* But that lie changes **"the grace of our God into a license for immorality"** (Jude 1:4).

That lie lurks in every heart. We would rather be cool than contend. We'd rather stand out than stand up for Jesus: we dress provocatively, talk suggestively, joke coarsely, drink excessively, swagger, and brag. And when guilt pricks, it's tempting to wave around God's grace like a get-out-of-jail-free card.

Jude says, contend for the faith! Take holiness seriously! That's our calling as Christians. As long as we live on the earth, fellow saints, face down, push back, and out-maneuver temptation! Each day pull on your gloves and fight for the faith that God entrusted to us. Sometimes sin's fist drops us. But in Word and sacrament, our triune God pulls us to our feet. He dresses our wounds with mercy, peace, and love. He reassures us that Jesus already dealt sin and Satan the knock-out punch. The outcome of this fight is sealed: Christ wins! And heaven is our prize. Contend!

Faith is not blind

Jason Nelson

It doesn't bother me if some of you reading this are not convinced. In fact, I pray that these books might end up in the hands of lots of people who just aren't sure; people who are looking for something missing in their lives and are exploring Christianity. That would mean we're not just writing for the choir. It would also be evidence that the Holy Spirit is already drifting in your direction.

Would it help you to know that faith is not blind? I wouldn't be interested in a blind faith either. There's nothing blurry about believing in Jesus Christ. Because of faith, believers see very real things that other people miss.

Believers can see where faith comes from: **"Faith comes from hearing the message, and the message is heard through the word about Christ"** (Romans 10:17).

Believers experience faith as a living and growing conviction nurtured by Christ himself. So we continue to look to Jesus, **"the founder and perfecter of our faith, who for the joy that was set before him endured the cross, despising the shame, and is seated at the right hand of the throne of God"** (Hebrews 12:2 ESV).

And believers have seen over and over again that our faith in Jesus produces good results: **"The prayer offered in faith will make the sick person well; the Lord will raise them up. If they have sinned, they will be forgiven"** (James 5:15).

Please, God, heal!

Sarah Habben

Doctors gave my brother a 20 percent chance of remission. God chose to heal him.

Doctors gave my unborn son a 20 percent chance of survival. God chose not to heal him.

"Please, God, heal!" I've begged it. You have too. Sometimes God says yes. Sometimes, "Not now." Hardest of all is when God says no.

So what do you think when **"the Lord, who heals"** (Exodus 15:26) will not heal? Do you wonder: "Does God really love me? Is my faith lacking? Am I praying hard enough?"

Knowing we would ask such questions, God gave us the example of the apostle Paul. You remember Paul's "thorn"—a source of torment and weakness that he begged God to take away. God loved his servant Paul. He knew his faith. He heard Paul's prayers. And yet God said no.

It wasn't, however, the empty no of an earthly physician who has exhausted every medical option. It was a no fastened to a mighty promise: **"My grace is sufficient for you, for my power is made perfect in weakness"** (2 Corinthians 12:9). It's like a father refusing his son's request to borrow the family van . . . handing him the keys to a brand-new car parked in the driveway and saying, "Here's something better."

"Please, God, heal!" We can pray it confidently. We should pray it with a "Thy will be done." We can pray it peacefully, knowing that even God's no connects us to something better: his grace and our heavenly home.

Getting the right information
Pastor Jared Oldenburg

I recently read that the amount of information you take in each day is equivalent to the amount of information a person living one hundred years ago processed in a lifetime. I don't think that stat is too hard to believe. Because of television, internet, newspapers, billboards, and smartphones, our lives (and brains) are inundated with information. If we *receive* that much information in one day, how much do we *forget*?

As the Israelites were about to enter the Promised Land, Moses was concerned that God's people just might forget what was important. He said about God's Word, **"Fix these words of mine in your hearts and minds"** (Deuteronomy 11:18). Even though they lived 3,500 years ago, they had similar distractions to you and me. They were moving. They were going to need new houses. They were getting new neighbors, new routines, and new jobs. What Moses didn't want was for them to find new gods.

No doubt your life is filled with distractions and things to take care of. You're not alone. Obviously, our biggest problem is not that we don't have enough information. Our biggest challenge is remembering the *right* information. The right information is where we stand with God through his grace and how we can live within that grace on earth.

Fix these words on your heart and mind today . . . because there's more information coming tomorrow!

Nobody to blame but me

Jason Nelson

It took a cartoon character to point it out and set us straight. On April 22, 1970, Pogo declared, "We have met the enemy and he is us." His indictment came in the context of the first Earth Day and reminded us that we alone are responsible for air pollution, water pollution, and litter in the streets. Pogo nailed the fatal flaw in people. We are always our own worst enemy. The problem is compounded because we hate to admit it. We have developed incredible facility for explaining how our problems are someone else's fault.

Blame shifting was the first evidence of sin and is still the red flag that we just don't get it. Honesty is liberating because when we admit we have a problem, we stumble toward a solution. Honesty triggers hopefulness. But it never occurred to our first parents to say, "Lord, it was our fault. Please forgive us. We are sorry we let you down." God gave them an opening to own their mess themselves when he asked, **"Where are you?"** and **"Who told you?"** But they deflected. Adam said it was **"the woman you put here with me."** And Eve said, **"The serpent deceived me"** (Genesis 3).

We botch an opportunity for repentance if we sing the same old song and blame everyone else when we're put on the spot. In order to turn anything around, we need to sing a much different refrain: "I have nobody to blame but me."

Rescued from the pit

Linda Buxa

A cave-in at the San José Mine in Copiapó, Chile, trapped 33 miners 2,300 ft underground. After 17 days, one of the drill bits used to drill exploratory boreholes came back to the surface with a note taped to it. The men were alive! Above ground, even though rescuers worked around the clock, it took almost two more months of drilling to be able to rescue the men. On October 13, 2010, after 69 days of being trapped, all the men were safely brought to the surface.

When Adam and Eve (the first two people on this earth) sinned, the world caved in. What was supposed to be a place of light and perfection became a pit that trapped them—and all future generations. There was no way we could crawl or dig our way out. Without someone to search for us, we would die—forever. Thankfully, God is good. He knew how desperate we were, and he put a rescue plan in place.

When the time had fully come, when everything was just right, Jesus left the glory of heaven to come to the darkness of earth. He lived perfectly in our place and then took the punishment we deserved. Now we get to tell everyone how successful his rescue was.

"He has rescued us from the dominion of darkness and brought us into the kingdom of the Son he loves, in whom we have redemption, the forgiveness of sins" (Colossians 1:13,14).

Pay attention to God's warnings

Pastor Mark Jeske

Cain has no fan club. Nobody sees him as a hero. Like the words *Hitler* or *Nazi*, *Cain* has become a byword for a violent, evil person. The first murderer, he treacherously jumped his brother Abel in a field and killed him.

You won't find much to imitate in studying Cain's life, but you do find the insight that Cain was not destined to kill his brother. He wasn't locked into fate. The murder wasn't inevitable. It was *evitable*! There was another path that Cain could have chosen which did not lead to a bloody corpse. No less an advisor than God himself spoke to Cain personally as the man sat stewing with rage: **"If you do what is right, will you not be accepted? But if you do not do what is right, sin is crouching at your door; it desires to have you, but you must rule over it"** (Genesis 4:7). Cain chose to ignore God's warning. Sin did have its way with him, and Cain allowed it to rule him.

You may never have heard the warning voice of God directly, as did Cain. But you have heard his warnings—from a friend, from your parents, from the Bible. Sin crouches at the door of us all. It desires to have us—to feed our resentments, stoke envy, fan the flames of hatred, and goad impulsive actions.

Pay attention to God's warnings. He speaks not to cheat you out of things you deserve. He speaks to keep you from spiritual suicide.

God's deep compassion
Sarah Habben

In 1960 the US Navy sent the *Trieste*, a submersible vessel, into the deepest part of the Mariana Trench—a valley called Challenger Deep. If Mount Everest were plopped down into this ocean valley, there'd still be a mile of water over its peak. During the *Trieste*'s descent, the extreme pressure caused one of the outer windowpanes to crack, violently shaking the entire vessel. But the *Trieste* succeeded in parking for 20 minutes in the diatomaceous ooze on the ocean floor, seven miles below the ocean's surface.

The prophet Micah lived about two thousand years before anyone knew of Challenger Deep, let alone had the technology to reach it. Such depths were impossibly far. But that's the picture Micah paints when he describes how God deals with our sins: **"You will again have compassion on us; you will tread our sins underfoot and hurl all our iniquities into the depths of the sea"** (Micah 7:19).

All your iniquities. The sarcastic way you spoke to your spouse the other day. That thing you did in high school that still makes your cheeks burn. The anger you aimed at your child last night. The boredom you fought during church last week. The nonchalant way you took Lord's Supper. Filled with compassion for you, God's Son trod your sins under his mighty heel when he paid for them at the cross. The Father flung your wicked deeds into the dark, cold ooze of Challenger Deep, never to be hauled to the surface, never to be seen again.

Stalker?

Pastor Mark Jeske

One of the most terrifying plot lines in a TV drama is to watch a nasty criminal stalking his victims. He secretly studies their life patterns, monitors their communications, and patiently bides his time to strike.

Does it creep you out to know that God studies your life? listens to your talk? tracks your travels? **"You have searched me, Lord, and you know me. You know when I sit and when I rise; you perceive my thoughts from afar. You discern my going out and my lying down; you are familiar with all my ways. Before a word is on my tongue you, Lord, know it completely"** (Psalm 139:1-4). Does that make God sound like a stalker?

Not if you know that all his activity comes from a heart of love for you and that all his efforts are to make your life better. What a comfort it is to know that he cares enough to pay attention! Though you are just a speck on the blue planet, he knows your name, follows your progress, invests gifts and resources, sends helpful people, deflects disasters from your head, protects you from demonic assault, and whispers guidance in his Word. He finds delight in you as you grow and mature in your faith just as any good father beams with pride on his children as they do well in life.

He's not stalking you. He's taking care of you.

Control your body

Sarah Habben

When it comes to sex, the world doesn't mince words: "My will is to be happy. My sexuality is my business. My desires should be satisfied."

When it comes to sex, the apostle Paul doesn't mince words: **"It is God's will that you should be sanctified: that you should avoid sexual immorality; that each of you should learn to control your own body in a way that is holy and honorable, not in passionate lust like the pagans, who do not know God"** (1 Thessalonians 4:3-5).

When it comes to sex, you might feel like you're in the middle of a tug-of-war. You want to be self-controlled, but lust is on the menu. You want to save sex for marriage, but your peers are hooking up. You want to keep your marriage bed pure, but your mind strays to unworthy pleasures.

It would be so easy to slacken the rope of self-restraint and let the world win. But that would be so very, very dangerous. Not just because our sexual sins cause damage in this life but because, unrepented, they lead to eternal damage.

Child of God—dig in your heels. Dig into the Word. And pray, because you aren't fighting alone. Standing alongside you is the Trinity: the Son, who lived a holy life and died a holy death in your place; the Father, who calls you his forgiven child; the Spirit, who fills you with the desire to live God's way and, when you stumble, pleads for you before God's throne.

Where did your money come from?
Pastor Mark Jeske

Is it good to be proud of your job and the work you do? Absolutely! There are too many workers who are just mailing it in and have no work pride. Is it good to be self-reliant? Absolutely! There are too many people willing to let someone else carry them. Is it good to think of yourself as a self-made man or woman? Absolutely not. Because you didn't make yourself or your income or your personal wealth.

It is good to work hard, live smaller than your income, accumulate assets, buy property, invest, have a long-term view, and exercise discipline in your financial matters. But behind all of these things that seem to be all you is the smiling face of the God who loves you. He is the ultimate driver and provider of all your financial successes.

Moses wanted the Israelites to understand where their future prosperity was going to come from: **"You may say to yourself, 'My power and the strength of my hands have produced this wealth for me.' But remember the LORD your God, for it is he who gives you the ability to produce wealth, and so confirms his covenant, which he swore to your ancestors"** (Deuteronomy 8:17,18).

When you look over your personal balance sheet, remember to thank the Lord. When you buy your first home, remember to thank the Lord. When you calculate that you can afford to retire, remember to thank the Lord.

He gave you your stuff.

The firefighter
Linda Buxa

"'Look! I see four men walking around in the fire, unbound and unharmed, and the fourth looks like a son of the gods.' Nebuchadnezzar then approached the opening of the blazing furnace and shouted, 'Shadrach, Meshach and Abednego, servants of the Most High God, come out! Come here!'. . . The fire had not harmed their bodies, nor was a hair of their heads singed; their robes were not scorched, and there was no smell of fire on them" (Daniel 3:25-27).

On 9/11, firefighters did what most people consider inconceivable—they ran *into* the buildings' heat, smoke, and flames while everyone else was rushing to get out. They came to save lives, knowing they would probably lose theirs. (In fact, 343 died instantly when the towers collapsed. Others are still dying from the health issues caused by that day.) Knowing the risks, firefighters do the same thing every day around the world.

There is One who has stepped into the fires of hell for us—and won. He saw that we would spend an eternity in the flames of hell, and he came running into this world to save us. He knew that ultimately he would die. But he did his job—endured the cross and scorned its shame.

As soon as he rose from the dead, he went into hell and declared victory for all who believe in him. Now, we don't even have a smell of death or hell on us. Not a single hair on our heads will be harmed.

Silence is consent

Jason Nelson

"But, you didn't say anything." It's a classic rationalization for doing something questionable. Children use it on their parents. Husbands and wives say it to each other. It's why acquaintances assume they are on the same page in their politics or values. People interpret the silence of others to be agreement with their opinions or preferences. We view silence as consent.

And that's how we got here. That's how so many things we don't agree with became accepted. We didn't say anything. We are accomplices to moral decay because we didn't say anything. Or we said it only among ourselves. But it's not too late. We don't have to be contentious about everything. But we can respectfully speak up in defense of God's truth.

"Let your love, GOD, shape my life with salvation, exactly as you promised; then I'll be able to stand up to mockery because I trusted your Word. Don't ever deprive me of truth, not ever—your commandments are what I depend on. Oh, I'll guard with my life what you've revealed to me, guard it now, guard it ever; and I'll stride freely through wide open spaces as I look for your truth and your wisdom; then I'll tell the world what I find, speak out boldly in public, unembarrassed" (Psalm 119: 46-48 MSG).

"The only thing necessary for the triumph of evil is for good people to say nothing"—Edmund Burke, adapted.

Reacting to failure

Linda Buxa

"But in keeping with his promise we are looking forward to a new heaven and a new earth, where righteousness dwells" (2 Peter 3:13).

Pixar is known for its animated success. From the *Incredibles* to *Finding Nemo* (and *Dory*). From *Up* to *Toy Story* (1, 2, and 3). What they aren't known for is failure. However, Pixar's cofounder Ed Catmull says failure is absolutely part of their creative process: "There are two parts to any failure: there is the event itself, with all its attendant disappointment, confusion, and shame, and then there is our reaction to it. It is this second part that we control."

For Christians, we want to be known for our successes. For the way we live faithfully, suffer trials patiently, pray unceasingly, and share the gospel boldly. However, failure—sin—is absolutely part of our lives. So how do we react?

Martin Luther, a reformer who lived five hundred years ago, said that though we can't help but have lives tainted by sin that we "believe and rejoice in Christ even more boldly. For he is victorious over sin, death, and the world. As long as we are here, we have to sin. This life is not the dwelling place of righteousness but, as Peter says, we look for a new heaven and a new earth in which righteousness dwells."

Failure is unavoidable; we aren't home yet, so let's control our reaction. Don't beat yourself up, because Jesus was beaten in your place. Instead, believe in the One who overcame and is preparing heaven for you.

Make the most of your moments

Pastor Jared Oldenburg

I don't know how big your town or city is, but mine is about 50,000 people, or the same size as the ancient city of Ephesus. Just imagine that you live in Ephesus and you receive this letter from the apostle Paul. The letter says, **"Make the most of every opportunity, because the days are evil"** (Ephesians 5:16). I don't think we have to argue too much that the days are evil. We truly live in troubling times . . . wars and terrorism and abuse and scandal.

Literally Paul says, "make the most of time." The word he uses is not *Chronos*, like *chronological*. He uses a different word, *Kairos*. The basic idea is "moment." Not only do we have a limited number of days, but we have a limited number of moments on this planet.

The average working person spends less than 2 minutes a day in meaningful conversation with his or her spouse or significant other and less than 30 seconds a day in meaningful conversation with his or her kids. The survey where I read this information didn't say how much time the average working person spends in God's Word.

As humans, we have the same amount of moments each day. So let's make the most of them. Spend time with people you care about and express God's love to them. Remember, not only do we have limited days, but we have limited moments.

Thanks for spending a moment on things that matter.

Recovering up front

Jason Nelson

I have a front row seat to addiction and recovery. My son is battling back one more time. He must remain sober and take the meds that treat the disorders for which he was self-medicating with substances. We can never stop praying for him, never stop supporting him in this effort.

There are many addictions, and the process is similar. The substance or activity causes the brain to feel much better than it usually does. People like feeling high, so they do it again. Then they chase the high over and over, and it takes more of whatever to get high again. And then they can't stop.

During Daniel's captivity, Babylon was a society of excesses. They chased a high life and treated themselves to wonders of the world. A young Jewish man would defile himself if he consumed their diet of meats, rich desserts, and alcohol. Daniel couldn't partake, and he was very up front about it: **"Daniel resolved not to defile himself with the royal food and wine, and he asked the chief official for permission not to defile himself this way"** (Daniel 1:8).

Call it a disease or not, but every addict faces enormous challenges. It takes tremendous willpower to fight urges. It takes tremendous willpower to leave using buddies behind and avoid things that could trigger a relapse. And it takes tremendous willpower to hold up a hand to people you just met and say up front, "Don't get me started because I can't quit."

Prayer killers: Amnesia

Pastor Mark Jeske

A mom is proud of her kid in college but pained by the empty nest. "Why doesn't my daughter ever call? I'm dying to hear from her." A boyfriend drifts off and the girl wonders, "He doesn't return my calls and texts. What's wrong?" Amazingly enough, those heart pains are felt by God himself. He invented the marvelous process of communication his Word calls prayer. He opens up his Word with its amazing and inspiring stories of his great works, and he opens up his heart to hear us, but so few messages are incoming. Why doesn't he hear from his children more?

A great question—why don't we pray more? And with more enjoyment? It's because of the prayer killers, the first of which is amnesia. We forget who we are, imagining that we built everything in our lives. Especially those who have lived as Christians for a long time forget how bleak and horrible life is without the forgiveness of sins and assurance of heaven. We don't think enough about the phenomenal work of Jesus Christ to redeem us and how death and hell and Satan have been defeated.

The cure for amnesia is remembering: **"Sing to him, sing praise to him; tell of all his wonderful acts. Glory in his holy name; let the hearts of those who seek the Lord rejoice. Look to the Lord and his strength; seek his face always"** (Psalm 105:2-4).

"Lord, your works are astounding. Let me tell you about my day."

Prayer killers: Shame

Pastor Mark Jeske

On this particular day, our family dog was not glad to see us when we got home. She slunk away. And then we figured out why: she had left a special present for us behind the couch, and she was ashamed.

Shame drains the fun out of a relationship, and it is a prayer killer too. How can you come to the Lord and pretend that everything's fine when you know things aren't? How can you ask for things when you've been ignoring him? How can you say "I'm sorry" when you are still doing the things you know are wrong? Shame paralyzes us spiritually, and that's just fine with Satan, who keenly enjoys putting his foot on our necks when we're down. What to do?

The key is not to try to do this on your own. You can't clean up your own messes any more than a dog can get urine out of a rug. When you are feeling ashamed before God, call on *his mercy*: **"You, Lord, are forgiving and good, abounding in love to all who call to you"** (Psalm 86:5). Let your starting point be the steady love that comes from God's heart, not yours.

It is the gospel that alone can wash away the guilt of your foolish past. It is the gospel alone that breaks Satan's grip on our willpower. And it is the gospel alone that gives us incentive and power to make the life changes we know we need to make.

Prayer killers: Pride

Pastor Mark Jeske

Most girlfriends and wives sooner or later run into male pride and stubbornness when it comes to asking for help. Men would rather drive around for half an hour than ask for directions. (Stupid, right?) Why do men do that? Pride. We place great value in figuring things out on our own, taking care of ourselves, not being dependent.

Women have pride too—unable to say, "I was wrong," "It was my fault," "I'm sorry." As hard as pride is on our human relationships, it is very hurtful to our faith lives as well. Pride is a prayer killer because proud people don't want to ask anybody for help. They want to work on their own situation all by themselves, and even when their lives are going poorly, they prefer a miserable status quo to humbling themselves and asking God for his help.

And so God waits. Sometimes he gently invites his struggling children to come home and talk to Daddy. Sometimes he uses his divine two-by-four upside their heads to get their attention, to show that they really can't get out of the hole they're in all by themselves.

Pride is a prayer killer. Here's a better attitude: **"My heart is not proud, Lord, my eyes are not haughty; I do not concern myself with great matters or things too wonderful for me. But I have calmed and quieted myself, I am like a weaned child with its mother; like a weaned child I am content"** (Psalm 131:1,2).

Prayer killers: Doubt

Pastor Mark Jeske

To choose to pray, your confidence level in three aspects of God have to be in positive territory. You need to believe he is *omnipotent*, able to make happen the superhuman things that you are asking. Second, you need to believe in his *wisdom*. You have to trust that his decisions will benefit you in the long run. Finally, you need to trust that he *loves* you. Prayer is impossible if you imagine even for a minute that he is sitting on his throne laughing at you or making fun of you to the angels in attendance.

Jesus doesn't despise us for our doubts, but neither does he tolerate that kind of thinking. His sacrifice on the cross brought God's favor and righteousness on us. Through faith in him we receive the priceless status of "Child of God." That makes his Father our Father and the Savior our Brother. Jesus once told his fearful disciples, **"If you, then, though you are evil, know how to give good gifts to your children, how much more will your Father in heaven give good gifts to those who ask him!"** (Matthew 7:11).

The powerful God who created the world in six mighty blasts of his word has not lost a step. The brilliant Designer and Engineer of this planet does not have Alzheimer's. And there can be no higher measure of love than that of Jesus Christ, who showed the world that he would rather suffer and die than lose us.

Prayer killers: Laziness

Pastor Mark Jeske

Prayer is work.

It requires concentration, humility, collected thoughts, content, a rationale, and a purpose. We should not be surprised at all that laziness is a persistent prayer killer. Laziness certainly is a drag on every other phase of our lives, from our work lives to student lives to taking care of our homes: **"Through laziness, the rafters sag; because of idle hands, the house leaks"** (Ecclesiastes 10:18). Why would this "I don't care" attitude not spill over into our spiritual lives too? If we are unwilling to expend energy to take care of material things that we can see, imagine our slowness to approach our God.

Lazy people are often completely aware that they're lazy, but they have played some mind games to justify their torpor. That's the value of Christian social capital— we can be a valuable buddy system for one another. Our Christian friends or family members can call us out on the fact that we haven't gone to church in a while, haven't been detected reading our Bible or participating in prayers.

If you hear someone close to you giving you the business about your sluggish spiritual habits, don't lash back defensively or mumble promises you have no intention of keeping. Let the rebuke sting your heart; let God know you want your life situation to change; and then accept the invitation from God's agent to get moving again.

Drop what you're doing and talk to God right now.

Prayer killers: Fear of rejection

Pastor Mark Jeske

A lot more romantic dates would happen if it weren't for males' fear of rejection. When we're young, many of us can't look squarely into a girl's face and make that first move. When we're home, we can't make our hand go to the phone. Filled with self-doubts, we are terrified of rejection. It would be better not to go to the dance than get rebuffed when you ask.

Doubting God is a prayer killer. But so is *self*-doubt. It's good to be mindful of your sinful unworthiness, but not to the point that you think you are hopeless. You might be so interested in protecting your feelings that you don't want to get your hopes up enough even to ask God for something you clearly need. Why not? "He'll just smack me down and say no."

That's Satan talking. Here's Jesus talking: **"Ask and it will be given to you; seek and you will find; knock and the door will be opened to you. For everyone who asks receives; the one who seeks finds; and to the one who knocks, the door will be opened"** (Matthew 7:7,8). God won't pray for you. He patiently waits for you to answer his invitation, remind him of his Fatherly obligations, and call on him to keep his promises. Through Christ the door to the throne room of heaven is open and the great King is smiling and gesturing at you.

Go ahead—Ask! Seek! Knock! Do it now.

Trick or truth

Sarah Habben

My kids get a little jumpy around Halloween—nervous to take out the trash in case something spooky is hiding behind the garbage bins. Or maybe they're just scared of chores.

Someone IS prowling around who means us harm—Satan. He won't jump out from behind a bush. He's content to bring about our spiritual death by deception. His trickery starts with, "Did God really say . . . ?"

"Did God really say he'll give you a way out of temptation? Then why do you keep falling into it?"

"Did God really say that heaven is yours by faith alone? Are you sure you believe hard enough?"

"Did God really say that Jesus' death paid for *all* your sins? Better play it safe and work on winning his affection."

Of course October 31 isn't just Halloween. It's the anniversary of when Martin Luther nailed his "95 Theses" to the door of the Castle Church in Wittenberg, which some mark as the beginning of the Reformation. The former monk toppled Satan's lies with one little word. That word could be *grace*—God's undeserved love.

God's *grace* made a promise in Eden. His *grace* gave us Jesus in Bethlehem. *Grace* won forgiveness on Golgotha. *Grace* made us right with God, for free and forever. *Grace* raised up Luther in Germany to rediscover this saving truth.

"For it is by grace you have been saved, through faith—and this is not from yourselves, it is the gift of God" (Ephesians 2:8).

november

Let the peace of Christ rule in your hearts,
since as members of one body you were
called to peace. And be thankful.

Colossians 3:15

Some kind of smart

Jason Nelson

Harvard professor Dr. Howard Gardner looked at human potential in his Multiple Intelligence Theory. He said everyone is some kind of smart. Some people are good with words, others with numbers. Still others are good with music, understanding other people, or good at creating artistic designs. He hoped teachers would create lessons so all children could learn according to their strengths. But everyone is some kind of gifted too.

"The evidence of the Spirit's presence is given to each person for the common good of everyone. The Spirit gives one person the ability to speak with wisdom. The same Spirit gives another person the ability to speak with knowledge. To another person the same Spirit gives courageous faith. To another person the same Spirit gives the ability to heal. Another can work miracles. Another can speak what God has revealed. Another can tell the difference between spirits. Another can speak in different kinds of languages. Another can interpret languages. There is only one Spirit who does all these things by giving what God wants to give to each person" (1 Corinthians 12:7-11 GW).

The Holy Spirit gives all Christians unique abilities. He wants us to serve others according to our strengths. That's how the body of Christ is built up. Everyone is some kind of smart and some kind of gifted. "Your gift is the thing you do the absolute best with the least amount of effort"—Steve Harvey.

What kind of smart and gifted are you?

Be a birdbrain
Sarah Habben

There's a reason why the roly-poly chickadee is a popular mascot for no team ever. They're just too . . . cute.

But God has equipped the chickadee to survive a northern winter. Chickadees spend their days foraging. At night they go into controlled hypothermia to reduce their metabolism. Excess body fat is used up overnight as they shiver to keep warm. (Picture a 165-pound man spending a frigid night outside and emerging 15 pounds lighter in the morning.)

Yet when the winter sun comes up, those little birds are singing. No wonder Jesus used birds as an antianxiety "mascot"! **"Look at the birds of the air; they do not sow or reap or store away in barns, and yet your heavenly Father feeds them. Are you not much more valuable than they?"** (Matthew 6:26).

Worry plucks our feathers. It steals our song. Worrying can't add an hour to our lives. And yet we all do it! Hence Jesus' advice to "be a birdbrain." (I'm paraphrasing.) Jesus actually said, **"Do not worry about your *life"*** (Matthew 6:25). Not your first day of school. Not the last breath you'll take. And nothing in between.

Then Jesus gives his cast-iron reason why no present or future predicament is worth our worry: because we are valuable to our Father. We are treasured by God for Jesus' sake, who ransomed us from sin and Satan with his holy, precious blood.

What peace there is in that truth! When worry rises like a winter wind, we can make like a chickadee and sing out loud.

Give up or give in?

Pastor Jared Oldenburg

Whenever we talk about time, it has a way of making us feel pretty guilty, doesn't it? We look at stats about how little time we spend with our spouses and how little time we spend with our kids. Then we hear about how much time we burn on TV and the internet. It's surprising that we get anything worthwhile done ever.

There isn't anyone who has ever lived who has not wasted time. Well, there is one person. Galatians 4:4,5 says, **"But when the set time had fully come, God sent his Son, born of a woman, born under the law, to redeem those under the law, that we might receive adoption to sonship."**

Everyone born on this planet is obligated to follow God's law. We're supposed to make the most of our lives, our time, and our opportunities. . . . We just don't. So do we give up or give in?

We give in and confess our time-wasting to God. We give in and lean on the very One who came to this earth with a job to do. At just the right time, God sent his Son.

His Son had a job to do. His real job was not a carpenter or a farmer or an accountant. His real job was making the most of every opportunity so he could bring you close to him. To redeem you and adopt you into his family.

You're valuable to God

Pastor Mark Jeske

Satan masquerades as your friend, but in fact he is your bitter enemy. He despises you, and though he tempts you with promises of freedom and excitement, the sin he promotes leaves you only with guilt and depression. Unhappy sinners always try to share their misery with others, so it's no surprise if fellow students, peers, coworkers, or even parents try to make you feel worthless. The worst is when your own self-talk becomes self-hatred.

Jesus had words of soothing and healing for all who have been beaten down by the evil one. He wants believers to know that they have great worth in God's eyes: **"Are not two sparrows sold for a penny? Yet not one of them will fall to the ground outside your Father's care. And even the very hairs of your head are all numbered. So don't be afraid; you are worth more than many sparrows"** (Matthew 10:29-31). Can you imagine the level of detail in God's daily inspections of life on earth? He counts birds! Not a one can fall ill or die without his permission. And think of it—you are worth more than many sparrows to God.

As just one example of the intensity of his interest in you—he keeps a running total of the hairs on your head. Seriously! And if he cares about your hair, surely he cares much more about your struggles, your needs, your hopes, your dreams.

You are precious to God.

God's odds

Pastor Mark Jeske

When a job is too big or too risky or too dangerous, the worker bees lose heart and start looking for the exits. An NFL team that lost 14 games in a season should not be telling the press that they will be in the Super Bowl next year. The odds are massively against them.

But when God gets involved in a project that matters to him, the odds change. The Israelite nation was encamped on the east bank of the Jordan River. On the other side were entrenched Canaanite nations, busily preparing a nasty welcome for the Israelites: **"When the Lord your God brings you into the land you are entering to possess and drives out before you many nations—the Hittites, Girgashites, Amorites, Canaanites, Perizzites, Hivites and Jebusites, seven nations *larger and stronger than you* . . ."** (Deuteronomy 7:1). But Moses urged on the Israelite armies in spite of how outnumbered and out-weaponed they were because they had God's odds on their side. Israel prevailed against them all.

When Jesus commissioned his disciples to make disciples of all nations, one or more of them may have thought it an absurd challenge, absolutely out of the realm of possibilities. But they tackled it anyway, and just during their lifetimes the number of believers exploded exponentially. Over the centuries the church has been planted in every country on earth. And with the technology of today, a truly worldwide reach of the gospel is doable. God's odds indeed.

Children by choice
Jason Nelson

I have three amazing "children-in-law." I love each of them and really appreciate what they add to our family because they weren't one of us to begin with. I thank them often for marrying the ones I have no choice but to love. It has been a lot of fun getting to know them and growing close to them. The first awkward moments of meeting each other are distant memories, and we are comfortable with each other.

Joining two families through marriage can be like bringing together aliens from different planets. Jokes, comedies, and dramas have been made at the expense of the in-laws. The Bible tells some in-law stories too.

Moses lived with his wife's family for a while and developed deep respect for his father-in-law, Jethro. When the stress of trying to lead over two million people to the Promised Land was getting to Moses, he learned something from his father-in-law he never learned from his father, how to delegate responsibility (Exodus 18).

The book of Ruth is an in-law story. Ruth didn't have the same faith as the family she married into, but that's how she became a believer. She grew very close to her mother-in-law, Naomi. When the family became just the two of them, Naomi urged Ruth to move on and start a new life. Ruth hated to leave, but her new family line gave us Jesus.

God gives us in-laws to make our families more complete.

I got away with it

Pastor Mark Jeske

"If a tree falls on an island and nobody is around to hear it, did it really make a sound?" The *Chautauquan* magazine posed that question in 1883 and answered its own question with a no. A year later the *Scientific American* concurred: "If there be no ears to hear, there will be no sound." Some people eagerly embrace that logic for moral questions. "It's not really a lie if you aren't found out." "It's not a crime if you don't get caught."

Just because people say such things does not make them so. Even if no one is on the island where the tree fell, sound waves were generated; God's ears could hear them. Even if nobody else discovered your lie, God heard it. Even if nobody saw your theft, God's eyes did.

Every day criminals who didn't get caught gloat that they got away with their crimes. Moses warned the Israelites (and us) not to succumb to the "it never happened" mind game: **"If you fail to do this, you will be sinning against the LORD; and you may be sure that your sin will find you out"** (Numbers 32:23).

Every day confess your sins to God without excuses, blaming, or minimizing. Confess the ones you remember and dump out all the rest as well. Show God the respect he is due for his universal presence, memory, and principles.

Claim Christ's forgiveness and resolve to sin no more.

No one should appear before the Lord empty-handed

Pastor Mark Jeske

I have some very strong memories of what Sunday church was like for me when I was a small boy. I loved the music and singing; my mother would pinch me *real hard* if I squirmed too much, and she would give me a dime to put in the collection plate.

I don't know if I reflected too much in those boyhood years on why it was that God needed a dime from me. Surely I needed that dime more than he—that was *two* packs of baseball cards (with gum). But I am mighty glad my mother taught me early. Giving is worship, intense worship. Singing "Hallelujah!" costs you nothing. Giving a gift of money to the Lord is a sacrifice.

But what a small sacrifice compared to what the Lord Jesus did for us. The magnificence of God's grace is a powerful motivator to want to give all of myself back to God. The giving of financial gifts has always been an important part of the worship life of believers. Moses instructed the Israelites: **"Three times a year all your men must appear before the LORD your God at the place he will choose. . . . No one should appear before the LORD empty-handed: Each of you must bring a gift in proportion to the way the LORD your God has blessed you"** (Deuteronomy 16:16,17).

Because of inflation, parents, I now suggest giving your kids at least a buck for the offering basket.

Pity the fool
Sarah Habben

Ever yelled at a chair for stubbing your toe? Ever blasted your horn when someone doesn't instantly react to a green light? Ever hit "send" on a scathing email? Ever seethed over someone's actions? Ever used your bigger size and voice to intimidate the smaller people in your family? Yeah. Me too.

So often we feel one of two ways about our anger: 1) We can't help it. Or 2) We're entitled to it.

But the Bible offers another opinion on reckless anger: **"Foolish people let their anger run wild. But wise people keep themselves under control"** (Proverbs 29:11 NIRV).

Our uncontrolled anger is foolish. How so? It can alienate us from our loved ones. It can ruin our reputation. It can damage our health. We might say of our anger: "Well, that's just the way God made me." But such an excuse is not only foolish; it's also a lie. Think back to your baptism. In those waters God remade you. Your sinful nature with its short fuse and sharp tongue was drowned. Your reckless temper was replaced by the Spirit's fruit—patience, kindness, gentleness.

Or remember Good Friday. The Son of God—wisdom himself—suffered the flames of hell for our foolish anger. Christ earned our forgiveness. We are remade: no longer slaves to rage.

So let's not live as fools to be pitied. Let's step off the path to destruction. Let's exercise true wisdom by thankfully, peacefully, gently imitating Jesus—our Way, our Truth, and our Life.

Swing it carefully

Jason Nelson

The Word of God is the sword of the Spirit. We need to swing it carefully, or someone will get hurt.

The Bible has two powerful messages, law and gospel. This is a double-edged sword, and we have a tendency to brandish the hard edge over the healing one. We like laws because they allow us to cut to the chase. Let's just post the Ten Commandments in every courthouse and enforce them strictly, and this will be a better world. The hard edge puts backbone in our social contract with one another. But the hard edge also leaves people bitter and resentful and can cut them off from Christ and one another.

This is noteworthy: God reviewed his acts of love before he prescribed his law. **"You have seen for yourselves what I did to Egypt and how I carried you on eagles' wings and brought you to my mountain. If you carefully obey me and are faithful to the terms of my promise, then out of all the nations you will be my own special possession"** (Exodus 19:4,5 GW).

People obey because they are loved. God wants us to apply his Word lovingly as we teach, parent, and witness. The law is best used sparingly, spoken in a no-nonsense way and with a serious tone. But we can let loose with the gospel, which is **"a new promise, a spiritual promise, not a written one. Clearly, what was written brings death, but the Spirit brings life"** (2 Corinthians 3:6 GW).

Stand and clap

Linda Buxa

"We can't all be heroes because somebody has to sit on the curb and clap as they go by."—Will Rogers

Happy Veterans Day! This is the day Americans across the country prove that Will Rogers, the famous cowboy, was right. We sit—no, we stand—on the curb and clap because we want veterans to know we are grateful, no matter how long ago or how recently they served. We acknowledge these strangers who were willing to put their personal comfort and safety to the side. We thank those who still walk into recruiting stations and sign up to put their lives on the line. All of them are willing to sacrifice their lives for someone else's freedom.

Only one warrior had his parade before his battle. His name was Jesus. On Palm Sunday, he rode through town as citizens cheered along the road. His battle came at the end of the week when he fought on our behalf—not as a stranger, but as our brother. He chose to put aside his comfort and safety. He willingly sacrificed himself, fighting death and Satan, because he knew we couldn't. He rose from the dead and gives us the victory so we can enjoy freedom. Forever.

Time to stand and clap for him. **"The Lord is my strength and my defense; he has become my salvation. He is my God, and I will praise him, my father's God, and I will exalt him"** (Exodus 15:2).

Hardship is not abandonment

Pastor Mark Jeske

Nobody loves comfort more than me. I work and save so that I won't experience financial stress. I eat only foods I like. I seek out the most comfortable chair in a room. Why on earth, then, would my heavenly Father, who professes to love me, sometimes make me so uncomfortable?

Moses explained to the Israelites he was leading that their hardships were not a sign of abandonment by God: **"He humbled you, causing you to hunger and then feeding you with manna, which neither you nor your ancestors had known, to teach you that man does not live on bread alone but on every word that comes from the mouth of the Lord"** (Deuteronomy 8:3). Wow! Out of *love* (seriously!). God actually let his children get hungry. Why? So that they would remember how much they needed him, cry out to him, experience his generosity, and love him back. Their hardships served to strengthen their relationship with their Father.

Do an audit of your hardships right now. Yes—right this minute. Yes, you. How are you being squeezed right now? How much pain (of mind and body) are you in right now? Realize that the One who didn't hesitate to send his Son to the cross for you could not love you more and that he might be using your hardship *only to draw you closer to himself*.

We live by the Word that comes from his mouth. Let him speak to you today.

Just breathe
Sarah Habben

Martin Luther once said, "The whole Christian life is a life of repentance." That's hard to hear. Repentance suggests guilt, which we'd rather not admit. Repentance assumes we want to change our ways, which is exceedingly difficult. But as long as we inhabit our sinful bodies in this sinful world, we're like pigs in a barnyard—we can't keep ourselves free of mud. Sin will stick to us until the day we die.

But doesn't this cycle of sin and repentance have a positive side? Confessing our sin squashes our pride. Sorrowing over sin makes us crave the grace of God. It drives us to Christ for forgiveness and for the power to live holy lives.

For Christians, repentance is like breathing. In repentance we exhale our sins, breathing out our guilt. And then we take a deep, sweet breath of Jesus' forgiveness, won for us by his death on the cross. **"Repent, then, and turn to God, so that your sins may be wiped out, that times of refreshing may come from the Lord"** (Acts 3:19). Keep seeking that refreshment!

We don't breathe just once a day, much less once a week. Without a regular exchange of oxygen and carbon dioxide, we'd quickly turn blue and die. Nor do we resent our need to breathe—our entire lives depend on it.

And so too with our spiritual breathing.

I'm sorry, Lord. *I forgive you.*

I'm sorry, Lord. *I forgive you.*

Our eternal life depends on it—so just breathe.

I want to be useful, Lord
Pastor Mark Jeske

Children are takers by instinct before they learn to be givers. Being interested in other people's lives and points of view is learned behavior, and it is one of many parent jobs to disciple children to care about the well-being of others.

Christian newbies naturally spend their initial energy as believers in processing their relationship with God. They need to absorb the incredible stories of what God has done for them and take them to heart. But as people grow in their faith, they will start to look outward and look for ways in which they can give back. How the Father's heart must be thrilled to hear the prayers of his believers as they express a desire to be useful to him.

He wants them to know that they each have been given a unique set of skills and gifts for a particular purpose: **"Now to each one the manifestation of the Spirit is given for the common good"** (1 Corinthians 12:7). No believer can say, "I got nothing." It is a source of continuing amazement to me to watch God's gifted children learn to be servants. Congregations benefit enormously from volunteers who care for the building and grounds, keep the books, seek ways to connect with people in their communities, befriend the lonely and troubled, tend to the aging and those with disabilities, disciple children, and make thrilling worship music.

How are your God-given gifts going to give him glory today?

It's my life

Sarah Habben

In 2000 Bon Jovi released the chart-topper song "It's My Life." When that siren song starts belting—tie me to a mast. Not just because I'm a horrible dancer, but because it's an international anthem that I want to sing with everyone else: "It's *my* life!"

But 1 Corinthians 6:19,20 puts the lie to those lyrics: **"Do you not know that your bodies are temples of the Holy Spirit, who is in you, whom you have received from God? *You are not your own*; you were bought at a price. Therefore honor God with your bodies."**

We are temples! At great expense, we recently renovated our church. We would never decorate its walls with skanky posters. We wouldn't rent out the pews for a clandestine affair. It's a temple of the Spirit!

At great expense, at the cost of his life, Jesus transformed us into temples. But sometimes we choose to be cheap motels. We hurry the Holy Spirit into the lobby and open our window to sin. We invite lust between our bedsheets, upload it on our computer screens, find it in books. And after the thrill, we shudder with shame.

Thank God that he doesn't shrink from our ugly confessions. That he doesn't withdraw from our hearts. That he assures us of his forgiveness with his own body and blood in Lord's Supper. That he enables us by the Holy Spirit to honor him with our bodies. That we can daily unwrap Jesus' Good Friday gift:

"It's my life," he says. "It's for you."

God is here now

Pastor Jared Oldenburg

Remember being a kid and thinking about all the cool things that the future would hold? My understanding of the future was that things were supposed to get easier. So if the future was like the *Jetsons* cartoon, you wouldn't have to park because your flying car would fold up into a briefcase, full meals would come out of a machine, and you'd just fly around to where you wanted to go.

I suppose *now* is the future, at least compared to when I was a kid. I guess cooking has gotten easier with gas and electric power, but on most levels, our lives are more and more complex. We aren't working less; in fact, we're working more. Our jobs are more and more difficult—it's harder to be a student, harder to be a parent, and harder to be an employee or boss. So what's the result of all this?

It's pretty easy to feel completely overwhelmed. I've been there, and I think you've been there too. I also think that it's a beautiful thing that we don't need to keep holding out for some future technology to make our lives easier. God is here now, and he wants to help. In fact, he commands us to place our troubles with him! In the book of 1 Peter it says, **"Cast all your anxiety on him because he cares for you"** (5:7). I don't know about you, but I'm a big fan of delegating my problems and concerns to the Lord of the universe!

Disobedience is death

Pastor Mark Jeske

Americans love rebels, and, no surprise, they love movies with rebellious lead characters. James Dean, Clint Eastwood, Keven Bacon, Matthew Broderick, and Jennifer Lawrence all played people who pushed against the status quo and were fearless about the consequences.

It's one thing to rebel against societal rules you don't like. it's another entirely to rebel against the will of God. Disobedience to God is death. It is a capital crime, and only the pure may live in heaven. There will be nothing sexy or glamorous on judgment day about the people who have set themselves against God.

The bad news is that each of us has chosen that path of rebellion. We may have excuses and rationales for our actions, but the curse remains. That's why the death of Christ matters so much—he alone bore the punishment meant for us. He alone offered his perfect obedience in place of our tattered record: **"For just as through the disobedience of the one man the many were made sinners, so also through the obedience of the one man the many will be made righteous"** (Romans 5:19).

Admitting that you are a sinful rebel doesn't mean that you should excuse it or, worse, glorify it. That painful self-realization should lead you to only one place, the cross of Christ, and to only one conclusion—gratitude for grace.

Keep your clothes on

Pastor Mark Jeske

Jesus used some really unusual metaphors to describe himself and his work: a hen gathering her chicks, the gate to a sheep pen, and the first and last letters of the Greek alphabet. One of the strangest comes from Revelation chapter 16 where he compares himself to a criminal: **"Look, I come like a thief! Blessed is the one who stays awake and remains clothed, so as not to go naked and be shamefully exposed"** (verse 15).

Yes, a *thief*. Why? Thieves study their prey and strike when they are not expected. The coming of judgment day will be sudden. When Jesus becomes visible as the returning King and Judge of all the earth, it will be too late for Bible study, church attendance, and earnest prayer. There will be no time even for quickie repentance. You will be locked forever in the spiritual state in which Jesus finds you. In his metaphor, will you be wearing the rags of your own shabby, sinful life? Or will he find you in the beautiful robes of his righteousness, given to you through your baptism (Galatians 3:26,27)?

No one, not even God himself, will force those shining garments on you. When you came to faith, your will was reborn and you now can make crucial spiritual decisions. Without Jesus, you will stand naked and defenseless in the final court. The beautiful clothes he bought you cost him his life to purchase.

Keep your clothes on!

God shows up

Pastor Mark Jeske

As he addressed the Israelite nation near the end of his life, Moses realized that he was talking to a young crowd. The older generation by now had almost completely died off, and most of the people listening to him hadn't seen or couldn't remember their former lives as slaves, the ten plagues that devastated Egypt, or the parting of the Red Sea.

Moses knew that the people would be sorely tempted by the religious beliefs and practices of the Canaanites, into whose land they would be moving. Canaanites worshiped the god Baal and the goddess Asherah and had developed a complex set of rituals and beliefs around them. But Baal and Asherah never did anything for anybody because they do not exist.

Moses wanted the Israelites to know that their God loved them and cared for them. And—their God showed up: **"There is no one like the God of Jeshurun [i.e., Israel], who rides across the heavens to help you and on the clouds in his majesty. The eternal God is your refuge, and underneath are the everlasting arms"** (Deuteronomy 33:26,27). His power not only soars above but stoops down to help his children in their time of need. When the storms of life howl, you can rest in the embrace of his everlasting arms.

The God of Israel is eternal. He still loves you. And he still shows up to bring you what you need.

Appreciate your blessings
Pastor Jared Oldenburg

Author Lynne Twist says that what we appreciate appreciates. It's pretty hard to appreciate what you have when you're constantly looking to the next thing. There's always something in our homes to upgrade: new carpeting, dishwasher, roof. And what about new clothes, new shoes, new job, new car, new relationships?

Sure, everybody feels that way, but it's not a big leap from disappointment with our carpeting to disappointment with the people God has put in our lives. Have you ever asked yourself, "Why aren't my kids better behaved?" "Why don't my parents support me?" "Why don't my friends call me as much as I call them?" "Why isn't my spouse super-crazy beautiful, or why isn't my husband as empathetic and romantic as the protagonist in a Nicholas Sparks novel?" This isn't a good place to be in.

The best way to get over being upset about what you don't have is to be thankful for what you *do* have. It's hard to be angry when you're thankful. The Bible puts it this way: **"Rejoice always, pray continually, give thanks in all circumstances; for this is God's will for you in Christ Jesus"** (1 Thessalonians 5:16-18).

In other words, let's appreciate the blessings God has given to us. Even more so, let's appreciate the people God has put into our lives. Once we find the beauty and love in the gift, strangely we start seeing the beauty and love of the Giver. That Giver of gifts is the God who literally gave up heaven so that he could come to make a relationship with you.

Joyful doing

Jason Nelson

Holidays are among the few play dates left for grown-ups. We get to set aside our mind-numbing routines and the problems at work and engage in some joyful doing. If they become stressful days of obligation, we aren't doing them right. Commemorating a bountiful harvest should be more like coloring a picture for Grandma's fridge and less like getting on task before the boss walks in. Stuffing a turkey should be more like craft time at summer camp and less like pushing the limits of productivity. Decorating the house should be like getting out the Legos and assembling something special. If we're grumbling under our breath instead of humming, "Come, You Thankful People, Come," we need to summon our inner child.

And our inner child can sing with David, who knew how to rock some joy. **"Come, let's shout praises to God, raise the roof for the Rock who saved us! Let's march into his presence singing praises, lifting the rafters with our hymns! And why? Because God is the best"** (Psalm 95:1-3 MSG).

Holidays are holy days because God is the best. So when the timer goes off and the pie is perfect, point heavenward and holler, "Yeah, Lord!" Break into your happy dance when you take a peek and the bird looks like it just flew out of a magazine and landed in your oven. And when the doorbell rings because the guests are here, hook your arm in theirs and march them into the presence of God.

God is good—even when life is not

Linda Buxa

As part of our mealtime prayers, my family occasionally says, **"Give thanks to the Lord, for *he is good.* His love endures forever"** (Psalm 136:1).

At one church my family attended, every worship service began with the pastor saying, "God is good." Then the worshipers replied, "All the time."

When people I love talk about healing, recovery, restored relationships, and seeing God say yes to their prayers, they say, "God is good."

I love when we give God the glory for the way he is working on this earth. Still, a nagging voice makes me wonder if we really believe that he is good—all the time. Maybe it's the loss of a job or struggles in church or battles with temptation that make you silently question his goodness. At every natural disaster, hurting hearts question, "If God is good, why did he let this happen?" This year, we might be gathering around a Thanksgiving table with breaking, grieving hearts. That's when we need the reminder that even when the situation is not good, God still is.

Sometimes we proclaim, "God is good!" with confidence, believing he will work good from hardship. Sometimes our voices shake, because we know he is good but are struggling to see how. However we say it, faith trusts that God will work all these hard things for the good of those who love him. *For your good*.

Because he is good, and his love endures forever.

Pretend you didn't hear

Pastor Mark Jeske

Good teachers know that they cannot correct every bad word or action from every student. There just aren't enough hours in the day. Sometimes you just have to pretend that you didn't hear. Good parents know that some sassy remarks mumbled under the breath by their children should just be left alone. Husbands and wives should probably not go digging for trouble either, as in, "What did you just say?"

We are all works in progress. Just imagine how patient God has been with us. Wowser! It pleases him when we show that same discerning mercy to the other fools and sinners around us: **"A person's wisdom yields patience; it is to one's glory to overlook an offense"** (Proverbs 19:11).

People often know right away that the words that just came out of their mouths were a mistake. They shouldn't have been uttered. But getting corrected when you're really upset only intensifies the conflict. Pretending you didn't hear allows the emotion in the room to die down. You can model and teach the right behaviors another time.

Overlooking an offense might preserve a friendship when the angry person didn't really mean the words he or she just said. The gospel of Christ that forgives our sins doesn't stimulate us to sin even more; in fact, it inspires us to amend our lives. Overlooking an offense gives a friend a chance to back down rather than defiantly throwing even more verbal darts. Go ahead. Try it.

Perceived scarcity

Pastor Jared Oldenburg

If you ever watch TED talks, you may have heard of researcher Brené Brown. She's a TED talk star. In her research she discovered that Americans struggle with what she calls a viewpoint of scarcity. This isn't hard to imagine once you start thinking about it. You wake up and feel like you didn't get enough sleep. You go to work and feel you don't have enough hours in the day to get your stuff done. You need coffee because you don't feel like you have enough energy. You want to buy something, but you don't have enough money. You fall into bed exhausted, empty. Time, money, energy—it seems like all our resources are scarce.

I don't think it's a big leap to question if God has given you a short end of the stick. Like you simply don't have enough. Is this true? Not even close.

I'll be frank, this kind of self-talk about our lives of scarcity is an absolute lie. Perceived scarcity and the worry and frustration that come along with it are hand-delivered lies from the devil. The reality is this: As a believer, you can have confidence that you have a God whose love and provision for you are not scarce. Philippians 4:19 says, **"My God will meet all your needs according to the riches of his glory in Christ Jesus."**

That's the truth. God will meet all your needs, and you can push this idea of perceived scarcity out of your life and instead rejoice in the blessing and abundance that the Lord has provided for you.

Forgiving has a limit

Sarah Habben

Forgiving. It's not so hard, in theory.

But then someone close blindsides you. Their offense lurches around in your mind like a horror-movie villain who refuses to die. The memory of it leaps from the shadows as you try to sleep.

"Forgive?" you think. "Forget it! I have my limits."

That's when Jesus sets new limits. Divine ones.

"'Even if they sin against you seven times in a day and seven times come back to you saying "I repent," you must forgive them.' The apostles said to the Lord, 'Increase our faith!' He replied, 'If you have faith as small as a mustard seed, you can say to this mulberry tree, "Be uprooted and planted in the sea," and it will obey you'" (Luke 17:4-6).

Forgiving an offense might seem harder than yanking a mulberry from the ground. Pain has long roots. Resentment is a hard soil. But when we think our faith isn't up to the task, Jesus says, "Forget the size of your faith. Remember the size of your Savior!"

Our small faith connects us to our super-sized Savior. He went to the cross for our sins: our selfishness, our short fuses, our lukewarm attitudes toward God's Word. But Jesus didn't hang from the cross plotting his revenge or nursing a grudge. No, on its planks he flexed his muscular love. A love that powerfully forgives you—and everyone around you.

Seven times a day and counting.

Thank you, Lord. Empower me to forgive with your limits: divine ones. Amen.

No cheating
Pastor Mark Jeske

In days of old there was no Bureau of Weights and Measures. No government agency regulated commerce. The Latin slogan applied: *caveat emptor*, "let the buyer beware." Customers were at the mercy of the merchants who weighed out their purchases, because the merchants owned the weights and the scales.

Cheating is not hard. There are thousands of ways to take advantage of people besides shaving metal off the weights, but sellers should realize that someone is watching their commercial behaviors: **"Honest scales and balances belong to the Lord; all the weights in the bag are of his making"** (Proverbs 16:11). It's not hard to lie about your products and services; it's not hard to pass on shoddy goods; it's not hard to overcharge or bill for work not done. But it is wrong, and those who do those things rot out their souls.

Here is a great way for Christian businesspeople to live their faith. Honest trade not only honors the Lord, but it is good for business too. Who wants to go back to a shop where she suspects she has been cheated? Honor your contracts. Tell the truth. Keep your promises. Put your customers' needs and interests ahead of your own. Go the extra mile. Accept responsibility for things that were your fault. Accept responsibility for things that were your company's fault, even if not yours personally.

You might make less money. But God will smile.

Why we obey
Linda Buxa

The church leader told the congregation, "I just want to encourage every one of us to realize when we obey God, we're not doing it for God. . . . We're doing it for ourselves, because God takes pleasure when we are happy. That's the thing that gives him the greatest joy."

Before we get upset at those words, we realize at some point we've all gotten the concept of obedience wrong. At times we obey because we don't want to get into trouble. Other times we obey God because we think it will make us look better. Sometimes we obey God and then expect that the rest of our lives will be easy and we'll be happy finally.

The good news for all of us is that Jesus came to earth to take the punishment for the times we obey out of selfish motives. He lived his entire life with a pure heart of obedience to his Father's will. We get the credit for that and can stop carrying around the guilt that comes from pretending to be obedient.

With hearts at peace, here's why we really obey God: because he loved us first. We obey him because we love him back. We obey him because he handmade us to do his work here on earth. We obey him because we know his plans really are best. We **"obey your statutes, for** [we] **love them greatly"** (Psalm 119:167).

The power of inclusion

Jason Nelson

Have you ever noticed what Jesus didn't do when he called his first disciples? He didn't say, "Now, boys, I want you to sit on these rocks and pay close attention while I give you a three-year lecture about the movement I am starting." Rather, he saw two brothers, Peter and Andrew, and said, **"Come, follow me . . . and I will send you out to fish for people"** (Matthew 4:19). Then he saw two more brothers, James and John. **"Jesus called them, and immediately they left the boat and their father and followed him"** (Matthew 4:21,22). Then they all hit the road, found some more people, and learned from Jesus along the way. Jesus was a street teacher, and Christianity was a pedestrian faith that grew by including ordinary people.

When the movement began, there was only one requirement for being included—following Jesus. But since then, Christianity has morphed into something like algebra. There are formulas to know, proofs to demonstrate, and equations to keep balanced. There are standards to meet and tests to pass before people can advance to the next level. And people are dropping out because they just don't get the math.

We may need to hit the reset button. There are lots of people out there who don't know Jesus but would love to be part of something special and life changing. The come-to-Jesus moment is a simple invitation to follow him. Everyone can be included as long as they stay on the road with Jesus.

The power of participation

Jason Nelson

As the movement progressed, there were enough followers that Jesus could send out 72 people to represent him. He gave them a sense of urgency and told them not to dillydally. **"Go! I am sending you out like lambs among wolves. Do not take a purse or bag or sandals; and do not greet anyone on the road"** (Luke 10:3,4). He made them full participants in his cause to redeem mankind. **"Whoever listens to you listens to me; whoever rejects you rejects me; but whoever rejects me rejects him who sent me"** (Luke 10:16).

See if this makes sense. Jesus' ascension to the one who sent him came at the end of his three years on earth. In that moment, his best-trained disciples still didn't fully grasp what the Jesus movement was all about (see Acts 1). So, it stands to reason that the 72 people he sent out before that were far from experts. They couldn't have understood it all either. Certainly, they made mistakes. They probably misspoke a few times and embarrassed themselves. Jesus knew they weren't fully prepared. Yet he made them full participants in his ministry.

One thing we know from the whole episode is the effect that being able to participate had on those people: **"The seventy-two returned with joy."** And the effect it had on Jesus: **"At that time Jesus, full of joy through the Holy Spirit, said, 'I praise you, Father, Lord of heaven and earth'"** (Luke 10:17,21).

The power of persuasion

Jason Nelson

The movement grew one precious soul at a time. Some people joined because they had a life-changing conversation with Jesus. We know the names of individuals who were persuaded to follow Jesus because of what he said to them.

Nicodemus was a part of the religious establishment, and he had some clout. He was on the ruling council and was a traditionalist strictly devoted to the laws of Moses and all of the additional laws the Pharisees added to them. Nicodemus was a genuine expert. But he saw signs that Jesus knew something he didn't and went to Jesus under the cover of darkness to find out what it was.

John chapter 3 records their conversation and includes the most persuasive words found in the Bible, or in any book: **"For God so loved the world that he gave his one and only Son, that whoever believes in him shall not perish but have eternal life"** (verse 16).

Nicodemus was an elite teacher in Israel. He knew things others didn't. He knew oral laws and written laws and prophecies about a peaceable kingdom, but he didn't really understand the kingdom of God. He didn't understand that the kingdom of God is within us. Still, he was persuaded to follow Jesus. Later, after Jesus died on the cross, Nicodemus risked everything and stepped out in broad daylight to help bury Jesus. Nicodemus was reborn by what Jesus said to him. Nicodemus entered the kingdom of God because God so loved him into it.

december

This will be a sign to you:
You will find a baby wrapped in cloths
and lying in a manger.
Luke 2:12

God's sufficient grace

Sarah Habben

Anxiety. For most it's circumstantial: a backseat driver who gets shrill when the way forward is uncertain. But for 40 million others in the USA it's clinical. It can plow a path of destruction through your sleep, digestion, and social interactions.

Are you dealing with anxiety? You probably know that therapy and medication help manage anxiety and that using such tools shows good stewardship of God's gift of life. But even with help, anxiety sometimes rears its head and roars. Perhaps you've prayed, "God, if only you would just take it away! How much better I could serve you then!"

God hears. And across anxiety's dark and roiling waters he shines the steady beam of his promises. Here's one: **"My grace is sufficient for you, for my power is made perfect in weakness"** (2 Corinthians 12:9). Your anxiety may never be "cured," but your weakness cannot dilute God's strength. Anxiety is complicated . . . but God understands it. It's ugly . . . but God's love will not falter in its face. Anxiety cannot crush your faith beyond God's ability to rebuild and reinforce it with his Word and sacraments. It cannot undo the truest truth your faith has taught you: that when Jesus made himself weak on the cross, it was to win your salvation. You have a home in heaven where every weakness will be healed.

When anxiety cripples you, lean on the cross. It's God's power made perfect—for you.

Now you know

Pastor Mark Jeske

We are all born outside God's family. Every new baby already has the terminal disease of sin, and the mortality that hangs over our heads is only the harbinger of a worse fate in hell to come. Spiritual corpses can't revivify themselves.

God not only needed to come in person as the incarnate second person of the Trinity to purchase your salvation; he needed also to inject your brain and heart with the Holy Spirit so that you could actually come to faith. Everything changed when you became a believer. Now the Word makes sense; now God's ways look good; now you have spiritual strength to detect Satan's workings and resist him.

God expects you to use your knowledge, discernment, and spiritual power to recommit to him and choose to follow him. Moses challenged the Israelites: **"This day I call the heavens and the earth as witnesses against you that I have set before you life and death, blessings and curses. Now choose life, so that you and your children may live and that you may love the Lord your God, listen to his voice, and hold fast to him"** (Deuteronomy 30:19,20).

I was once pulled over for speeding 15 mph over the limit. All I could offer the sheriff's deputy was the excuse that I didn't know. Pretty lame. I had to pay a hefty fine. When Christ returns to judge the living and the dead, that excuse won't work for you either.

Now you know. Choose life.

The gift of forgiveness
Pastor Mark Jeske

Do you spend a lot of time on your Christmas gift list? Sadly I am a procrastinator. Most of my purchases are made at big-box retailers where I can get 'er done in one afternoon. But the gifts I am proudest of are those I thought about and planned for way in advance, the one-of-a-kind presents I find at unique specialty shops or things I made by hand.

In all the busyness of buying, making, giving, and receiving this month, I invite you to pause for a minute right now and think of the great Christmas gifts that God has given to you. Like all the best gifts, they were planned way in advance, are one-of-a-kind, and were "handcrafted" personally for you.

The first of these gifts is your very salvation: **"It is by grace you have been saved, through faith—and this not from yourselves; it is the *gift* of God"** (Ephesians 2:8,9). You and I *need* saving, remember? Just as fetal alcohol babies are born addicted, we are born with sin and death in our very bones. Those FA babies can't change their condition by themselves—they are totally dependent on their medical team.

God *gave* you what you couldn't do for yourself. What a great Christmas gift you have in the unconditional forgiveness of your sins through the person and work of your Savior Jesus Christ! Thank you, God!

Remain in me
Sarah Habben

When we lived in Malawi, my family had some hand-carved wooden furniture. It was sturdy. It withstood the equatorial seasons. But a silent, tiny enemy could weaken it from the inside out, destroying its beauty and structural soundness. Termites. No matter how beautiful or strong, a chair chewed by termites eventually amounts to firewood.

That's also true of any good thing we do apart from Christ. We might carve out a life of good works that looks impressive. We might strive and sacrifice to win the favor of people and God. But if we do these things without Christ, we're like a chair riddled with termite holes. All our efforts will only end in collapse. That is the terrifying judgment of Jesus himself. **"If you do not remain in me, you are like a branch that is thrown away and withers; such branches are picked up, thrown into the fire and burned"** (John 15:6).

Jesus' warning comes from his great and tender love for us. He does not want to see our lives end as firewood. How precious, then, is his promise: **"I am the vine; you are the branches. If you remain in me and I in you, you will bear much fruit"** (John 15:5).

Alone we are dead wood, riddled with sin and self-righteousness. No good thing can be carved from our lives. But Jesus has pulled us from God's fiery judgment. He wants to graft us to his side and make us new people—forgiven, fruitful, and useful.

The heavenly host: Mighty spirits

Pastor Mark Jeske

Only a few fortunate human beings in history have ever been allowed to see the angels. God made them in the form of spirits, and thus they are invisible to us. Though they have appeared to people in human form, they do not have flesh and blood as we do. And yet they are not just a faceless army of drones and clones. They have names, identities, individual willpower, unique gifts and missions.

And immense strength. God invests them with some of his almighty power when it pleases him to use them as instruments of his will. The apostle John was allowed to see a vision of them at work, and though the vision is in part a metaphor, it is based on reality: **"Then a mighty angel picked up a boulder the size of a large millstone and threw it into the sea, and said: 'With such violence the great city of Babylon will be thrown down, never to be found again'"** (Revelation 18:21).

God's angels are *mighty* spirits. It is a great comfort for anxious believers to know that they are on our side. Satan and his demons seem so strong and ubiquitous that we fear we will be overwhelmed. There is so much evil, so much violence, so much terror pouring from the pits of hell! But God's holy angels are stronger still. The saints will be preserved, the church will prevail, and the Grand Reunion will take place on schedule.

In the meantime, r-e-l-a-x.

The heavenly host: Worshipful congregation

Pastor Mark Jeske

Angels have the ability to exercise individual willpower. They are not robotically controlled from a giant radar dish somewhere. They choose to be in service to God. Those who chose to rebel and seek life without God were granted their wish and expelled from God's presence. These demons now huddle with Satan in hell and try to destroy as much of God's creation as they can before time runs out. They know they are doomed, and that just drives them more feverishly to their dirty work.

But those angels who chose to stay enjoy the daily thrill of the glory and peace that radiate from God's throne. They delight in the beauty and light and peace of heaven. Like us on earth, they love to worship God: **"All the angels were standing around the throne and around the elders and the four living creatures. They fell down on their faces before the throne and worshiped God, saying: 'Amen! Praise and glory and wisdom and thanks and honor and power and strength be to our God for ever and ever. Amen!'"** (Revelation 7:11,12).

The saints who have passed away now get to join that angelic chorus for their worship times in God's immediate presence, and soon you and I will shuffle off the stage and join them. The angels genuinely appreciate God's mighty acts in history and love the love coming from his face.

So do we.

The heavenly host: God's agents

Pastor Mark Jeske

Does God *need* the angels? I suppose not. God could create and run his universe without them simply by expressing his will through his word. His word alone could suffice to translate his thoughts into reality.

But it pleases God to work his will through agents who love to be on his team. The angels view executing his plans and designs as a privilege, not punishment. It is service, not slavery. It is a holy mission, not just dull mandate. They are almost as passionate about their work as God is. Scripture tells us that they shout with joy over one sinner who repents.

In some ways they seem way above us: they shine in holiness while we have sinful dirt on our faces; they fly at the speed of light while we limp one step at a time; they airily dart back and forth between heaven and earth while we are still heavy and earthbound. But we are God's family, and they are not. Christ was incarnate to save people, not the evil angels. And thus God's heavenly host is working not just for God but *for us*! **"Are not all angels ministering spirits sent to serve those who will inherit salvation?"** (Hebrews 1:14).

The armies of heaven who attend you are one more immense example of how valuable you are to God and the lengths to which he will go to get you home safely.

The heavenly host:
Our protectors

Pastor Mark Jeske

Every citizen owes a debt of gratitude and appreciation to the men and women in uniform who risk their lives in the military. Civilians have only a hazy idea of the rigors of physical conditioning they must go through, the complexity and immense power of the weapons in which they are trained, or the heart-pounding experience of being under live fire from an enemy trying to kill them.

God has sent his heavenly hosts against the hordes of hell, whose cruel desire is to maim, kill, and destroy. The angels are led by Michael the archangel, the great prince. You and I and all believers are being protected from savage attacks we can't see, by angelic forces we can't see either. **"At that time Michael, the great prince who protects your people, will arise. There will be a time of distress such as has not happened from the beginning of nations until then. But at that time your people—everyone whose name is found written in the book—will be delivered"** (Daniel 12:1).

This is the only war in human history where the outcome is known in advance. No matter how broken things get on earth, God, working through his heavenly host, will bring the believers safely home. Through Christ we have already triumphed over Satan. Through Word and Baptism you have been brought to faith, and through that faith your name is entered into God's heavenly ledger.

It is the guest book of heaven.

The heavenly host: God's messengers

Pastor Mark Jeske

We live in an age of astounding communication advances. The power and complexity of ways to share information and connect with people have exploded in our lifetimes. Words, images, and videos fly around the globe at near instantaneous speeds.

In the biblical era, there were only two ways to communicate: orally and through handwriting. God's Word was transmitted and spread outward through patient human-to-human communication. On special occasions God used a third channel: angels. Interestingly enough the word that God chose for his heavenly assistants from which we derive the word *angel, ángelos* in the Greek New Testament, means "messenger." Perhaps communication was the angelic function God most prized.

The angels' most famous message was given to some livestock handlers working third shift and heralded the stupendous events in Bethlehem on Christmas Eve: **"An angel of the Lord appeared to them, and the glory of the Lord shone around them, and they were terrified. But the angel said to them, 'Do not be afraid. I bring you good news that will cause great joy for all the people. Today in the town of David a Savior has been born to you; he is the Messiah, the Lord'"** (Luke 2:9-11).

God could have told the shepherds the news himself. But it pleased him to let the Christmas gospel come from his *ángeloi,* his heavenly messengers.

They were talking to you too, you know.

The gift of faith

Pastor Mark Jeske

If you've lived a while, you've had the experience of having a gift rejected. Perhaps you cooked a fabulous meal for somebody who wasn't hungry. Perhaps you bought a ring for somebody who didn't want it. Perhaps you overcommitted to a relationship and gave yourself totally to someone who just wasn't that into you.

God's grace is pure, perfect, accomplished, and all his doing. The manger, the cross, and the empty tomb guarantee God's unconditional love and forgiveness for the whole world. But here's the thing—if people don't know about it, or if they know and don't believe it, that grace will be of no value to them on the great day of judgment. Ignorance of the gospel and contempt for the gospel both condemn the sinner.

We are saved by grace *through faith*. And here is another gift of God—he *gives* you the very faith you need through his mighty Word. Faith can't be self-synthesized in the human brain or heart. God alone converts unbelievers into believers: **"Don't be deceived, my dear brothers. Every good and perfect gift is from above, coming down from the Father of the heavenly lights. . . . He chose to *give* us birth through the word of truth"** (James 1:16-18).

The first birth gave you a toe tag for hell. Your second birth makes you a candidate for heaven. Thank you, God!

Sorrowing saints

Sarah Habben

Are you a sorrowing saint? Perhaps you've lost count of your sleepless nights, of the prayers that have unraveled from your heart as you drag a load that God seems unwilling to lift.

Another sorrowing saint once wrote this lament in Psalm 77: **"Will the Lord . . . never show his favor again? Has his unfailing love vanished forever? Has his promise failed for all time? Has God forgotten to be merciful?"** (verses 7-9).

Maybe you've asked those questions too. They are questions that elbow forward when God shrouds his will, when trouble follows trouble, and when tomorrow sounds worse than today. The sorrowing saint of Psalm 77 likely longed for God to poke his head through the clouds with a rumbling pep talk about the future. But instead, faith pointed him to the past: **"Then I thought . . . 'I will remember the deeds of the Lord; yes, I will remember your miracles of long ago . . . and meditate on all your mighty deeds'"** (verses 10-12).

Inside the psalmist's hurt was room for praise. Today was painful. Tomorrow was unknowable. But the past was proof of God's miracles and might.

Inside *your* hurt is room for praise. Start at the cross where Christ worked his mightiest deed—the winning of your forgiveness and salvation. List God's daily faithfulness. Praise and thank God for each item on your list. Be convinced anew of the truth that God's favor and love and promises and mercy are all YES in Christ—yesterday, today, and always.

The terrible risk of prosperity

Pastor Mark Jeske

When we think of the phrase *money troubles*, our minds jump immediately to things like job layoffs, huge credit card balances, heavy student loans, investment crashes, house foreclosure, or huge medical bills. We don't generally use the phrase *money troubles* to describe wealth.

But maybe there are times when we should. Having too little money is a problem, but so is having a lot. Wealth is a wonderful tool to make things happen, but it easily becomes an idol. The chase for it is consuming, and the power that comes with it is seductive. Be careful of asking God for wealth. Moses observed that prosperity was a problem for the Israelites. They **"grew fat and kicked; filled with food, they became heavy and sleek. They abandoned the God who made them and rejected the Rock their Savior"** (Deuteronomy 32:15).

God loves to be generous with his children. He would give us even more if he dared, but believers have a terrible track record of coping with too much wealth. Imagine his crushed heart as he watched his children prosper because of blessings he sent them only to see them abandon him and lose their faith.

Have you been blessed with many years of stable income, steadily growing assets, and many comforts in your home? Ask God for discipline, balance, and wisdom. Cultivate a spirit of generosity so that you honor the Giver.

And be grateful, not boastful.

God is sovereign over all governments

Pastor Mark Jeske

Just because our eyes do not pick up infrared or ultraviolet rays does not mean that those rays don't exist on the wave spectrum. Just because our eyes cannot see God at work governing the affairs of earth doesn't mean he isn't.

Our world seems in perpetual chaos. There are either many small wars going on or some large wars going on at all times. The strong take advantage of the weak; weapon technology makes it possible to kill more and more people; terrorists glide invisibly across borders and seem to get away with their deadly work more often than they're caught. Where is peace? Where is justice? Where is God?

He's right here. Nebuchadnezzar, emperor of Babylonia and the entire Mideast, was given behind-the-scenes information from courier angels. As a wielder of power, he needed to understand who was really in command: **"The decision is announced by messengers, the holy ones declare the verdict, so that the living may know that the Most High is sovereign over all kingdoms on earth and gives them to anyone he wishes and sets over them the lowliest of people"** (Daniel 4:17).

Nebuchadnezzar had to endure a spell of insanity before he was given back his mental clarity. You have the opportunity to learn and believe straight from the Word: The God of the Bible is sovereign over all the earth. All human history works out for his glory and his agenda. His Word is the last word.

Speak forgiveness

Linda Buxa

We pay attention to celebrity news the same way we gawk at traffic accidents. We are outraged by sports stars who beat their girlfriends or party themselves right out of a promising future. We are disgusted by elected officials whose sex scandals ruin their careers. We are indignant when we discover celebrities have abused children.

So sometimes it's baffling that we continue to give them our attention—and our money. A radio commentator captured this phenomenon perfectly: "In our society forgiveness is not for those who truly repent; it's reserved for those who still have something to offer."

We forgive famous people usually because they have something to offer—victories, entertainment, the promise of better living conditions. Really, though, *forgiveness* isn't the word for that. We overlook, rationalize, minimize, judge. So we give the impression that to earn our "forgiveness," people have to perform.

I am so thankful our God doesn't forgive that way. In fact, he forgives because he knows we have nothing to offer. Jesus is the only one who can bring us back into a relationship with our Father because he is the only one who earned it. Through faith, the rest of us just get all the benefits of forgiveness. Now that we have that peace and joy, we get to pass along that kind of forgiveness to the people we know. Not because they've earned it or have something to offer, but out of gratefulness to Jesus.

You're worth something to God

Pastor Jared Oldenburg

How do you know you're worth something? Have you ever stood in a checkout line and gazed upon all the celebrities on the magazine covers? Their lives seem perfect, with nanny in tow on a stroll around Martha's Vineyard. And what are you doing? You're wrestling kids at 10:00 A.M. at Walmart, trying to get milk and some cornflakes.

However, have you ever checked out other people, the ones who aren't famous? You log in to Facebook and think, "I should be skinnier. I should be smarter. I should be prettier. I should be more successful at my work or taking awesome vacations or have kids who win awards or who always listen." The truth is we don't want to be better than celebrities; we just want to be better than the people we know. Then we'll be worth something. We think, "I won't be worth something until I am skinnier, richer, funnier, have more hair, have less hair, or am more successful."

It's true: you're not valuable *until* . . . but it's a different *until* than you think. **"In Christ Jesus you are all children of God through faith"** (Galatians 3:26). The most valuable thing that you possess, the thing that makes you worthwhile is that *through faith in Christ, you are God's child.*

So you can look in the mirror and say, "In spite of my past and in spite of my shortcomings, in God's eyes, I am valuable. In God's eyes, I'm his child."

Not just for Mars

Jason Nelson

My daughter attended a leadership conference that focused on team building. The speaker was an expert on understanding personalities and how different types of people can work together to accomplish a common purpose. He is helping NASA identify the qualities of astronauts with the right stuff for the first manned mission to Mars. How cool is that? In a Q & A session, he was asked what he was looking for in people who must work in close quarters on a long voyage to achieve a distant goal. Without hesitation, he said, "Humility."

From here this thing wants to write itself. Jesus has humility swaddled all over him. We love the story of Christmas because there is humility everywhere. There is a humble husband and wife staying in a stinkin' barn. There is a lowly manger serving as the crib for the almighty God who humbled himself to begin a life of service and sacrifice as a little baby. And the first admirers on the scene were low-class shepherds. Even the cattle were lowing. Nothing makes us appreciate humble like Christmas Eve. It is one night every year that we love humble. Oh, that we were there and could be that humble too!

Isn't it amazing that a Christ-like virtue transcends a stable and stained glass and is embraced by the larger culture? Humble people have always been God's first choice to accomplish his mission. And now humble people are the first choice for the mission to Mars.

The gift of security

Pastor Mark Jeske

Way back in 1924, a national marketing campaign encouraged people to buy phonographs for their loved ones because it was "the gift that keeps on giving." Get it? They will enjoy your gift over and over and over every time they play a record. That phrase has been reused countless times, including as encouragement for people to register as organ donors.

The birth of Jesus Christ is the ultimate gift that keeps on giving. His life's mission was fulfilled as he changed God's verdict on humanity from "Guilty!" to "Innocent!" But in addition his intercessory presence at his Father's right hand means that the Father's every interaction with us will be loving, positive, and helpful: **"He who did not spare his own Son, but gave him up for us all—how will he not also, along with him, graciously give us all things?"** (Romans 8:32).

If the Father put his Son through crucifixion for us, he will certainly not hold back on the far littler things we need. It means that all our needs and troubles are noticed. It means that our Father's heart cares what's happening to us. It means that he pays particular attention to our prayers and fast-tracks them for action. It means that he adjusts his management of the universe with us in mind.

All these things are gifts. He loves to give us all things for Jesus' sake. Thank you, God!

Comfort my hurting people

Jason Nelson

"'Comfort, oh comfort my people,' says your God. 'Speak softly and tenderly to Jerusalem, but also make it very clear that she has served her sentence, that her sin is taken care of—forgiven! She's been punished enough and more than enough, and now it's over and done with'" (Isaiah 40:1,2 MSG).

The tidings of the season are comfort and joy because the Savior is no longer on the way—he has come. And it's all taken care of. All of the uncertainty about where we stand with God and all of the hurting from our self-inflicted wounds are taken care of. The times of stress from every soulful trauma are over. Christ has paid our dues for us and served our sentence. We have spent enough time in the seasons of our own distress.

"'Comfort, comfort all my people; speak of peace,' so says our God. 'Comfort those who sit in darkness, groaning from their sorrows' load. Speak to all Jerusalem of the peace that waits for them; tell them that their sins I cover, that their warfare now is over" (Johannes Olearius).

I don't know anyone who doesn't want more comfort and joy. Who's going to say, "Enough already"? I don't know anyone who doesn't need reassurance from the calming voice of a prophet looking ahead or a hymn writer looking back on the Savior sleeping like a baby. Merry Christmas to all of God's hurting people. Grab as much comfort and joy as you can get.

Build on the rock

Pastor Jared Oldenburg

Time management guru Stephen Covey tells the story of a professor who brought a jar and box of rocks into his classroom. He put big rocks in the jar and filled it to the top. He then asked the class if the jar was full. Some said yes, thinking he couldn't fit in another big rock. That's true. However, he then added smaller rocks to it and asked again if the jar was full. The class, catching on, started to wonder. Finally, he added sand into the small empty spaces. The point? It's not about squeezing the most out of your day, but instead prioritizing your day. You have to put the big rocks in first.

What are your big rocks? I'm guessing that your big rocks and my big rocks would be pretty similar. We desire a relationship with Jesus, we want time with our family and friends, we enjoy meaningful work, and we probably invest in ourselves physically and emotionally. My guess is that your list doesn't somehow include burning the day on Facebook or eye-guzzling the latest Netflix series. That stuff is not so important; that stuff is sand.

Jesus uses a metaphor in the Bible about building our lives on things that matter versus things that don't. **"Therefore everyone who hears these words of mine and puts them into practice is like a wise man who built his house on the rock"** (Matthew 7:24). In the end, things that don't matter (sand), will never hold you up when real trouble comes. There is only one thing that can do that—a life built on Jesus' promises!

Seeing the future
Linda Buxa

Most of our stress is because of the unknown. How will the kids turn out? What will retirement look like? Will I be able to make rent this month? Will our relationship survive?

So much is unknown that our prayers get a little panicky. "Dear God, what am I going to do? How is this going to work out? Please just fix it."

Really, we are asking God to let us see the future. That's not how it works. You know what though? We can see the past.

In his Word, God reminds us of the great things Jesus has already accomplished: living a perfect life (and giving us credit for that), dying a painful death (so we don't have to), and rising from the dead (so we can be with him forever). Which, really, gives us a glimpse of our eternal future.

"In his great mercy he has given us new birth into a living hope through the resurrection of Jesus Christ from the dead, and into an inheritance that can never perish, spoil or fade. . . . In all this you greatly rejoice, though now for a little while you may have had to suffer grief in all kinds of trials. These have come so that the proven genuineness of your faith—of greater worth than gold, which perishes even though refined by fire—may result in praise, glory and honor when Jesus Christ is revealed" (1 Peter 1:3-7).

Teach us to count
Sarah Habben

Adults don't need to be taught to count. Monday's alarm blares, and we start a countdown until Friday. We count down to birthdays, anniversaries, and retirement. But if we're only numbering earthly milestones, our counting doesn't add up.

"Teach us to number our days, that we may gain a heart of wisdom," so Moses prayed in Psalm 90:12. God had called Moses to lead millions of rebellious Israelites through the Sinai Peninsula. For their sin, many would die in the desert. Their days were numbered.

Just like those Israelites, I treat my daily "manna" with arrogance—as if my children, my job, my home, my health are blessings that will last forever. What if I did a better job of measuring my mortality? I'd be more inclined to pray like Moses: pleading for wisdom as I use my days, for forgiveness when I misuse them.

But even as Moses suffered under God's justice, he refused to let go of God's grace. He boldly prayed, **"Satisfy us in the morning with your unfailing love, that we may sing for joy and be glad all our days"** (Psalm 90:14).

Marvel again at that unfailing love! God put skin on to suffer hell in our place. Christ stepped from the grave on Easter morning, ending death's reign. Though we misuse our time, every morning brings fresh forgiveness. God's unfailing, satisfying love fills us with daily joy and purpose until he calls us home.

In the light of that love, make every day count. Even Mondays.

I have problems, Lord

Pastor Mark Jeske

In my experience, women are far ahead of men in the area of prayers for help. We men are stubborn creatures. We go as long as we can stand it trying to do everything on our own. Somehow we get it into our heads that if we ask for help, we are *weak*. We lose the game. We might forfeit our "man card." There is a long-running story about men preferring to drive in circles for half an hour when they could have gotten help in three minutes. It's true.

There is no point in suffering any longer than you have to. God not only accepts our calls for help; he encourages them. The Bible's book of Psalms gives many examples of believers, males included, who had exhausted their own resources and needed divine help. **"The cords of death entangled me, the anguish of the grave came over me; I was overcome by distress and sorrow. Then I called on the name of the Lord: 'Lord, save me!'"** (Psalm 116:3,4).

What burdens are you carrying right now that you need help with? (*Psst*—guys, there is no shame in asking for God's help.) He who did not hesitate to send his own Son to the cross has demonstrated beyond all doubt that he loves you. If he did the Big Thing, he will surely do the littler things to help his children.

He has resources to send into your life, *but he's waiting to be asked.*

The gift of usefulness
Pastor Mark Jeske

It's generally considered bad taste to give someone a gift that comes back to benefit the giver in a big way. For instance, if I want to impress my wife, I should probably not give her NFL tickets or a chain saw for around the house. She should not give me scented candles or new cookware.

Ironically a big part of God's giving activity with us comes back to bless his agenda in a big way. The Bible teaches us that all of the aptitudes and passions and skills that we have really come from God and are intended for his purposes: **"Each one should use whatever *gift* he has received to serve others, faithfully administering God's grace in its various forms"** (1 Peter 4:10).

In other words, God has saved us not only *from* something—from sin, from death, from Satan, from hell. He has saved us *for* something—for service, for evangelism, for teaching, for loving other people, for modeling a joyful Christian life. All of the parts of you that other people like best—your humor, memory, skills with cloth or wood or spreadsheets or food or guitar—really come from God. And he wants us to know that we will find our greatest fulfillment in life by using those gifts to make other people's lives better.

He saved us not only so that we could go to heaven someday. He saved us so that we feel useful *now*. Thank you, God!

Christmas Eve

Your best Christmas present

Pastor Mark Jeske

Sin alienates people from God and from one another. When it dawned on Adam and Eve how badly their fruit-tasting experiment had gone, they tried to escape the Father who had been so kind to them. So great was their guilt that they hid naked in some bushes, trembling and aghast at what they had done.

Whenever holiness and heaven broke into people's day-to-day existence in Bible times, they had the same experience—fear, even terror, that the hammer was finally going to drop. Zechariah and Mary both had to be calmed down before the angelic Christmas message could be delivered to each.

And so did some shepherds working third shift in the fields outside little Bethlehem: **"And there were shepherds living out in the fields nearby, keeping watch over their flocks by night. An angel of the Lord appeared to them, and the glory of the Lord shone around them, and they were terrified. But the angel said to them, 'Do not be afraid'"** (Luke 2:8-10).

Here is your best Christmas present, this year and every year—that the Christ Child came to earth to take away your fear. Because that little Child will bear your condemnation and the consequences of your sin, there is no judgment or punishment left for you. You can live every day of your life absolutely certain that you are loved, forgiven, and immortal.

No fear. Merry Christmas!

december 25

Christmas Day

The perfect gift

Sarah Habben

It's finally Christmas. Maybe you have high hopes for it: a perfect church service, a perfect gathering, a perfect turkey, a perfect tree, the perfect gift.

But what if the choir is flat, loved ones are missing, your turkey is dry, your tree droops, your gift is another toaster . . . what then?

If the Christmas season leaves us feeling a little empty, weary, or sad, perhaps it's not because our hopes are too high but because they aren't high enough. What if we raised our Christmas standards—not to HGTV heights, but to heavenly heights?

Listen to the angel choir: **"Glory to God in the highest heaven, and on earth peace to those on whom his favor rests"** (Luke 2:14).

Glory. Peace. Favor. Those are the ingredients of a perfect Christmas. They are embodied in the baby who lies in the manger—and who will die on a cross, rise from his tomb, and reign on our behalf. They are ingredients that never disappoint.

So take a moment. Honor God for the evidence of his *glory* in your life. Start with your God-given faith.

Praise God for extending you *peace* for the sake of his Son. Your sins are covered. This isn't a peace *from* trouble and sorrow, but peace *in the midst* of trouble and sorrow.

And thank God for his *favor*. You didn't earn it, yet he has loved you and adopted you in Baptism.

Glory. Peace. Favor.

Now that's a perfect Christmas gift.

Using the ordinary

Linda Buxa

God doesn't work like we think he would, does he?

It was finally time for the Savior to come to the world. Instead of a grandiose entrance, a baby was born in the middle of the night. Birth is such an ordinary event that it happens every night of the year all around the world. Mary didn't have the world's most-renowned obstetrician. Instead, Joseph did his best. She didn't recuperate in a palace, which would have been fitting for the King of kings. Rather, she and her newborn shared space with animals.

What's most surprising though is the first people who heard the news. Instead of spreading the word to leaders in the temple, angels announced it to shepherds. Admittedly, the angels' part is extraordinary. But the shepherds were absolutely ordinary. In fact, they often worked nights and weekends and couldn't spend much time at church.

Still, God chose ordinary people to **"spread the word concerning what had been told them about this child, and all who heard it were amazed at what the shepherds said to them"** (Luke 2:16-18).

God still doesn't work the way we think he should. Though he gives pastors to preach, their main job is to equip us—the ordinary people who work days, nights, and weekends—to go and spread the word concerning what has been told us about this child.

We, the ordinary, have been given a job that is extraordinary. Let's hurry off.

Immanuel

Pastor Mark Jeske

"Born as man with man to dwell, Jesus, our Immanuel."
—Charles Wesley, 1739

Wesley's magnificent Christmas carol celebrates one of the most precious names that Scripture gives to our Savior. As Joseph was waking from his incredible angelic dream, the evangelist Matthew links the stunning news to messianic prophecy from Isaiah chapter 9: **"All this took place to fulfill what the Lord had said through the prophet: 'The virgin will conceive and give birth to a son, and they will call him Immanuel' (which means 'God with us')"** (Matthew 1:22,23).

Here is more Hebrew: *Im* means "with." *Immanu* means "with us." *El* is the name of our God. The name that Isaiah and the angel wanted you to know and appreciate and use is based on God's powerful promise never to leave or forsake you. Jesus' "Immanuel" name celebrates the astounding fact that God came in person to bring about the rescue of the human race. Without Immanuel, all people caught up in Satan's rebellion would also be caught up in the devastating condemnation and punishment that are hanging over his slimy head.

When you are fearful and depressed, call out Immanuel's name. When you feel guilty and unworthy, call on Immanuel. When you feel overwhelmed and alone, call on Immanuel and rejoice at the absolute certainty that because he came here for us in person, we will spend eternity with him. In person.

A little bit more?

Pastor Jared Oldenburg

Someone asked America's first billionaire, John D. Rockefeller, how much money is enough, and he said, "A little bit more." Sure, money is just a tool, but it's such a powerful tool. Few things in our world change our mood, change our perspective, and cause more stress in relationships than money. People, it seems, will do just about anything to get more.

What is the godly way to handle money? Ask yourself this question: "What good could I do if I had a billion dollars?" Really, what would you do? My guess is that you would want to help people, support the gospel, right an injustice, or even change the world.

Rockefeller's response seems pretty ridiculous, but would your answer be any different? How much money would you need to try to change the world? How much money do you need to look out for friends and family? How much money do you need to advance the truth of Christ with unbelievable generosity? Is your answer, "A little bit more"?

Yet God says in Ephesians 3:20, **"[God] is able to do immeasurably more than all we ask or imagine, according to his power that is at work within us."**

Well, how about that! You don't need a billion dollars to change the world. In fact, you don't just need "a little bit more." God can do more than you can imagine with what you have. Change the world? Sure. Support the gospel? You bet. Right an injustice? Why not? God can do more than we ever imagined!

Tweet last

Jason Nelson

As a younger man, I was so sure about everything. But there are many things I would like to take back because I spoke too soon. For starters, I now realize students wearing jeans to class did not signal the end of civilization. In fact, I wear some nice clean ones to church like nearly everyone else I see there. Too often, there was not a long enough delay between what entered my mind and what came out of my mouth. I should have taken more vows of silence and given things much more thought. You know what they say about trying to get the little word ponies back once they bolt out of the barn.

I've spent some energy trying to execute the first half of this passage: **"My dear brothers and sisters, take note of this: Everyone should be quick to listen . . ."** The back half deserves equal attention: **". . . slow to speak and slow to become angry"** (James 1:19). We're going through a social phase where people are talking past each other in a fevered pitch. I think the fever will break eventually. But if James were writing today, he might say, "Especially Christians, please take some time to hear everything out, think it through, and tweet last." A knee-jerk remark is usually saddled with anger. It is for me. When I see red, I pop off. We could rewrite world history if people would have kept their mouths shut just a little longer. And I could rewrite my own.

Kindness, not judgment

Linda Buxa

"When you, a mere human being, pass judgment on them and yet do the same things, do you think you will escape God's judgment? Or do you show contempt for the riches of his kindness, forbearance and patience, not realizing that God's kindness is intended to lead you to repentance?" (Romans 2:3,4).

He needs to watch his mouth. She should put more clothes on. I can't believe they can't get their act together! If they just went to church, things would work out for them.

Multiple times in my life, I have been guilty of thinking someone needs to change his or her external behavior to become a "better" person. Maybe you're guilty of that too. I think it's because judgment is easier than getting to know someone. The more people meet our standards, the better we can feel about ourselves.

Still, as I meet people each day who need Jesus, these words from Paul put me in my place. Who am I, a mere human, to spend more time judging the sins of others while completely discounting mine? I'm simply a beggar showing other beggars where to find bread. I show the love of Jesus sincerely and share the kindness of Jesus with patience. I talk to others with gentleness and respect. I tell them about the Savior who has changed my life.

Then I watch the Holy Spirit work. He'll change hearts. And he'll help them change behaviors. Not because God is angry. Because God is kind.

Homeless

Pastor Mark Jeske

The Bible's stories of divine intervention on behalf of believers are truly inspirational, aren't they? For a brief, shining moment, everything is perfect and in order and just so *right*, right? With a little imagination, you can fantasize that you were there, enjoying the moment of the revelation of God's power and purpose.

But let's be real for a minute. After Elijah's triumph on Mt. Carmel, evil Ahab was still king and his dragon queen Jezebel was alive and steaming with murderous rage. Sarah got her miracle baby boy, Isaac, but now she had to raise a toddler at the age of 90. The Israelites were freed from Egyptian slavery by an extraordinary string of punitive miracles but now they were all—homeless. **"After leaving Sukkoth they camped at Etham on the edge of the desert. By day the LORD went ahead of them in a pillar of cloud to guide them on their way and by night in a pillar of fire to give them light, so that they could travel by day or night. Neither the pillar of cloud by day nor the pillar of fire by night left its place in front of the people"** (Exodus 13:20-22).

But even though they didn't know for sure where they were going or what difficulties would arise tomorrow, they knew they had the Lord's favor upon them and the Lord's power with them. The pillar of cloud gave them direction, and the pillar of fire gave them protection.

His Word is our cloud and fire today.

Devotions for Special Days

Good Friday

Because of love

Pastor Matt Ewart

Today is a somber day of remembrance. Usually we respond to the announcement of Jesus' death with joy. But today that joy is somewhat muted due to the fact that he didn't just die *for* us. He died *because of* us.

Had it not been for our sin, there would be no need for those nails to pierce him. Had it not been for our rebellion, there would be no need for those dark hours on a cross. Had it not been for our wandering, there would have been no need for him to chase us down. His search for us led him right into the clutches of death.

But there's another side to this day. While our *sin* was the factor that *called for* Christ's death, his *love* was what motivated him to *answer* that call. His death was not forced upon him as one who was left with no options. He chose the path that would lead to suffering and death because this was the only path that would lead him to you.

So while it is accurate to say that Jesus died because of your sins, it is even more accurate to say that Jesus died because of his love for you. Throughout the day, repeat in your mind the first six words of Hebrews 12:2: **"*For the joy set before him* he endured the cross, scorning its shame, and sat down at the right hand of the throne of God."**

The resurrection changes everything

Pastor Mark Jeske

Overuse of words trivializes them, does it not? Turning the word *hell* into a throwaway cussword makes people not think about its terrible threat. Turning God's personal name into merely a conversation intensifier (OMG) trivializes his majesty and rank. And using *Easter* as a modifier with *bunny, ham, outfit, vacation,* and *eggs* runs the risk of emptying that grand word of its crucial meaning.

What happened in Jerusalem on the original Easter morning changed everything. Literally changed everything. **"If Christ has not been raised, your faith is futile; you are still in your sins"** (1 Corinthians 15:17). If Jesus Christ had failed his divine mission in any way, even in some small detail, his dreadful death would not have achieved its saving purpose and his body would have turned to dust like ours. Our guilt would remain, our hope of eternal life would evaporate, and our longing for God's smile and favor would become a joke.

But he did rise. His resurrection guarantees that the blood price he paid was sufficient and acceptable to his Father. His resurrection guarantees the forgiveness of our sins, and we are no longer threatened by their gloomy curse. His resurrection also guarantees our own. We too will rise, just as he did.

So have an egg hunt with your children and grandchildren this year. Bake a ham for your family. Peel the foil off a chocolate bunny and enjoy the sweet taste that God invented.

But never forget the real Easter.

Mother's Day gift

Pastor Matt Ewart

Suppose for a moment that you had to compensate God for all he has done for you. Go ahead, put a number on it. How much would you have to give him?

No amount can possibly compensate God for all he has given and all he has done. Consider the imagery God gave through Isaiah: **"I will extend peace to her like a river, and the wealth of nations like a flooding stream"** (Isaiah 66:12).

Just like you can't measure a stream that continually flows; you can't measure God's goodness. That means there's only one way to respond to what he does. The best we can do is to let our gratitude overflow with these three words: *God, thank you.*

Mother's Day reminds me how moms are one of the greatest blessings God has given to this world. They're not perfect. They have up days and down days. But God uses moms—imperfections and all—to make a difference in this world. Through Jesus, God takes their sins away. Through Jesus, God takes their best efforts and considers them perfect. Moms are a dear gift from him.

If you're a mom, it's difficult to express adequately how grateful we are for you. Like a river, your love is immeasurable. There is no way to compensate you for all you've done. No gift can testify adequately to the impact you've made. So if you're a mom, the best we can do is let our gratitude overflow today with these three words: *Mom, thank you.*

Fathers are needed to provide for their families

Pastor Mark Jeske

People know that fathers are needed to provide for their families. Or do they? Single moms who say they can raise their children without a man are being brave, but their lives are going to be hard, really hard. To Jesus it was so obvious that fathers are depended on as providers that he made it an assumption in a little story about the wonderful providing that God the Father did for his children: **"Which of you, if your son asks for bread, will give him a stone?"** (Matthew 7:9).

The obvious and expected answer is, "Duh, nobody." Any father worthy of the name is dialed into his children's needs. In my experience, marriage is God's number-one anti-poverty strategy. Dads are not just optional equipment or accessories; they are essential to a thriving and happy home life. And while I have met some phenomenal single mothers who accomplished miracles, single parenthood should not be allowed to become the new normal in our society. We need our dads at home.

When a mother and father split up, they have to establish two complete households. That means that all the money the man now has to spend on his own rent, utilities, and upkeep is not available for investing in his children. Staying together is not only pleasing to God; it is pleasing to your financial situation.

Has your dad been a steady provider for you? Take time today to thank God for him, and you might just thank Dad too.

A tummy full of turkey

Pastor Mark Jeske

I am glad for an annual day for giving thanks, just as I need calendar reminders to remember the significant people in my life on their birthdays and remember to celebrate my marriage on its anniversary date.

But should we need to be reminded to give thanks to God? I know why I need it. Because I'm quicker to complain than rejoice. I'm quicker to look to myself for solutions than pray to God. I'm quicker to credit myself for good things in my life than see the connection to heaven. I'm quicker to feel cheated and envious than blessed and rich in everything that matters.

I need the Word's encouragement to see and acknowledge the Source of everything good in my life: **"Be joyful always; pray continually; give thanks in all circumstances, for this is God's will for you in Christ Jesus"** (1 Thessalonians 5:16-18). The Word opens my eyes to be aware of the holy angels who protect me, the Spirit who lives in me, the Father who daily forgives me, and the Son who loves me unconditionally.

A tummy full of turkey is only one example of the constant stream of blessings that I enjoy. Today, God will be hearing from me more than usual. But, you know, really every day is a day of thanksgiving.

About the Writers

Pastor Mark Jeske brings the good news of Jesus Christ to viewers of *Time of Grace* in weekly 30-minute programs broadcast across America and around the world on local television, cable, and satellite, as well as on-demand streaming via the internet. He is the senior pastor at St. Marcus Church, a thriving multicultural congregation in Milwaukee, Wisconsin. Mark is the author of several books and dozens of devotional booklets on various topics. He and his wife, Carol, have four adult children.

Linda Buxa is a freelance writer and Bible study leader. She is a regular speaker at women's retreats and conferences across the country. A regular blogger for Time of Grace Ministry, her first book, *Dig In! Family Devotions to Feed Your Faith*, was released in August 2014. Linda and her husband, Greg, have lived in Alaska, Washington D.C., and California. They now live in Wisconsin, where they are raising their three children.

Pastor Jon Enter has served in West Palm Beach, Florida, for over ten years. He also serves as a regular speaker on *Your* Time of Grace video devotions. He is married to Debbi and has four daughters.

Pastor Matt Ewart and his wife, Amy, have been blessed with three young children who keep life interesting. Matt is currently a pastor in Lakeville, Minnesota, and has previously served as a pastor in Colorado and Arizona.

Sarah Habben resides in Antigua, where her husband, Dan, became a missionary in August 2017. Since their arrival, Sarah has spent a lot of time sweating, slapping mosquitoes, dodging hurricanes, and adjusting to life in the Caribbean after 18 years in Alberta, Canada. She has four daughters, three of whom are in uniform on the island and one who is at Luther Preparatory School in Watertown, Wisconsin. Sarah is the coauthor of *The Bloodstained Path to God* (2012, Northwestern Publishing House) and the author of *The Mom God Chose: Mothering Like Mary* (2015, Northwestern Publishing House).

Diana Kerr is a certified professional coach, writer, and blogger on a never-ending chase for a life focused on what matters most. Her business and life's passion are all about equipping goal-oriented Christian women with the tools and truths they need to get unstuck and make the most of their time and life. You can find out more about Diana or read her motivational and transparent content on her blog at dianakerr.com.

Pastor Daron Lindemann is pastor at a new mission start in Pflugerville, Texas. Previously he served in downtown Milwaukee and in Irmo, South Carolina. Daron has authored articles or series for *Forward in Christ* magazine, *Preach the Word*, and his own weekly Grace MEMO devotions. He lives in Texas with his wife, Cara, and has two adult sons.

Pastor Jeremy Mattek has served as the lead pastor of a congregation on Milwaukee's urban north side since earning his seminary degree in 2004. He is also a regular speaker on *Your* Time of Grace video devotions. He is married to Karen and has five children.

Jason Nelson had a career as a teacher, counselor, and leader. He has a bachelor's degree in education, did graduate work in theology, and has a master's degree in counseling psychology. After his career ended in disabling back pain, he wrote the book *Miserable Joy: Chronic Pain in the Christian Life* (2007, Northwestern Publishing House). He has written and spoken extensively on a variety of topics related to the

Christian life. Jason has been a contributing writer for Time of Grace since 2010. He has authored many Grace Moments devotions and several books. Jason lives with his wife, Nancy, in Wisconsin.

Pastor Mike Novotny has served God's people in full-time ministry since 2007. He is currently at a congregation in Appleton, Wisconsin, and also serves as a *Your* Time of Grace speaker. Mike loves seeing people grasp the depth of God's amazing grace and unstoppable mercy. He and his wife, Kim, have two daughters.

Pastor Jared Oldenburg has worked with churches in urban and suburban Milwaukee; Seattle; Denver; and Santa Maria, California. He, his wife Aimee, and their three children currently live and serve a congregation in Castle Rock, Colorado. Jared is also a regular speaker on *Your* Time of Grace video devotions.

About Time of Grace

Time of Grace is for people who want more growth and less struggle in their spiritual walk. The timeless truth of God's Word is delivered through television, print, and digital media with millions of content engagements each month. We connect people to God's grace so they know they are loved and forgiven and so they can start living in the freedom they've always wanted.

To discover more, please visit timeofgrace.org, download our free app at timeofgrace.org/app, or call 800.661.3311.

Help share God's message of grace!

Every gift you give helps Time of Grace reach people around the world with the good news of Jesus. Your generosity and prayer support take the gospel of grace to others through our ministry outreach and help them find the restart with Jesus they need.

Give today at timeofgrace.org/give or by calling 800.661.3311.

Thank you!